FOOD
IN THE SOCIAL ORDER

Studies of Food and Festivities
in Three American Communities

FOOD
IN THE SOCIAL ORDER

Studies of Food and Festivities
in Three American Communities

MARY DOUGLAS, Editor

Russell Sage Foundation
New York

The Russell Sage Foundation

The Russell Sage Foundation, one of the oldest of America's general purpose foundations, was established in 1907 by Mrs. Margaret Olivia Sage for "the improvement of social and living conditions in the United States." The Foundation seeks to fulfill this mandate by fostering the development and dissemination of knowledge about the political, social, and economic problems of America. It conducts research in the social sciences and public policy, and publishes books and pamplets that derive from this research.

The Foundation provides support for individual scholars and collaborates with other granting agencies and academic institutions in studies of social problems. It maintains a professional staff of social scientists who engage in their own research as well as advise on Foundation programs and projects. The Foundation also conducts a Visiting Scholar Program, under which established scholars working in areas of current interest to the Foundation join the staff for a year to consult and to continue their own research and writing. Finally, a Postdoctoral Fellowship Program enables promising young scholars to devote full time to their research while in residence for a year at the Foundation.

The Board of Trustees is responsible for the general policies and oversight of the Foundation, while the immediate administrative direction of the program and staff is vested in the President, assisted by the officers and staff. The President bears final responsibility for the decision to publish a manuscript as a Russell Sage Foundation book. In reaching a judgment on the competence, accuracy, and objectivity of each study, the President is advised by the staff and a panel of special readers.

The conclusions and interpretations in Russell Sage Foundation publications are those of the authors and not of the Foundation, its Trustees, or its staff. Publication by the Foundation, therefore, does not imply endorsement of the contents of the study. It does signify that the manuscript has been reviewed by competent scholars in the field and that the Foundation finds it worthy of public consideration.

Library of Congress Catalog Number: 84-060262
Standard Book Number: 0-87154-210-2
10 9 8 7 6 5 4 3 2 1

*This volume is dedicated
to Audrey Richards and Margaret Mead
for their pioneering work on food habits.*

Contents

Contributors

MARY DOUGLAS holds the Avalon Foundation chair in the humanities at Northwestern University, where she teaches in the departments of Anthropology and History and Literature of Religion. Several earlier essays on food behavior and food meanings can be found in a recent collection of her work, *In the Active Voice.* In 1984, she presented four lectures at the Ecole Practique des Hautes Etudes, University of Paris, on symbolism in modern society, with specific reference to the case of food.

WILLIAM K. POWERS is professor and former chair of the Department of Anthropology at Rutgers University, New Brunswick, New Jersey. He received his B.A. from Brooklyn College, CUNY, in 1970; M.A. from Wesleyan University in 1971; and Ph.D. from the University of Pennsylvania in 1975. His writings include *Oglala Religion* (1977) and *Yuwipi: Vision and Experience in Oglala Ritual* (1982), both published by the University of Nebraska Press.

MARLA N. POWERS is a visiting research associate at the Institute for Research on Women, Rutgers University. She received her B.A. from Brooklyn College, CUNY, in 1971, and her M.A. and

Ph.D. from Rutgers University in 1982. Her published works include "Menstruation and Reproduction: An Oglala Case," which appeared in *Signs*, 1980.

The Powerses have collaborated on research at Pine Ridge, South Dakota, for 27 years and are presently writing a number of books and articles on Oglala kinship and marriage, images of American Indian women, sexual symbolism in the Sun dance, Lakota foods, music, and dance.

JUDITH GOODE is chairperson of the Department of Anthropology at Temple University. As an urban anthropologist, her interest in ethnicity brought her to the study of food systems. She now teaches and publishes in both urban and nutritional anthropology and has been active in organizing the Committee on Nutritional Anthropology. She is co-author of *The Anthropology of the City* (with Edwin Eames) as well as other books and articles.

KAREN CURTIS received her M.S. in urban studies and Ph.D. in anthropology from Temple University. She is currently working at Temple on the Metropolitan Philadelphia Machine-Readable Records Survey Project. She has held several research positions in applied anthropology relating to education, manpower training, and economic development. Her major research has been related to Italian-Americans and nutritional anthropology.

JANET THEOPHANO received her Ph.D. in folklore from the University of Pennsylvania. She was a founding editor of the *Digest* (an interdisciplinary newsletter on the study of food) developed at the University of Pennsylvania. She has worked on a child nutrition project for the New Jersey University of Medicine and Dentistry. She is currently a visiting professor of American studies at Pennsylvania State University, Middletown, Pennsylvania.

Contributors

TONY WHITEHEAD is an associate professor of social anthropology in the Department of Health Education, School of Public Health, University of North Carolina, Chapel Hill. Dr. Whitehead received his M.S. in hygiene and Ph.D. in anthropology from the University of Pittsburgh. His research interests include household structure and food habits, correlates of hypertension, gender constructs, men and family planning, family dynamics, African-American cultures and societies, cultural systems and health systems, and integrating qualitative and quantitative research methods for health program planning and evaluation. He has carried out research in the Commonwealth Caribbean, the rural South of the United States, urban America, and West Africa.

JONATHAN GROSS is professor of computer science and vice-chairman of the Computer Science Department at Columbia University. He is also a member of the Department of Mathematics and the Department of Statistics. For his research accomplishments, which include forty papers, he has been awarded fellowships by IBM and by the Alfred P. Sloan Foundation. He is the author of six books and serves on the editorial advisory boards of the Columbia University Press, *Computers & Electronics* magazine, and the *Journal of Graph Theory*. He is also a consultant to Bell Laboratories.

1

Standard Social Uses of Food: Introduction

Mary Douglas

The Food Problem

The idea is still widely held that the proper, the most direct, and indeed the only true way to prevent famine and hunger is to increase food production. The emphasis on the physical shortage of food materials has guided economic planning and dominated debates about global population and resources. It will be a difficult notion to correct, sustained as it is by convenient fictions and anchored in shared prejudices. But gradually a reaction is being expressed. Food policy is not merely concerned with production, storage, and conveyance to the kitchens of the people. The worst horrors of famines could be diminished and many famines even be averted if understanding the social, legal, and economic aspects of food problems was given priority. Amartya Sen (1981), in his study of the four great famines in Bangladesh, Bengal, Sahel, and Ethiopia, demonstrates that famines cannot be explained by food shortages: famines are liable to occur even with good harvests and even in prosperity. People die of starvation in front of food-filled shops. The causes are complex shifts in the legal entitlements which determine individuals' access to food. Administrators, like planners, are blinkered by their conviction that the causes lie in the physical supply of food. Unsuspecting of the extremes to which people will go in order to protect their own stocks when food shortages are rumored, they compound their initial misunderstanding with prolonged mishandling. There is extraordinarily little to guide them about the social uses of food. The dominant paradigm treats the human problem in the same terms as getting fodder into cattle troughs.

This volume seeks to present an expanded and humanist approach to food. Only observe how little is known about access to foods at the domestic level, about the cultural influences training tastes, or about the micro-politics that govern its distribution. Something about those blank places in our knowledge calls for explanation. Why is so little said on these particular scores? International agencies certainly know that unequal access to food is the result of social inequalities. They are discussing programs to improve the living conditions of the poorest segments of the developing countries. But, of course, authority tends to be most precarious in the poorest countries, so the very places where food is most unequally distributed are those in which politics are most sensitive to criticism. Plans for a new economic order meet political obstacles if receiving aid is conditional on interventions that threaten the sovereignty of the developing country (Fishlow et al. 1978). A concern to protect international collaboration may explain a tendency to keep political criticism out of the debates on world food problems.

Perhaps the extraordinary emphasis on production is a response to a need to depoliticize the subject of food. One might expect that this need would promote unpoliticized methods of thinking about food distribution.* But this is another blank space that needs explaining. The absence of serious research into the cultural and social uses of food is caused by a more fundamental separation between food sciences and social thought. It is the legacy of a process of intellectual compartmentalization corresponding to academic teaching and research divisions. The research reported here is intended to reach a more fundamental level of understanding. It attempts to examine some elementary relations between food sharing and social integration. The method has potential for bridging the gaps separating food

---

*Margaret Mead in 1964 observed that the anthropological work on food habits which she had initiated during the 1940s had not been further developed, nor the recommendations for research implemented.

sciences, cultural analysis, and sociology. It starts from the assumption that unlike livestock, humans make some choices that are not governed by physiological processes. They choose what to eat, when and how often, in what order, and with whom. The idea of approaching these choices through information theory has been aired before but never worked out, and this is what we here attempt.

Though dismay at the horrors of famine and hunger drives the rich industrial nations to advocate basic political changes, none of them seems to be a convincing solution to the problems. A revolution in favor of the socialist state could theoretically solve problems of production and maldistribution by planned direction of the economy and strict rationing of food. It has often worked for short, intensive periods: through the duration of a war or through the crisis period of an earthquake or flood disaster. But over the long term it is subject to well-known abuses. Moreover, the solution of imposing long-term control on individual choice is repugnant to the Western liberal tradition, even if it was considered to be efficacious. Another version of a radical political solution is reduction of scale: a turning back from the unwanted effects of high technology and the bureaucratic control associated with it. Small government is one thing, but rejection of the achievements of science reads too much like avoiding one kind of famine disaster by returning to the earlier famines and pestilence characteristic of preindustrial Europe. It is difficult to see how to make sense of it. A third political option is the one currently followed in the West: the system of private enterprise and sporadic and ineffectual rescue efforts.

Lacking political solutions to that part of the world food problem which is inherently political, professional food theorists understandably turn to low-level solutions based on improved administration and further research. Food policy and planning deal with production, storage, and distribution as management problems. Researchers directed by administrative priorities study the food sciences, human biology, agriculture, and stock raising; and improved official standards of nutrition, health education, welfare support services, and marketing. But this major effort of research hardly touches on consumer behavior. Instead of solving problems, the research reveals mysteries about human behavior. There is the mystery of why nutrition education fails. After much expenditure of time and work the nutritionists are left believing in consumer irrationality, berating the public for wrong choice of foods, or bewailing its conservatism in food preferences. The consumer in modern industrial societies is painted to be just as stubbornly conservative and blind to his own advantage as the fabled peasant in the third world or in our own historic past. Where food is concerned, the consumer is far from being seen as the optimizing rational agent of economic theory. Considering that we are in the midst of a notoriously swift-changing market in food—where pizza has swept its manufacturers into a multi-million-dollar market, where kiwi fruit from the Antipodes has become a fashionable accompaniment for fish, and where frozen yogurt competes with ice cream—the real mystery is the sturdiness of the belief in consumer conservatism.

There is another more fundamental mystery about tastes. Just at the point at which the technology of the chemical senses has become capable of producing any taste or smell or texture or combination of these on demand, the food technologists are smitten by frustration; they do not know what flavors to copy and what textures to reproduce in easily manufactured cheaper substitutes for existing known food stuffs. There is also the mystery of waste: careless waste, conspicuous waste, careful but ignorant waste. The private consumer is arraigned again and again as a person totally unfitted to be left in charge of his own food preferences, an awkward approach for liberal philosophy.

And then there is the mystery of exclusion, even more galling for the philosophers who would defend our civilization. In societies based on primitive technologies, so Marshall Sahlins (1972) would argue, hunger is shared, whereas in modern industrial societies food flows in divergent streams: a trickle of less nourishing stuffs to the poor and unprivileged and huge quantities of highly nourishing stuffs to the rich. The scandal that hits home most squarely is that of undernourished children living in the next street to overfed ones. If we knew the springs of our behavior, we would be in a better position to understand that part of the starvation which follows on lack of social contact and lack of social concern. It is often argued that the sheer urgency of the great food problem directs attention to immediate short-term solutions rather than fundamental rethinking, but there is yet another reason why our worries about the food of the world only turn up scandals and mysteries.

In the sense that the whole of society has been secularized by the withdrawal of specialized activities from a religious framework, so food has also been taken out of any common metaphysical scheme. Moral and social symbols seem to have been drained from its use, at least in the opinion of professional food theorists. However, this theoretical bias may be due less to the secularization of food habits among ordinary folk in the Western Hemisphere than to the secularization of social theory. On the one hand, the official theory of food is exclusively concerned with physical nourishment, it being assumed that consecrated food taking is either a thing of the past or one of minority religions. On the other hand, the ordinary consuming public in modern industrial society works hard to invest its food with moral, social, and aesthetic meanings. The actual current meaningfulness of food is being overlooked by professional food theorists because their thought is doubly restricted, partly by antique metaphysical assumptions about the separation of spirit and flesh and partly by an intellectual tradition which has desocialized the individual.

Theories about human needs, if their assumptions were to be made explicit, would show disapproval of social expenditures (Douglas 1978). The assumptions seem to rest on a postulated good human nature, with physical and spiritual components which should deploy physical resources only to reach some modest level of comfort. At some time past spiritual resources would have supplied an all-encompassing religious system, and defined appropriate physical comfort within coherent theories of life, death, and destiny. In default, the central assumption now seems to be that corrupt society always tempts the individual to misuse material things either for greed or to serve envy and pride by rivalrous display. The assumption still carries forward the religious distinction between godliness and worldliness. It allows that in a secular world without religion the physical needs for survival, work, and leisure are still the same. Furthermore, though the spiritual and intellectual supports of religion have gone, its accouterments remain: music, poetry, and visual and plastic arts count as spiritual activities because they are enjoyed for their own sake, unlike food and shelter needed for base physical reasons.

This division of human needs into instrumental material things and self-justified spiritual things leaves a gap. The goods which are used for extended social intercourse are without justification. Festivities are then treated as illegitimate demands on the world's productive system, the source of social inequalities and ultimately responsible for the maldistribution of food. Although this has the ring of ultimate truth, it is too simple to treat all the demands of society as unacceptable. Unless we still subscribe to the religious denomination which teaches this particular doctrine of incompatibility between salvation and society, it should have no place in our inquiry and indeed may have nothing to say to us about the great food problem. Worse, the doctrinally derived judgment distracts our vision by insinuating that what is needed is a change of heart: conversion of minds to an anti-institutional attitude instead of correction of institutions to the mind's purposes.

Our contemporary view of the problem is fogged by another intellectual legacy, the model of the desocialized individual which now dominates our social thought. As Dumont (1977) has skillfully shown, the individual had once been seen as a partially autonomous subunit, gaining full significance from his part in a hierarchical whole. In contemporary philosophizing he has become a separate, self-justified unit, locked in individual exchanges with other such self-seeking, rational beings. The switch to thinking about humans in this way changes the attitude of the investigator to the range of communications available between individuals. Whereas food, like other material things, may be used to communicate, all the possible messages are now treated as originating between private individuals, direct commands or instructions or guileful signals about self-identity, intended to further the sender's private objectives.

In consequence, two things are missing now from our repertoire of explanations of behavior: society as well as religion. An unfavorable judgment on social life follows implicitly from moralizing against material pleasures whenever they are pleasures of social intercourse. The bias is reinforced by a further moralizing judgment against social life, seen as the arena of individual self-seeking. Given this background of implicit assumptions, no wonder advertisers believe that the symbolic meanings of foods in modern society are all comprised in messages about individual role definition and role performance. It is as if the best mother, the best wife, the most caring persons all press food into the social competition by using it relentlessly for grading one another's role performance. Briefly, the assumptions current about the social uses of food are patronizing, sometimes moralizing, sometimes exploitative, and always incoherent. There is scope for a fresh approach to understanding food habits, especially by way of comparison between different civilizations.

Anthropologists' Work on Food Habits

Having a privileged position for cross-cultural comparison, anthropologists also have a responsibility to exercise it. Indeed, anthropologists have always been very interested in the subject of food. They have much to say about food as part of the analysis of domestic and local organization. Some have written about its place in public policy. Audrey Richards (1939) pioneered the study of food in its full relation to agriculture and political economy in Africa. Margaret Mead (1943, 1964, 1965) pioneered the study of food habits and social change in the United States during World War II. At that time, immigrants and displaced persons having lost their access to their habitual foods often rejected those offered them. A good theory would have been valuable for directing the appropriate food supplies to threatened regions, for feeding refugees as well as making the best use of existing resources in the homelands. Mead's theory was based upon a core/periphery model of the components of any culturally distinct food system: the core elements, identified by their greater frequency of use, were held to be less liable to change than the peripheral elements. The snag in this approach is that the frequency count of foods appearing in household menus or shopping lists overlays the actual patterning of the food. When the core selection corresponds to what is most cheaply and easily available, it gives an unjustified impression of assimilation of an immigrant population's food habits.

Apart from this sustained work on applied problems, the research of anthropologists on food has gone in several directions. There is an impressive development of interest in nutritional anthropology (Jerome et al. 1980) which applies social and cultural frameworks to problems of nutrition. Excellent work in this field is nevertheless limited by lack of a general theoretical structure. Also, there is fascinating work on food semantics, the meanings of food in different civilizations. Generally conducted in places where food is invested with strong religious significance (Vogt 1976), work in this tradition tends to highlight the secularization of food in our own society. Thus, it re-inforces the sense that we are uniquely different, so that nothing that may be learned about food habits of earlier generations or of other societies is going to help us to understand the place of food in our own modern industrial society.

The meanings of food need to be studied in small-scale exemplars. Attempts to generalize by using linguistic theoretical assumptions tend to produce explanations of tastes and preferences that seem too trivial or too bizarre (Leach 1960; Lévi-Strauss 1970) to have much bearing on current food problems. Another dilemma confronts an-thropologists: if research is designed according to the prevailing so-cioeconomic categories of our own culture, it is too deeply biased to claim the advantage of cross-cultural perspective; on the other hand, if research is structured according to conceptual categories of the particular culture being studied, it cannot emerge with results that apply elsewhere. It is intrinsically difficult to learn something of gen-eral applicability about how tastes are formed from small-scale studies of remote, exotic places. We can get exquisite miniature por-trayals of all the specificities of a particular historic case of adjustment between values and resources, without getting a theoretical grip on the forces that brought that case into being.

Anthropology works on a macro-scale with an evolutionary frame-work of thousands of years. While this very scale would seem to allow opportunities for experimenting with new perspectives, theoretical investigation tends to stay within the paradigms prevailing in the bio-logical and social sciences: the supply/demand model and the in-come/expenditure model. Marvin Harris's work (1971) exemplifies this approach, which has potentially powerful insights for interpret-ing long-term changes. But the method is inevitably weak for observ-ing short-term relations between social factors and perceived needs. Furthermore, it assumes rational economic choice for explaining cul-tural adaptation, but we have seen that this is precisely the assump-tion that is challenged in the current thinking about food tastes. The modern consumer has lost credibility as a rational agent in the eyes of food theorists. So this distinctively anthropological approach lacks fine-tuned relevance to the way that the great food problems are posed.

If the modern consumer is not behaving convincingly as a mar-ket-minded individual, neither seeking nor using education about food values and food costs, perhaps the explanation is that the symbolic aspects of food in the system of social class really get in the way of optimizing expenditures for health and hygiene. Two distinguished anthropologists, Marshall Sahlins and Pierre Bourdieu, have given us independent analyses of the social class structure underlying food tastes in modern industrial society. Bourdieu (1979) treats food as part of the general analysis of dominance and subordination of aesthetic judgment within the French class system. As far as food is concerned, the contrasting principles that he abstracts—such as formality/informality, exotic/homely, traditional/experimental— are valuable guides to understanding the process of social ranking. Sahlins (1978) adds another factor, the metaphors of inner/outer social dimension which are projected upon food, inner being closer to nature and outer being more civilized. In such a symbolic structure, no wonder that intestines are reckoned inferior to steak and no wonder that offal is regarded as uncivilized, low-class food.

Both of these anthropologists use the process of social exclusion to explain the contemporary distribution of tastes. Probably no one after reading Sahlins can order a steak or after reading Bourdieu enter a gourmet restaurant without a sense of guilt. Both exercises are fired by the same just anger against modern industrial society that is characteristic of professional social thinkers of our day. Sahlins and Bourdieu show how apparently innocuous food tastes are guilty of mean social striving. Economists treat all tastes and especially food tastes as purely individual matters, based on physiological needs or ultimate private preferences. Satirists have always known that this is untrue. But the exact mechanisms of metaphor, comparison, and social grading of events and food which make for cultural competence have not been established. It is easy for politically radical critics and satirists to see that something is wrong with modern industrial society and that it shows in the abuse of food. But it may be premature to pin the fault on industrialism as such—as if nonindustrial society never used food for extravagant personal rivalry, letting its lower ranks hungrily watch the spectacle of waste. Individual competition occurs quite widely in the world. The gourmet cruise and the monster steak are only mild symbols of social competition compared with the feasting described by Petronius or, to be contemporary, with the beef-eating orgies of the Gurage Men's Societies in Ethiopia (Shack 1966) or certain New Guinea pig festivals (Pospisil 1972).

Neither Sahlins nor Bourdieu stands outside or above the prevalent judgments against food's social uses. Far from unprejudiced, each exposes an implicit hankering for some other time or place where humans treat humans more generously. But alas, each knows enough of other cultures to hesitate to recommend a model for our modern predicament. Just because they give the current prejudice such powerful expression, they pose acutely for us the problems of a balanced and unpoliticized approach to food uses.

The political criticism invites us either to abandon the experiment of living in modern industrial society or to remake it. The first recourse is too drastic; for the second we are given no guidance. A radical approach to food's place in civilization would require the whole range of food's social uses to be considered.

Even social animals in the wild use food to create and maintain their social relations. So a first step to rectify thinking about food is to recognize how food enters the moral and social intentions of individuals. Nutritional needs can be seriously at odds with the demands of hospitality in which these moral intentions are actualized. Hospitality is part of a system of reciprocal exchanges. Giving food away unilaterally makes an asymmetrical relation. The lopsided food gift loads the recipient's status with demeaning signs. If no reciprocity at all is allowed, the gift is outright alms and the receiver is labeled a beggar (Douglas 1978). This is partly why the subject is so sensitive that food planners profess that all problems have to do with production.

Suppose we try to discard the sectarian residues in our tradition. The individual would not be regarded as a flawed, divided being, deplorably prone to envy and gluttony, sacrificing a spiritual heritage either to physical nature or to corrupt society. Suppose we start with the individual as a moral being, with his own moral ends, expecting to be treated by others as an end in himself and not an instrument of their purposes. Suppose that his essential human concern is to build up a society in which all members treat each other as moral agents. Because this same Kantian position underlies the moralizing of commentators on the world food problem, it makes a good shared starting point for thinking about culture. It stands also in a certain old anthropological tradition (Beattie 1964; MacBeath 1978) which never separates cultural analysis from analysis of moral principles.

Assume that the individuals who are constructing their society together, expecting to live for some time and to die eventually, entertain something like a lifetime moral program (Fried 1970), so that they judge themselves and each other on success in pursuing moral objectives coherently over their lifetime. The moral program cannot be defined negatively in terms of specific faults to be avoided, but can be defined positively as aiming at a life-span coherence so that the individual, adjusting sights all the time, can see himself as a particular kind of person who would always do this sort of thing and never do that. "Moral style" is set collectively. At any given time the pervading cultural environment provides moral standards affecting every kind of resource. Food is inevitably brought within the moral perspective. It is easy in a stable, homogeneous society to say what is a wasteful and what is a necessary and appropriate way of using food. Indeed, to be able to know these things is part of the definition of such a society and a test of cultural competence. For everyone to be uncertain about them indicates social change and mixture.

A plural society has plural cultural values. No wonder we are so confused about how food ought to be used. On this subject of food we are like Richard Niebuhr's Christian sects who know that their calling is to a knife-edge equilibrium between living in the flesh and rejecting the world. No wonder that the nutritionist needs to define narrow professional responsibilities and does not try to draw lines of general moral responsibility for the public at large. It is appropriate within professional boundaries to ask employers whether their workers are adequately fed and to provide scales for testing, to ask parents whether their children are adequately fed and provide scales for testing, and likewise to ask nurses and doctors on behalf of their patients. The nutritionist does not take it on himself to say, "Why do you turn beggars from your door? Why is your conscience sleeping while you stuff yourself with food in the sight of starving people?" If he were to extend his professional concern for nutritional well-being to relations of friendship, he might ask, "Why do you heap your guest's plate with noxious fats and fill his glass with liquor that will shorten his life?" He does not ask because of another moral concern that praises the lavishness of the generous host and the cheerful gathering in the well-ordered, well-stocked home.

Many of the important questions about food habits are moral and social. How many people come to your table? How regularly? Why those names and not others? There is a range of social intercourse which is based on food, on reciprocity, on frequency of exchange and other patterns. We ought to know more about patterns of social involvement so as to understand rejection, since it appears undeniable that starvation and undernourishment are the result of social rejection more than of physical deficiency of food supplies.

Food is not only a metaphor or vehicle of communication; a meal is a physical event. After a year or a decade, the sequence of meals can be counted, as real as colonnades through which people can walk. Food may be symbolic, but it is also as efficacious for feeding as roofs are for shelter, as powerful for including as gates and doors. Added over time, gifts of food are flows of life-giving substance, but long before life-saving is an issue the flows have created the conditions for social life. More effective than flags or red carpets which merely say welcome, food actually delivers good fellowship.

Food Patterns

There are policy reasons for giving food patterns more systematic attention. A rural population once adequately fed by multiple small resources tapped at different points in the seasonal cycle, when it turns over to imported foods or to cash-cropping and a less complex diet, loses its delicate balance with the environment. Grave nutritional disorders frequently result. Nowadays there is a widespread concern about imposing alien foods or introducing even small changes too hastily. The local food system needs to be understood and appreciated in the context of its relationship with the other family institutions, and the interlocking of the family with the larger social institutions of the community.

Some of those who recognize the global food crisis urge that certain food supplies once despised be reinstated in esteem. It may be easier to improve a traditional staple than to control the consequences of introducing a new one. But attempts to improve the quality of traditional foods may meet resistance from the local population. Some new nutrients slip into the traditional system very easily, while others (with only minute taste differences) are emphatically rejected. There are, therefore, direct nutritional reasons for concentrating on cultural aspects of gastronomy.

Policies which foster major changes in the division of labor between the sexes have an impact on the household, on cooking, on timetables, and on food. On the one hand, the policy which seeks to free women to play a fuller part in a wider community is bound to change the hours women spend in the kitchen. On the other hand, the movement to promote better nutrition criticizes the quality of mass-produced foods. But the advance of women's status will hardly be effected without mass production. At least we can be sure that it will involve a parallel change in food habits, and even a radical change in the size and function of domestic units. And yet there is little research on how food habits are formed, how they become resistant to change, or on how conservative they really are.

The Russell Sage Foundation explicitly includes among its objectives a concern to understand the causes of poverty in America. Under such auspices an anthropological program of research on culture could do worse than study the meanings and uses of food. Poverty leads to destitution which leads to food vouchers or even to doles of hot soup. The work that is reported in this volume represents the collaboration of three teams of anthropologists who were already involved in work of this kind.

At an early juncture, Judith Goode wrote that with colleagues at Temple University she had been studying expressions of distinctive Italian ethnicity in food in a suburb of Philadelphia. She already knew the local culture well and requested support for further work on ethnic patterns in food. About the same time, Tony Whitehead at the University of North Carolina asked for assistance from Russell Sage. He was interested in assertions about the absence or presence of distinctive cultural identity of American blacks, particularly with respect to food habits.

Natalie Joffe (1943) had asserted a common view when she declared: "There are no American Negro food habits. The rural Negro in the South eats substantially the same food as does his white neighbor of similar circumstances, while the Negro school teacher or physician reared in the North eats the same food which his white counterparts serve." Whitehead wanted to develop a way of checking whether this was correct. The University of North Carolina's Department of Public Health had been conducting a series of studies on hypertension and its causes among black populations. The causes could be genetic; they could be cultural; they could be environmental. If it was true that there were no behavioral differences between blacks and whites in the same income and occupational brackets, the case for genetic differences making blacks more prone to hypertension was strengthened. But the exercise of systematically examining the food habits of white and black Americans in the same socioeconomic bracket in the same neighborhood had not been convincingly attempted. Whitehead was looking for a method for comparing food styles and food quality within and across income groups.

Edward Montgomery, another anthropologist, who had already contributed to nutritional anthropology, was looking for support for research in Tennessee to test a hypothesis about how food habits change in response to industrialization in a rural area. William and Marla Powers joined the research, both being conversant with Lakota (Sioux) culture and interested in the cultural importance of food in defining ethnic identity. With research covering suburban Italian-Americans, rural Tennessee, blacks and whites in North Carolina, and American Indians—the future conversations promised plenty of contrast. Each project was to last for one year (in some cases less according to the time they had to spare). Each team was to pursue its own particular field interest, but in the course of the year each was also to give four months of intensive fieldwork in collaboration with the others, according to a common plan. The design of the research that was to be done collaboratively was to be argued out together at meetings. The teams would enrich the common project by experience from their separate field sites. Each team would help to force the terminology and conceptualization of the project out of any local mold of assumptions into an overarching scheme, sufficiently general to apply to very disparate cultural types.

When it assembled in September, the group had been further strengthened by the addition of Jonathan Gross, computer scientist in the department of mathematics and statistics at Columbia University, and by collaboration from the Monell Center for Research in the Chemical Senses (see end of chapter note). Gross had been working in the summer on an overall design for comparison of food habits and social structure. This design was clearly going to demand from all the teams a much more exacting, closer collaboration than anyone had expected on entering the project. If they were to standardize the collection of data, they would have to argue energetically about concepts and terms. Furthermore, since the whole project was very experimental, they were asked to gather much more data than would have been necessary if a problem and method had been precisely determined in advance.

The general set of problems put to Gross for incorporation into the research design was about structure in food patterns. If a community is using food for affirming publicly the standard social categories that it knows and accepts, food will work as calendrical markers as well as social markers. Earlier research by Michael Nicod on food patterns in four English families had found an extraordinarily high degree of structure, corresponding to the time of the day and the day of the week or the festival season of the year (Douglas 1974, 1975, 1982; Douglas and Nicod 1974). Structure appears as the result of strict rules governing the presentation of food, the varieties permitted at a given occasion, and rules of precedence and combination. Such an elaborate structure clearly facilitates the expressive functions of food. Variations on the rules are used for discriminating fine meanings. In other societies, food may be less structured. One could say that in different cultures food may be more or less encumbered with social significance. For a fictional account of eating habits entirely free of standard meanings, read Toni Morrison's description of the three women who lived at the edge of the black community in her novel *Song of Solomon.* Their relatives considered that they ate like children:

> No meal was ever planned or balanced or served. Nor was there any gathering at the table. Pilate might bake hot bread and each one of them would eat it with butter whenever she felt like it. Or there might be grapes, left over from the winemaking, or peaches for days on end. If one of them bought a gallon of milk, they drank it until it was gone. If another got a half bushel of tomatoes or a dozen ears of corn, they ate them until they were gone, too. They ate what they had or came across or had a craving for. . . .

Their food carried no symbolism at all except its power to satisfy private and spontaneous whims. Being unencumbered with other meanings, their food was able to be totally unstructured; or one could say that so long as it remained unstructured it could not carry meanings. The food was part of a chosen life style. The grandmother, Pilate, could be a consummate chef if she cared.

Apart from menu changes, there is another way of using food to give meaning to an occasion: by changes in quantity. A feast would have to be more lavish than ordinary food and changes in volume could be a measure of perceived differences in importance. As soon as one starts to reflect, the difference between these two ways of conveying meaning suggests the possibility of their being incompatible.

An enormous quantity of food is expensive in prime costs. An enormously fine attention to intricate rule changing is expensive in time and thought since special varieties must be laid by, special sauces and accompaniments prepared. Possibly, one form of expression can be developed only at the expense of the other. The two extremes would appear as expressions of totally different cultural styles affecting much more than food. For example, according to Ruth Benedict's division of cultures (1934), in the Apollonian culture a rule-bound food presentation would unfold over long and orderly ceremonial sequences, sacralizing all the social institutions; in the Dionysian culture, dramatic changes in volume would appropriately express values of a culture that honored individual endurance in privation and exuberance in feasts. Not everyone can empathize with the Fijian culture of which Hocart (1916) reported legends of great eating contests: each side is bound to eat all that the other provides; it is a disgrace "that the report should go that they have been overwhelmed or weak in war or in exchanges, or in eating or drinking. It is better that they should die in battle than run away; it is better that they should be poor rather than that their contribution of stuff to the exchange should be small; it is better that their bellies should burst, and their stomachs be rent than that food and water should be left."

In the face of the wide range of cultural variation represented by the separate teams, discussions of how to research into the structuring of food provoked more ideas than this report can ever do justice to. The mathematician had a clear idea of structure; the anthropologists knew the limitations of their materials. Before the two approaches could be combined, there had to be agreement on how to choose and define the elements to be compared.

The anthropologists in the common project wanted to take nothing for granted. They could not countenance imposing on the materials a culture-bound concept of what the family is, who its members might be, what it does for them or what they do for it, or even whether the idea of a family unit was to be relevant at all. The same doubt applied to the vaguer notion of a household, the unit for which most national statistics of consumption are gathered. Conceivably the majority of eating functions might be limited to the interacting of one individual with coke and cake-vending machines; how badly the facts would be distorted if they were crammed into the conceptual pigeonhole of household consumption. A relentless pressure to widen the research categories came from knowing that what might apply to the American Indians might not work for the people in North Carolina, either as to identifying the social units or as to identifying elements in the structure of the food.

The research went to the heart of the well-known difficulties of cross-cultural comparison, even though all the subcultures were North American. It seemed reasonable to expect each team to be able to discover quite early in fieldwork what is the normal commensal unit, that is, whatever cluster of people normally consumes food together or apart. But the idea of consuming food together instantly became problematical: how much togetherness counts? Among certain homes in Tennessee, it was absolutely normal for each member to take his or her plate of food and to retire with it to continue whatever occupation he or she was engaged in; yet, it was prepared by one person, the mother, in one place, the kitchen. Could the definitional problem be solved by shifting from the idea of commensality to the notion of the kitchen? The researchers could each identify the place from which food was normally produced and trace the network of persons habitually fed from it. Such openmindedness seemed like very hard work for the field researcher, but was it worth it? After all, a kitchen is itself an imposed researcher's category. The Lakota like to eat certain berries on horseback after gathering them from bushes—where then is the kitchen? In anticipation of nearly insuperable problems of identifying a baseline, the focus shifted to the idea of the cook. After all, someone could be identified as responsible for the food in some decisive way that would be relevant to the interest in meanings and rules. Of course, the cook might not be the mother, nor be a member of the household, nor necessarily share in any normal commensal unit.

The concept of the "key kitchen person" eventually provided the most elementary unit on which the common projects could be based. The same kind of discussion had to be worked through for the concept of "meals." What is a "meal," after all? Does every folk taxonomy include the idea of a meal? What about "food varieties"? Most of these anticipated difficulties dissolved in the next stage of work. The Italian-American culture in Philadelphia and the Lakota culture in South Dakota were already very intimately known to the respective project directors. On request they quickly produced the local folk taxonomy of the calendrical ordering of big and little feasts, weekday and weekend arrangements for food. It turned out that the words "meal" and "feast" corresponded so closely to local usage that it began to seem pedantic to stick to "food event" or to put the word "meal" in quotation marks. Paradoxically, the North Carolina and the Tennessee subcultures were much less well known than the Native Americans and the Italian-Americans as to food habits. Consequently, they always presented more difficulties in the fieldwork. Alas, Edward Montgomery, for this reason, withdrew in the last lap, but not before providing fascinating glimpses of a much less structured pattern than the others. Tony Whitehead stayed on and his essay in this volume testifies to the methodological difficulties encountered.

To sum up this preminary stage of question, challenge, and counterchallenge, the clue to discovering differences in the structuring of food between subcultures came from lifting the eyes above the everyday and weekend sequences. Micro-analysis reveals micro-differences; for a larger scale of comparison, attention needs to be focused on larger features of the system. If Tony Whitehead had been able to attend and record what was provided at all the home-comings, pig-picking parties, and church lunches in his field area, he would certainly have been able to give a picture comparable to the analysis of grand and minor feasts in Philadelphia and South Dakota. But it was quite enough of a burden to establish the baseline of daily practice from which the feasts were departing. These are some of the concerns for faithfulness to data that are condensed in Gross's report in this volume. It will be easier to follow the organization of the research and to see how problems of comparison were met after introducing the use of the concept of complexity.

Culinary Complexity

The mathematical idea of complexity is the combination of variety with logical order. If we had simply tried to stay with that idea, we might have contrasted a very complex pattern of food taking with a rigidly rule-bound system having few and simple patterns, without ever touching the social and policy problems mentioned above. Gross's design directed the research to focus on complexity within the order of food insofar as it corresponds to the order of society. This focus would mean that a high degree of complexity was expected to show up when people's eating was committed heavily to celebrating a complex pattern of social categories. Food was studied only as a medium for registering information about social categories.

The application of this idea of complexity to culture avoids the main difficulty in comparing structuredness. All human behavior is structured; there may be no end to the number of rules being observed by every individual every instant of the day. Consequently, the research that tries to compare structured behavior has to define a baseline, a time span, and the size of the mesh being applied to behavior across the board. Otherwise the results will be biased by arbitrary incompleteness and spottiness in the analysis. Were the investigator to be equally assiduous and systematic in pursuing his quest for structure in all the units which he is comparing, he would find inexhaustible layers of structured behavior which would tell him nothing about cultural variations. Were he to be less thorough and less consistent, he would find differences in his results that would say nothing about the level of structuredness in the cultures being compared, because the results would merely reflect bias and inconsistency in the research.

The pitfalls of arbitrariness and inconsistency were avoided by establishing the local norm for everyday eating and by using it as the threshold from which variations were assessed. A culture that is obviously, visibly, highly structured would not score high marks for complexity if the structure consisted of "always" and "never" rules which never changed during the selected time span. There are hundreds and thousands of rules of deportment which apply at all times. The English gentleman who was supposed always to dress for dinner, even when alone in the jungle camp, would certainly follow other invariant rules. He would probably never wipe his nose on the tablecloth and never eat peas off a knife; he would always use a butter knife and always sit bolt upright at table, always take mustard with beef and never with mutton. However strictly rule-bound he might be, there is no complexity here in the sense in which this research came to apply that idea. "Always" and "never" rules are merely a part of the solid, bedrock mass of patterned behavior. Even if our jungle traveler varied his everyday diet by drinking one pink gin at midday and two whiskeys at sundown, that counts for structure that accords with the diurnal movements of the sun, but not for complexity. If on the Queen's birthday he took two pink gins and if he produced his cigars only when he had company, that would count toward complexity because these switch points are socially defined. If he had a clean napkin and an extra serving on Sundays, that would count, and any other variation that he made regularly in recognition of social demands. He might also be so isolated that he had no visitors and did not even know the date. Then he would have a low score for complexity, his highly structured everyday rules notwithstanding. Again, if he could make only irregular changes which varied his menu according to the luck of the hunt, but did not signify any social categories, he would score very low complexity indeed. However many millions of fixed daily prescriptions of behavior the research might reveal, because they are fixed for every day they would not qualify in the comparison of complexity.

Of course, there is no guarantee or prior assumption that food is necessarily everywhere the domain in which social events are publicly celebrated. The menu might remain at the same level through the seasons, while all sorts of different social events were being signaled with standard gifts of flowers or sung calypsos or memorial recitations of verse. Knowing that, it is still useful to assess how much alertness to the social scene could be found in the treatment of food. Social responsiveness might turn out to be connected with variety in the menu, itself a point that interests nutritionists. And again, social responsiveness in its several modes may create forms of hospitality that demand nonnutritious foods. The criterion of complexity was devised to serve the project directors' common interest in the social uses of food for creating social separation or social involvement. The researchers did not seek to understand the meanings that are conveyed by food; they sought clues only as to the sheer *quantity* of discriminated meanings that the food could carry. This may sound ambitious, but it is a much simpler task than trying to generalize as to what any particular item of food means. The task of interpretation is much more difficult than careful counting of the number of changes in food rules that respond to a preselected list of cues from the social world.

Counting and summing the number of responses sounds like a natural history approach to food, as one might count and sum the movements of chimpanzees. Although changes in behavior are the subject matter, the approach via complexity is not strictly behaviorist. It assumes that changes in the complexity of food are made consciously so as to constitute a system of signs. It assumes that conscious intention generates the changes in the physical medium, food, and that conscious persons are able to read off the meanings, whatever they may be. The shared consciousness defines a subculture. Any category of people belonging to the same subculture but not showing consciousness of its categories is either marginal or has no membership in it. This method is a start toward thinking of the strength of a culture's hold on the minds of its members. If the comparison shows that some subcultures hardly call forth any individual response to the sequence of public events, the method could be a contribution to assessing states of anomie. It is also a start toward thinking about cultural inclusion and social separateness.

Perhaps we should emphasize even more strongly that the approach through complexity is not hermeneutic, by insisting that it is not a method for supplementing ethnographic knowledge. Quite the contrary, the method cannot be used at all in the absence of very thorough ethnographic competence. This is apparent in the research design, for it assumes that the ethnographers know from the outset the calendrical and other ordering of food in the culture. All cultures operate in a temporal sequence and must have some minimal calendrical ordering. The idea of the calendar is a cross-cultural concept; upon a seasonal cycle each population punches out its own special anniversaries and commemorations. The ethnographers know what they are and can grade them into series by importance or can clump them into big divisions. Furthermore, an elaborately organized culture will have apportioned different kinds of calendrical events among social units of different orders of importance.

Among the Oglala (the major Lakota division studied by William and Marla Powers) each feast has a regular commensal unit associated with it. A combination of households are involved in low feasts; for certain low feasts, however, the whole community is included, while other feasts are intended for a district-wide attendance (parties and picnics associated with school graduation and homecoming, church events, and Western notions of patriotism and religion). One type of high feast concerns the extended household unit; another involves the whole local community; and another involves the whole tribe. This clear public structuring of food celebrations by the Oglala was not exactly matched by the Philadelphia Italian-Americans, for there the ethnographers had to make their own classification of high, middle, and low feasts according to number and rigidity of rules, length of preparation time, and other criteria. But here, also, a clear association emerged between a class of event and categories of kin and friends expected to attend. Whether the event is a Lakota curing ritual or powwow feast, or Catholic Easter or St. Francis Day, it is clear that the major and minor feasts can be characterized by their attendance, the required kinds of foods, and the deviations from everyday food. Similarly, among the North Carolina black Americans, a line is drawn around a church lunch or a party to thank neighbors for support, a line which fluctuatingly defines the different segments of the community. Analyzing complexity in food behavior depends upon good ethnography and does not replace it.

Many people assume intuitively that complexity mainly depends on the variety of materials available. On this assumption a rich household would show more complexity just because it could add more varieties to the menu than a poor household limited to a monotonous diet. If this were inevitably so, the research on complexity could stop at once. Its results would laboriously show differences that could be anticipated by ranking according to income. But complexity depends on pattern order as well as on variety, and the way it involves socioeconomic factors is indirect. If the rich household used six sauces every day, its food system would be no more complex than the poor household using one sauce. Throwing in extra items is not in itself as complex as extra interlocking of a few items with others to produce patterns of "if . . . then" entailments, which also lock into the outside world. There is no reason to suppose that the domestic unit with huge food resources necessarily organizes them in more complex patterns any more than the rich household will necessarily organize its use of large spaces more intricately than the caravan dweller. The concept of complexity is logically independent of economic determination. It has a special strength in cultural analysis wherever we are interested in measures of behavior that are independent of income or wealth.

To illustrate the way that complexity is independent of wealth, Gross gives a theoretical example.* Let us suppose that a certain wealthy man has access to the letters A, B, C, D, and E, while his

*The example is repeated from Douglas and Gross (1981), which was an early statement about work in progress on this research.

poor neighbor has access only to the letters A and B. If the rich man constructs the pattern

ABCDEABCDEABCDEABCDEABCDEABCDE

while the poor man constructs the pattern

ABAABBAAABBBABAABBAAABBB

one would conclude, after a careful examination, that the poor man has achieved a more complex pattern.

The concept of culinary complexity in itself is independent of economic determinants. It depends on individual decisions about how much complexity or logical structure is desirable; of course, those decisions, as we will see, are affected by costs and social needs. In this example the rich man repeats the motif ABCDE over and over again, while the poor man reiterates the motif ABAABBAAABBB. If we imagine a computer that would construct these two patterns, its program for the rich man would be as follows:

1 Print A
2 Print B
3 Print C
4 Print D
5 Print E
6 Go to rule 1

The program for the poor man would be this:

1 Print A
2 Print B
3 Print A
4 Print A
5 Print B
6 Print B
7 Print A
8 Print A
9 Print A
10 Print B
11 Print B
12 Print B
13 Go to rule 1

It is not difficult to prove that the given program for the rich man's pattern is as short as possible, six instructions. When we say the poor man's pattern is more complicated, we really mean that the shortest possible program to produce it is longer than six instructions. Even a novice programmer could reduce the length of the program for the poor man's pattern by using loops. However, it would take a significantly more advanced level of mathematical skills to prove that a program of length six or less could possibly produce the poor man's pattern—and this is what happens to be true. Sometimes a simple rule can easily explain an apparently complicated pattern, if one could only infer the rule. Proving that the solution to a problem has a minimum level of complexity is a standard situation, known to be quite difficult in theoretical computer science.

Although the length of the main motif is often important, it is not the determining factor in the minimum program length. Consider, for instance, a pattern in which the main motif is 300 A's, followed by one B. Despite its length of 300 letters, it has a very short program:

1   Do 300 times rule 2

2   Print A

3   Print B

4   Go back to rule 1

The fundamental characteristic of a complicated pattern is a long program of instructions. Thus, the motif of 300 A's and a B is not complicated, just sort of boring. A food specialty is not to count as complicated merely because of the preparation time or the cooking time. Stirring steadily is merely tedious, and lengthy cooking requires attention only to the stopping time.

Representing a meal pattern by a sequence of letters is no easy task, but it is not beyond the skill of a good ethnographer. For instance, Nicod had reported the following main motif for a particular segment of the British working-class dietary system mentioned above:

ABCBCABBCABBCABBCABBCABBCAB

In this case, A = dinner, B = secondary meal, and C = tea and biscuits. On Sunday the submotif is ABC, and on each of the other six days it is BCAB. The entire pattern is produced by the following quite complex program:

> 1 Print A
>
> 2 Print B
>
> 3 Print C
>
> 4 Do 6 times rules 5 to 8
>
> 5 Print B
>
> 6 Print C
>
> 7 Print A
>
> 8 Print B
>
> 9 Go to rule 1

The Parallel with Linguistic Structures

Jonathan Gross designed his program in all innocence of linguistic analysis. Because he adapted Kolmogorov's informational theoretic approach to the problem in hand, he came out with something close to grammatical theory, which has a common origin—compare his method with the late Roland Barthes' *Le Système de la mode* (1967).*
In this book, Barthes used the analysis of a fashion magazine to give an account of nonverbal meaning by linguistic methods. The first difference between Barthes' method and the idea of complexity is that complexity does not relate behavior to speech. It is not intended for translating one medium into another. This might suggest that most of the questions resolved by Barthes would be irrelevant, but they are illuminating.

Barthes took up de Saussure's distinction between language—a massive, abstract, institutionalized aspect of speaking—and speech itself, a momentary and particular element drawn from language. By a large analogy, he could treat fashion, insofar as it deals with dress, as corresponding to language. Fashion is a vast, institutional-

---

*See also Marshall Sahlins' "Western Society as Culture," in *Culture and Practical Reason* (1976).

ized, abstract set of concepts; the term "clothing," by contrast, can be used for the individualized physical form of clothing actually worn, corresponding to acts of speech. In the fashion journal two distinct classes of interconnected and interacting statements emerge at once: the clothing described and the circumstances in which the clothing will be worn (for example, weekend, sport, office) or personality features (for example, features of the garment which declare it to be young or amusing). Barthes called this referent the "world" and found that fashion speech continually relates the clothing to the world: for a summer evening, muslin or taffeta; this sweater for town or country; for the city, dark colors, with touches of white.

The words "clothing" in the abstract and "world" in the abstract are never referred to as such in the fashion journal. These words are part of a meta-language Barthes had to produce for the requirements of his analysis. However, fashion is continually referred to, explicitly or implicitly. Fashion is the abstract concept which stands for an articulated set of principles about how the clothing system is supposed to relate to the world system. The speech of fashion refers to particular cases of this articulated relationship, but fashion itself stays as a background concept which can merely assert, "yes, that is the fashion" or "no, it is not the fashion."

The idea of information complexity as developed here by Gross also focuses upon the continual mutual reference of food and the world. Complexity traces a relation between particular instances of food-related behavior and the idea of the world, such that a change in the one is accompanied by a change in the other. All cultural analysis is faced with the problem of defining discrete domains of behavior. Any such domain that can be reasonably selected for comparison owes its discreteness to an immense pool of abstract ideas about an articulated system of relations that ought to hold between behavior in that domain (say food or clothing) and events in the world. So where do the events in the world come from? The world gets its elements and their discrete boundaries from the same intellectual activity that creates cultural categories such as luncheon, garden parties, and barbecues. Some meta-language concept, such as culture, custom or etiquette, comprises all these expected and approved articulated relationships between a medium and the world of events and personalities.

Every anthropologist knows that there is no obvious limit to structuredness. The analysis unguarded can easily slide from a wide mesh to finer meshes, to even finer ones. The analyst can self-indulgently pick out elements which seem to illustrate his favorite theory. Depths of structured behavior can go on for worlds without end. By taking account only of variations in one domain which manifest or correspond to variations in another, Barthes showed how to isolate a domain.

Choosing the fashion journal, Barthes had to distinguish between levels of writing about clothing: writing about fashion's judgment about clothing's response to the world's events (prints triumph at the races, pleats are right for the afternoon, city dress needs touches of white) is different from writing about the technology of producing the appropriate clothing. He warns against jumping from one level to another. If there is a clothing group which comprises hoods, toques, berets, turbans, and bonnets, the system of correspondences between fashion this year and fashion last year shows that what makes the toque the right item this year is just that it is not a bonnet or hood or beret. No one who knows gloves supposes that they can substitute for boots or collars. He expected that the variation and substitutions in themselves indicate natural groupings. Be careful, he says, not to be distracted by elements in the description which refer to the materials or process of manufacture; keep the levels clear. This is a task which he took more lightly than we can in our work on food. He writes as if the principles of transformation would automatically give him his groupings, without prior outside knowledge. Evidently, his easy recognition of fashion-meaningful elements is underpinned by a set of culturally given pseudo-natural categories which he, as a member of the culture, already knew. For example, he had been trained in his own culture to be aware of the difference between headgear and neckwear. The cross-cultural exercise is harder. An archeologist retrieving objects from an ancient tomb might easily confuse a diamond tiara with a diamond necklace or belt or anklet. Barthes is so confident about the decision as to what may be used for the hands, the feet, and the waist that he gives no clues as to how it is to be made. Because he stayed within one culture, he never had to practice the total openness to what the constituent elements of a system might be. This is a weakness in Barthes' thinking. He never anticipated the cross-cultural problem of how to recognize and control imported ethnocentric prejudice.

The crucial matter in cultural analysis is how to identify meaningful contexts and meaningful units of behavior. Barthes let his fashion journal do the first and he thought his method looked after the second (though he has actually drawn upon his culturally informed judgment here). This was right since his main intention was to show that linguistic-type analysis could be done. He was not aiming to develop a tool of inquiry into social problems. His objective was completely met when he had demonstrated the relation of different levels of meaning in one limited domain without trying to compare one set of responses with another. If food was little more than a medium of communication, like fashion, it would be less urgent to attempt comparison between cultures. But food sustains life, so the linguistic model does not go far enough.

Investigating complexity starts with selecting a class of behavior which makes regular responses to changes in the world. Our task is to select the interacting systems we wish to deal with and to specify precisely the elements that will throw light on the questions we have in mind. One of these questions has to do with ethnicity, the use of food to signal ethnic differences. Another has to do with hospitality, the changes in the social register. It is sufficient to start by observing three systems: a calendar, a social register, and a food system, each invested with an infinity of social meanings. All have reference to what Barthes called the world. The changes in the calendrical system are made physically manifest in many ways, and especially by food and a changing social presence.

Ethnic Food

Isolated food items in themselves do not make an ethnic diet; the ethnically distinctive aspect is in the patterning of a whole cycle of combinations (see the study by Goode et al.); for another, new food materials can be nativized and then perceived as ethnic. Some of our friends have scoffed at our terminology: food system sounds pedantic and pretentious. But it is precisely the concept that is needed for thinking about ethnic food. If there is a system at all, it has a regular pattern. Changes in one part relate to changes in the others.

Unless there are distinctive patterns, the food habits of immigrants cannot be compared with those of the host population once they have come to share the same resources. A count of what foods each group chooses to eat conceals the real distinctive element. Judith Goode and her associates have succeeded in moving the weight of attention away from individual items of food to series of menus. To develop their observations, they needed to coin another term, the meal format, which is a named, standardized pattern of dishes and food items. Naming the format in the course of discussing a proposed menu references a whole restrictive pattern of combinations. Menu negotiation is the essential process by which a commensal unit shifts its habits from one cultural pattern to a new one. The strong patterning which they uncovered in the Maryton minority group appears through long cycles in which a series of Italianate meal forms alternate with American ones, under the names of "gravy" (one-pot), and platter meals, respectively. A 1935 study of the diet of a group of Italian-American families in New Haven, Connecticut, showed a tightly structured menu cycle in which the two parts of the Sunday dinner were the basis for alternating meal formats for the two meals in the daily cycle of week days: one platter, one gravy each day. A clear pattern of alternation between the same formats nearly fifty years later is still recognizable in the menu cycle in contemporary Maryton, except that instead of alternating within the day, the same rule of alternation holds between days. Here is evidence of cultural continuity that would never have been picked up without the focus on patterning.

Menu negotiation starts from ideal expectations of what the food on a particular occasion should be like—for example, how much variation it should use to respond to social cues. The cultural ideal has to be accommodated to the realities of budget and work constraints and other limitations. Sometimes a message of strong ethnic traditions is to be conveyed, sometimes not. The Maryton case histories show the pull of different social networks upon families engaged in deciding on menus. It would seem that the survival of an ethnic food system depends on some degree of social segregation of the ethnic minority. Pressure to join the leisures and to interdine and intermarry with the host community shows in the process of menu negotiation as pressure to conform to host community meal formats. Ethnic difference in food seems to be fading out in some places, though much less speedily than Judith Goode's predecessors could have detected without her methodological focus on pattern. Where ethnic identity is a vital issue, ethnic foods are revived, new items are recruited to the old tradition, and some distinctive pattern is established.

In their essay on the place of food in Lakota culture, William and

29

Marla Powers show how ethnic awareness is as alive as ever and is expressed in food categories all the more now that other forms of ethnic antagonism are restricted. The Oglala, confined to the reservation, were forced to revise their diet drastically, but they did not lose the old food categories. New foods were first rejected; pork and beef revolted them, but eventually these foods were nativized and absorbed into the old category system. Cattle had to be hunted with bow and arrows or rifle, then skinned and butchered as if they were buffalo, before they could accept that beef was edible at all. Coffee was analogical to traditional, bitter-tasting medicine; bags of granulated sugar were analogical to maple sap. So it became possible within the space of ten years to eat the new food, give it native names, and even to count it as Indian food, contrasted with the concept of white food. As Indian ethnic distinctiveness became more and more an open political issue, so the distinction between Indian foods and white foods became more important. Changing the actual physical materials of food has little to do with eating ethnically.

The sum of this research is that distinctive ethnic diets disappear at the same time as the other ethnic boundaries disappear. Ethnic food is a cultural category, not a material thing. It can persist over fundamental material changes so long as the feeling of ethnic distinctness is valued. Food is a field of action. It is a medium in which other levels of categorization become manifest. It does not lead or follow, but it squarely belongs to whatever action there is. Food choices support political alignments and social opportunities. The concept of individual economic rationality is much too narrowly applied to such issues, as if food could be segregated from the major concerns of a person and as if these major concerns were not social.

Social Involvement

The research into complexity described in Gross's report suggests a method for assessing social involvement. To appreciate his results one has to recognize the hazards of analyzing information collected from observed behavior. The units of information have to be well defined and the structure of their relation to the research has to be clearly conceived before an analysis can even be set up. Several of the questions that had seemed interesting to pursue at the outset had to be abandoned because of prohibitive difficulties or incompleteness in collecting the material. The object of Gross's research was to show that formal models from information theory could be applied to culture. His essay explains how commensal units in the different communities were ranked according to how they used the selected submedia for transmitting information. The results, which we had not necessarily expected to find, showed that each household's ranking was consistent across the various submedia. Conceivably, a household that conveyed a lot of social information through the food varieties might not make significant differences for food equipment or duration of the meal. But one social unit within the Italian-American community scored more for information in all these submedia, and the same was true within the North Carolina and South Dakota communities. The social unit scoring top rank for information tended to operate a more active network in the Italian-American community or to be more alert to the political implications of maintaining Indian traditions in the Oglala community. This means that something else is going on when certain social units in a community are using the material arrangements of their lives to signal more complex cultural information.

The consistency of information rank within a household and differences among households suggest an index of cultural and social involvement. Would an old-age pensioner living entirely alone go to the trouble necessary for recognizing calendrical celebrations, even in a modest way? Do not bereaved persons show their withdrawal in grief by reducing complexity in their food and other cultural media? Some households involve themselves energetically in maintaining cultural ideas and values and developing new ones, but others are less concerned. Could it be because they lack a sense of belonging? Have they chosen or have they been allotted a peripheral place in the community life? One might surmise that if two families in one community, both at the same low level of income, ranked very differently in complexity of information in their food, this ranking would predict which of the families was likely to suffer economic failure, since low complexity would signify fewer and weaker social networks and more trouble in raising credit when needed.

The idea that low cultural complexity goes with low levels of social involvement is shown to be too simple by research contributed by Tony Whitehead to this volume. Recall that the whole research was organized from the start to recognize the locally relevant units of food sharing. In the southern community that Whitehead calls Bakersfield, the church has to be treated as the significant center for distributing food. This appears only when we change the focus from household kitchens where food is cooked and go beyond the everyday provision of food to take account of the many church festivities to which every effective parishioner contributed. These community-wide celebrations linked each parish to others sharing the same liturgical and social calendar. At that level, we find strong social involvement of members with each other. Contributing food to church occasions creates safety nets that protect the smaller family units from some of the disasters that afflicted them. Bakersfield shows low complexity and high social involvement, whereas in Maryton and South Dakota high complexity goes with being more deeply involved in community affairs. To make sense of this we look again at the festivities. In Bakersfield and in Philadelphia two quite different systems of hospitality emerge.

Information score is inherently a cross-cultural concept. To be able to rank the scores between communities, the research design should have included codings for all feasts, weddings, graduation ceremonies, July 4th picnics, and so on, right through each community through a year. But for the public celebrations and big feasts, the background of general knowledge about the standard festivities was supplemented only by truncated series and irregular observations.* Scanning the three reports in this volume, it does seem that the Oglala with their strictly prescribed ritual foods might compare with the Italian-Americans in complexity. Obviously, the Oglala use of ritual food speaks worlds about their solidarity and historic traditions, low regard for mixed-blood Indians, and utter rejection of white values. The Italian-Americans are speaking to each other about revered origins, church affiliation, and assimilation. While the North Carolina community would probably rank lower than either in the amount of precise information about the calendar and the social world that

---

*Official information about nutritional status is usually related to the socioeconomic categories of income, household size, occupation. Food on Sundays and feast days is often deliberately screened out of official record-taking. But feasts and the prevailing patterns of hospitality make a major difference to diet. Standard consumption research which does not include eating at feasts reifies highly artificial patterns of consumption.

could be read off from their food and its appurtenances, it does not signify less social involvement or community solidarity.

When a Bakersfield woman renowned as a skilled cook regularly delivers her most famous dish to the church lunches, she is building up the hospitality system we can call inclusive. It contrasts with the type of hospitality we call selective. For example, the list of who gets invited to a particular type of feast in the Italian-American community is selected from what anthropologists call ego-focused categories: kin, workmates, and neighbors are selected for their closeness to a particular person among the hosts. The guest list for Oglala and North Carolina feasts is not ego-focused so much as territorial and church-based: all the people who live in this district or all the people who worship here. Through inclusive hospitality, community solidarity is both demonstrated and actualized. When disaster hits a family in Bakersfield, the same inclusive guest list for the feast days shows who will rally round and keep the stricken family afloat. The contrast between selective and inclusive hospitality bears directly upon our interest in principles of exclusion in food distribution.

There may well be a negative connection between complexity of information and inclusive principles of hospitality. Regularly inviting the whole district or all the worshippers would impose difficulties of organization if there were strict rules about what is to be eaten, in what order, with what accompanying garnish. The easiest format is the potluck to which each guest contributes, and in which quantity tends to be the dominant concern. The same is true of the domestic unit that tries to keep open house: complexity tends to be exchanged for quantity and the keeping properties of foods. So we reach the heart of the nutritionists' problems. For people of low income, in precarious employment, to use their budgets so that smaller quantities of better quality food are allotted to each person in the household unit is quite inimical to a program of membership in a needy group practicing inclusive hospitality. To be honorably acquitted in such a group, no persons should draw in their network of reciprocal aid or communal food sharing. Nor would it work in one's own self-interest to do so. As Tony Whitehead (1978), with others, has argued, spreading consumption by wide links of reciprocity is a strategy for survival in economically marginal units. If children are expected to go from house to house, to pick up a meal when their own home kitchen is not functioning, the menus will be adapted to an unpredictable attendance list and nutritional values will take second place to filling hungry mouths on flexible demand.

Having identified two quite different patterns of hospitality, the first ideas about the relation between complexity and social involvement need to be elaborated further. Where a selective pattern of hospitality prevails, some social categories may be systematically dropped off the round of exchange. In that case relatively low complexity scores will surely indicate low social involvement. The ranking on information will point to the vulnerably isolated elements in the population. But where an inclusive pattern prevails, low complexity means something quite different: not that individuals are suffering from rejection or isolation from the more competitive and successful among their own kin and community, but that whole communities are excluded from some social competition whose rewards are greatly enticing other segments of the population.

Complexity in the food system needs to be related to social and economic conditions. Table 1.1 compares an inclusive hospitality system with a selective one; the economic status of individual kitchen units within each community is taken to be much the same. Differences of economic status between the communities are irrelevant for the moment. The significant difference is the last column. In case A the kitchen units that are engaged in selective reciprocal hospitality all enjoy sufficient economic independence to be able to issue the expected invitations on the recognized occasions and to produce the standard celebratory food for each kind of feast. Under such an assumption, everyone gets left off some invitation lists, but no one gets left off more than anyone else and the hospitality cycles round the prescribed channels of reciprocity. The culinary complexity, as well as social involvement, is likely to be at a very high level.

TABLE 1

Forms of Hospitality and Social Involvement			
	Complexity	*Social Involvement*	*Economic Independence*
Hospitality			
Selective A	+	+	+
Selective B	−	−	+
Selective C	+	−	+
Hospitality			
Inclusive	−	+	−

We can contrast this imagined case with one (not on the table) in which the system of marriage and social promotion is very competitive. Then the selectivity in the hospitality system will be an active principle for redefining boundaries according to local criteria of social success; the interest in gastronomic competence will be competitive, standards of hospitality and of complexity will go up; because of the rising costs of competitive high cuisine, the constituent kitchen units will not all be equally able to afford to belong to the circle of hospitality and some will drop out.

The first result for the dropouts will be case B. For the time being, economic independence is assured at the cost of cultural complexity and social involvement, but whether they can keep their economic independence, having withdrawn from the system of marriage and social promotion, is dubious. An example of case C would be the British families studied by Nicod in the early 1970s when unemployment was low, job security high, pensions and medical care assured by the national welfare system. Enjoying the occasional company of kin and friends but not all relying on their aid* their clearly structured menus of three daily meals with complex variation over the seven days of the week and the twelve months of the year reflected the stable self-sufficiency of these workers' lives. The inclusive system of hospitality contrasts with all of these three; the units are not economically secure or independent, they reduce complexity in favor of solidarity and share their last crust together.

Among these four types, the people who are least likely to pay attention to the nutritionist are those who cannot afford *not* to keep up a large network of reciprocal exchanges—that is, those who score high for social involvement—whether of the competitive selective kind involving smoked salmon and grouse in due order and due season or of the inclusive kind of potluck at the church lunch.

If we are right in suggesting that the incidence of hunger can be traced along these lines of solidarity and competition, we have justified drawing attention to food habits and food distribution. For however much production is increased, the extra food will not make hunger and malnutrition disappear. When social competition governs the patterns of hospitality, there will always be food abuse. The satirists are right who show food tastes being shamelessly trained by so-

---

*Goldthorpe and Lockwood (1971). This gives an example of family behavior that is clearly dissociated from the wider kinship of neighborhood networks.

cial competition. But the blame does not lie narrowly on the institutions of modern industrial society. It is dangerous to ignore the fact that uncertainty combined with competitiveness and rapid change always give a ruthless twist to selective patterns of hospitality.

The social critic does not want to be heard deploring out of one side of his mouth the consequences of social choices which he recommends out of the other side, or of choices which he makes in his own life. To be more effective in our good intentions toward the hungry we need to stop thinking of food as something that people desire and use apart from social relations. The idea of separate physical needs can be demythologized. Then we can stop wondering in amazement how hunger arises in the midst of plenty. We know enough about what happens to focus our concern on the stability and continuity of social relations. It is disingenuous to pretend that food is not one of the media of social exclusion.

Note

This is the place to acknowledge the collaboration with the Russell Sage Foundation Project on Food Patterns enjoyed, through Dr. Morley R. Kare, director of the Monell Chemical Senses Center, with Dr. Gary K. Beauchamp and Dr. Mary Bertino. This center is splendidly equipped to maintain a unique record in pioneering investigation of perception through the chemical senses. While organizing the joint research which is reported in this volume, it seemed a pity to neglect altogether the question of sensory preference for foods. The established approaches generally ignore the cultural influence, known to be so important in humans.

While major aspects of the sensory response to foods are established by the biology of the organism in humans, individual experience often plays a crucial role. For example, different cultural groups obviously define quite differently what is an acceptable or a highly palatable food. At a different level, sensory distinctions within a type of food may depend on the role that food has within a specific cultural group. Among people who prize potatoes, for example, small differences in flavor may be significant and the sensory responses may be alerted to subtle differences unnoticed by individuals with less interest in potatoes. Thus, Dr. Beauchamp proposed to evaluate different groups of people, with different food habits and experience, for the sensory responses to foods varying in chemosensory characteristics.

Several aspects of this project particularly attracted the investigators at the Monell Center. They hoped to find standardized cultural influences by working with ethnographers; they looked forward to investigating fine variations in the flavor (odors and tastes) of real foods rather than working exclusively with standard salt and sugar taste solutions; they expected that the measures of complexity in food habits would provide an index of informal training of the palate, which would be manifested in differential response to variations in flavor. Those hopes proved too ambitious.

Attention turned to a new ploy—developing a questionnaire which would show the complexity and strictness of culinary standards applied in the home, to use in conjunction with more conventional taste tests. Would a palate trained at home to distinguish minute differences in cooked greens or tomato sauce be quicker to distinguish differences in concentration of salt and sugar solutions? Is the trained palate like a trained musical ear or is that training specific to each kind of taste? After much hard work at all stages of the project, the team found that the general complexity of culinary standards, as determined from the questionnaire, was unrelated to any of the taste variables which were measured. It found that training in taste perception is very specific.

Because these results were tangential to the main direction of the project, no special report was included in this volume. However, the Monell investigators continued to investigate the role that cultural differences may have in determining sensory responses to foods.

Bibliography

Barthes, R. *Le Système de la mode.* Paris: Seuil, 1967.

Beattie, J. *Other Cultures, Aims, Methods and Achievements in Social Anthropology.* London: Cohen and West, 1964.

Benedict, R. *Patterns of Culture.* Boston: Houghton Mifflin, 1961.

Bourdieu, P. *La Distinction, critique social du jugement.* Paris: Minuit, 1979.

Douglas, M. "Food as an Art

Form." *Studio International,* September 1974.

———. "The Sociology of Bread." In *Bread,* edited by A. Spicer. London: Applied Science Publishers, 1975. (Republished in *In The Active Voice.* London: Routledge & Kegan Paul, 1982.)

———. *The World of Goods: Towards an Anthropology of Consumption.* London: Allen Lane, 1978.

———. "The Effects of Modernization in Religious Change." *Daedalus* (Winter 1982): 1–19.

Douglas, M., and Gross, J. "Food and Culture: Measuring the Intricacy of Rule Systems." *Social Science Information* 20, (1981): 1–35.

Douglas, M., and Nicod, M. "Taking the Biscuit: The Structure of British Meals." *New Society* 30 (1974): 744–47.

Dumont, L. *Homo Aequalis, genèse et épanouissement de l'idéologie économique.* Paris: Gallimard, 1977.

Fishlow, A.; Dias-Alejandro, C.; Fagan, R. R.; and Hansen, R.D. *Rich and Poor Nations in the World Economy.* New York: McGraw-Hill, 1978.

Fried, C. *Anatomy of Value.* Cambridge, Mass: Harvard University Press, 1970.

Goldthorpe, J., and Lockwood, D. *The Affluent Worker in the Class Structure.* Cambridge: Cambridge University Press, 1971.

Harris, M. *Culture, Man and Nature: An Introduction to General Anthropology,* 2nd ed. New York: Crowell, 1975.

Hocart, A. M. "The Common Sense of Myth." *American Anthropologist* (N.S.1916): 307–18.

Jerome, N.; Kandel R.; and Pelto, G., eds. *Nutritional Anthropology: Contemporary Approaches to Diet and Culture.* Pleasantville, N.Y.: Redgrave, 1980.

Joffe, N. "Food Habits of Selected Sub-Cultures in the United States." In Mead (1943).

Leach, E. R. "Anthropological Aspects of Language: Animal Categories and Verbal Abuse." In *New Directions in the Study of Language,* edited by E. H. Lenneberg. Cambridge, Mass: M.I.T. Press, 1964.

Lévi-Strauss, C. *The Raw and the Cooked: Introduction to a Science of Mythology,* vol. 1. Translated by John and Doreen Weighman. Chicago: University of Chicago Press, 1969.

McBeath, A. *Experiments in Living.* New York: AMS Press, 1978.

Mead, M. *The Problem of Changing Food Habits. Report of the Committee on Food Habits, 1941–43.* National Research Council, Bulletin No. 108. Washington, D.C.: National Academy of Sciences, 1943.

———. *Food Habits Research: Problems of the 1960s.* Washington, D.C.: National Academy of Sciences, 1964.

———. *Manual for the Study of Food Habits. Report of the Committee on Food Habits.* National Research Council, Bulletin No. 111. Washington, D.C.: National Academy of Sciences, 1965.

Nicod, M. "A Method of Eliciting the Social Meaning of Food." Master's thesis, University College, London, 1974.

Pospisil, L. *Kapauku Papua Economy.* Reprints Series No. 67. New Haven: Yale University Press, 1972.

Richards, A. *Land, Labour and Diet in Northern Rhodesia.* New York: Oxford University Press, 1939.

Sahlins, M. "The Original Affluent

Society." In *Stone Age Econom-ics.* Chicago: Aldine, 1972.

———. "Food Preference and Taboo in American Domestic Animals." In *Culture and Practical Reason.* Chicago: University of Chicago Press, 1978.

Sen, A. *Poverty and Famine: An Essay on Entitlement and Deprivation.* New York: Oxford University Press, 1981.

Shack, W. *The Gurage: A People of Ensete Culture.* Oxford: Oxford University Press, 1966.

Vogt, E. Z. *Tortillas for the Gods, A Symbolic Analysis of Zinacanteco Rituals.* Cambridge, Mass.: Harvard University Press, 1976.

Whitehead, T. "Industrialization, Social Networks and Food Flow: Survival Techniques in a Jamaican Sugar Town." Paper presented at the Tenth International Congress of Anthropological and Ethnological Sciences, New Delhi, December 1978.

2

Metaphysical Aspects of an Oglala Food System

William K. Powers and Marla M. N. Powers

Introduction

The purpose of this essay is to examine the relationship between food and culture among the Oglala Sioux of the Pine Ridge reservation in southwestern South Dakota. Our focus is on traditional Indian foods, and, in particular, the special way in which the Oglala regard buffalo meat, dog meat, and *wasna*. These foods derive symbolic importance from the manner in which they are prepared and eaten in ceremonies such as the sun dance, memorial feast, and *Yuwipi,* a modern curing ritual.

We hope to show that perceived differences between Oglalas within their own social boundaries, as well as differences between Oglalas and Euro-Americans, are expressed through the conscious manipulation of foods. We argue that because the Oglala today believe that Indian culture is best expressed through religious precepts and public participation in the rituals, one of the strongest symbolic statements about Indianness is expressed through ritual foods. At an earlier time some of these ritual foods were considered to be quite ordinary, but today they have taken on a new meaning that conjures up what the Oglala believe to be accurate reflections of their traditional culture and history.

Metaphysical Aspects of an Oglala Food System

The present food system is very much a reflection of Oglala social organization, particularly noticeable in the manner that foods are distributed. A brief recapitulation of this organization is therefore useful. (For a longer historical and cultural account, see Hyde 1937, 1956; Olson 1965; Powers 1977).

The Oglala represent the largest of seven divisions of the sociopolitical unit known as Teton, or Western Sioux. The Teton itself is the largest of seven divisions known as the Seven Fireplaces *(Oceti Šakowin)* that originally formed a loose alliance in Minnesota before being forced onto the Plains by the Ojibwa and Cree, the latter of whom were first to receive trade rifles and ammunition from the French and British, and who thus overpowered their traditional Sioux enemies.

The Oglala along with their other Northern Plains neighbors are regarded by Indians and non-Indians alike as being typical of all Indians; the stereotypes include nomadic buffalo hunting, unsurpassed horsemanship, warbonnets, tipis—in short, the Indian of buffalo-nickel fame. In tourist areas like the Southwest, even Pueblos are likely to dress up like "Sioux" in order to be unmistakenly identified by non-Indians as Indian. This popularity of the Plains Indian image, which, in fact, the Oglala do represent, has arisen out of a long historical relationship between the Sioux at large and the federal government, a relationship that has been in the past—and continues to be—strained.

For example, the Oglala were active along with other Teton in the famous Indian Wars of the West, culminating in the signing of the 1868 Fort Laramie Treaty, which marked the only time in the United States history that an Indian tribe was victorious. More spectacular was the involvement of the Sioux in annihilating George Armstrong Custer and most of the Seventh Cavalry at the Little Big Horn River. The Oglala became the subject of newspaper headlines again as the victims of an infamous massacre that took place on December 27, 1890, near a small creek on the Pine Ridge reservation called Wounded Knee.

And the Pine Ridge drama continues to unfold. Most recently the Oglala along with other Lakota* have been featured in the press with respect to the tribe's ongoing land dispute with the federal government. Of particular importance today is the status of the mineral-rich

---

*Lakota refers to both the native language and the political division more commonly known as Teton of which the Oglala are a part.

Black Hills which lie 80 miles northwest of Pine Ridge. The Hills were taken away from the Sioux in abrogation of their Fort Laramie Treaty, then returned. Although the Sioux still technically own them, a fact attested to by the United States government, they refuse to accept over 100 million dollars being offered to them by the government, and instead are opting for non-Indian encroachers to pay to the Sioux people "back rent" on the land, and also to give the Sioux jurisdiction over the various public lands which were taken away from the Sioux mainly by the National Park Service as a result of the Allotment Act in 1887.

It is unfortunate that the Oglala are so well known because of their "warlike" qualities. Even today little attention is paid by anthropologists, historians, or the press to the majority of 20,000 Oglala (and other Lakota-speakers) who are disassociated from the political and economic upheavals that so often characterize the state of the reservation to outsiders.

The Oglala perceive themselves to be and are perceived by others (both Indians and non-Indians) to be different. Part of this difference is achieved and maintained though a number of sacred and secular rituals that become the social basis for food sharing. There are perhaps no (or at least very few) peoples of the world who do not augment their social events with food. But what makes each social group different is their selection of foods to highlight the nature of the event: Christmas, Easter, sun dance, or powwow. At the same time special foods underscore the fact that the particular ceremony is pertinent to them and not others. Special kinds of ritual foods are prepared and eaten by the congregation in a way that serves as a symbolic statement about their sense of identity.

Most Oglala food events take place in small communities where almost everyone is related. We suggest that degrees of relatedness (or nonrelatedness) have some effect on the nature of each event and that the manner in which people prepare, distribute, and consume food is dependent on these kinship factors. We have found, and this is one of our major considerations, that the number of people who attend events and the manner in which they are related will partly predict the kinds of foods that will be served, how they will be prepared and distributed, and how the leftovers will be disposed of.

These kin groups and communities have come into being because of historical factors that placed the Oglala on the Pine Ridge reservation after the Treaty of 1868. The treaty was again drastically augmented by the Indian Allotment Act of 1887, which divided the Great Sioux Reservation into land in severalty. Furthermore, the reservation was divided, for administrative purposes related to the distribution of food annuities promised to the Oglala, into seven (then later eight) "districts." These were ration districts supervised by a "boss farmer," a non-Indian agricultural specialist. The Oglala's seven *tiyošpayes* (bands) settled on each of these districts; but as the population grew, the original *tiyošpayes* subdivided into smaller communities, called *oti*.*

Although some events involve the entire reservation or each of its districts, most events take place at the level of the community. These events include all feasts and "dinners" related to births, baptisms, school graduations, farewells, wakes and funerals, and memorial feasts for the deceased. At this level, particularly if the feasts are part of a religious ritual, the foods most frequently prepared are traditional foods.

Food and Religion

Oglalas distinguish traditional Indian from Euro-American culture partly (some Indians would say entirely) on religious grounds (Powers 1977). Young and old traditionalists regard Lakota culture as synonymous with religious culture. To be Indian, then, is to be a religious Indian, which requires participation in the public rituals as well as the private ones. The reason is that since the conquest by the federal government, the traditional political system under the leadership of "chiefs" and councils and traditional economics, mainly buffalo hunting, have succumbed to the dominant society, rendering the Oglala dependent on Euro-American forms of politics and economics. In the religious sphere, however, Christianity has not been as successful as its secular counterparts in spreading its dominion. Despite the presence of Christian denominations and ubiquitous churches, traditional Lakota religion continues to play an important part in the lives of the Pine Ridge people.

---

*Both *tiyošpaye* and *oti* are derived from the Lakota root *ti* (to dwell). The common term for dwelling *tipi* is also derived from this root.

We regard this form of native religion as one that has continued throughout the reservation period. At times, this religion has faced prohibition by the federal government. For example the sun dance and the ghost-keeping ceremonies were prohibited in the 1880s in an attempt to "civilize" the hostile Indians. In most instances the rituals continued surreptitiously.

In the past twenty-five years, a great resurgence of interest in traditional religion has been shown by those in their late teens and early twenties. This is partly owing to a reduction of religious restrictions by the federal government; also, traditional religion provided its adherents not only with a sense of spirituality, but with a sense of cultural identity, one perceived to be entirely distinct from that of the larger white society that engulfs the reservation.

Traditional religion contrasts with Christianity and can best be described as a belief in (1) the sacred pipe made with a catlinite bowl, a red stone perceived to be formed by the blood of the Lakota's antecedents when they died in a primal flood; (2) the cosmology, the most important aspect of which today is the creation story in which the Lakota emerged from a preexisting subterranean culture; (3) the rituals that were brought to the Lakota by the sacred white buffalo calf woman *(Ptehincalasanwin)* at a time when famine had swept over them. These seven sacred rites *(wichŏ 'an wakan šakowin)* are composed of the sweat lodge *(oinikagapi),* vision quest *(hanbleceya),* ghost-keeping *(wicanagi wicagluhapi),* making of relatives *(hunka),* sun dance *(wiwayang wacipi),* female puberty ceremony *(išnati awicalowanpi),* and ball game *(tapa wankayeyapi).* Of these seven rituals, it is clear that the sweat lodge, vision quest, and sun dance have continued intact, albeit modified, over the reservation period. The ghost-keeping ritual is still observed by some families, but it is now an integral part of the memorial feast, held within a year after a person has died. The *Hunka* had all but disappeared as a ritual by the 1930s but was revived again in the early 1970s (the first one we witnessed was in 1974). There is some possibility that the female puberty ceremony, also known as the white buffalo ceremony, will be revived, as well as the throwing of the ball ceremony, both of which have been defunct since the 1930s.

All the rituals that persist are underscored by a number of customs comprising special prayers, songs, recitations of the moral code, dancing, and sometimes special costumes and other accouterments. Of particular importance to our research is the fact that highly

44

charged symbols of traditional religion are loaded onto the food system.

We assume that every food system (like any system) comprises a number of components, all of which interrelate in such a way that any alteration of one component of the system affects other components. The number of components in a food system requires an operational definition because, depending on one's research interests, the components are likely to change. Many nutritionists and anthropologists focus exclusively on consumption of food, but we identify five components which reflect an idealized procedural model.

1. *Procurement* is the manner in which people select and collect their food stuffs, whether from their own garden, by hunting and gathering, or from the supermarket; it depends on a whole host of ecological and technological factors as well as strategies and techniques, which should be treated as components of the total food system, but which we do not treat in our present study.

2. *Preparation* is the manner in which people modify or maintain the natural state of their foods before serving and consuming them. Here the gamut runs from the raw to the cooked. The study of preparation also includes palatal preferences; symbolic statements about status; and technological considerations such as utensils, nature of the "kitchen" (or place where food is prepared), techniques, and selected varieties of foods.

3. *Distribution* is the procedure for getting food from its time and place of preparation to its time and place of consumption (unless, of course, people are picking foods off vines and consuming them on the spot, in which case the distribution and consumption components are identical). We are particularly interested in whether food is served by a host or whether people help themselves; whether people line up cafeteria style, selecting their own food from a common table, or sit in a circle and are served by a host. Trying to identify this component raises a number of issues, such as whether people sit at one table, on the ground, or at several tables—considerations obviously related to the other components, particularly consumption.

4. *Consumption* is the manner in which people eat—their physical behavior (whether they eat with their hands or with forks; whether they peel their own grapes or have a slave do it for them). This component also obviously includes the kinds of utensils used (if at all), and the nature

of the eating place and its setting, including functional as well as aesthetic components of the dining area. It also includes the times at which people prefer to eat.

5. *Disposal* is a component which for some people marks the end of a single food event. For others, it is a beginning. Whether people eat everything on their plate or whether more food is prepared than can be possibly eaten at one sitting is interesting to examine from the perspective of "leftovers." The question is not whether the contents of a doggy bag are really the master's late night snack, or Fido's, but why some people institutionalize surplus foods.

These five components are augmented by an array of rules, values, and meanings that are associated with food: for example, spiritual, social, economic, political. But we are more concerned with what can be called metaphysical aspects of the Oglala food system, aspects that are considered by the Oglala themselves to be a reflection of their traditional system of belief and ritual, albeit a changed one since the establishment of the reservation. Ritual foods are differentiated from others exclusively on the basis of their metaphysical aspects; there's a bit of the supernatural in each morsel.

In order to identify the metaphysical aspects we are partly guided by Wallace's "anatomy of religion" in which he poses the question: "How does one recognize a religion?" (Wallace 1966, p. 52). He provides us with the following answer:

It is the premise of every religion—and this premise is religion's defining characteristic—that souls, supernatural beings, and supernatural forces exist. Furthermore, there are minimal categories of behavior which, in the context of the *supernatural premise,* are always found in association with one another and which are the substance of religion itself. Although almost any behavior can be invested with a religious meaning, there seems to be a finite number—about thirteen—behavior categories most of which are, in any religious system, combined into a pattern that is conventionally assigned the title "religion."

Wallace's thirteen categories, which he acknowledges to be a "rough and ready classification" that may circumstantially require revision, includes (1) prayer; (2) music, including singing, dancing, and playing instruments; (3) physiological exercise; (4) exhortation; (5) reciting the code, including mythology, morality, and other aspects of the belief system; (6) simulation; (7) mana; (8) taboo; (9) feasts; (10) sacrifice; (11) congregation—processions, meetings, and convocation; (12) inspiration; and (13) symbolism.

Metaphysical Aspects of an Oglala Food System

In applying Wallace's guidelines to our own research we are aware that he regards "feasts" as an important religious category, and we, in somewhat the reverse, seek to understand how religious aspects are an important part of feasts. We find no contradiction inasmuch as all these categories are, as Wallace says, always in association with one another. Some foods, then, are part of a religious festival, but we are more concerned with foods (such as dog meat, buffalo meat, and *wasna)* that are capable of carrying a symbolic load both in and out of ritual context. Most importantly, we are interested in those foods which are seen as being necessary to the efficacy of the ritual. Stated another way, if the ritual food is absent, the ritual is seen to be inefficacious, or at least the absence of the proper food may partly explain why the ritual failed.

We believe that ritual foods are the most highly charged symbols of Oglala social and cultural identity both positively (they are irrefutably Indian) and negatively (they definitely are *not* Euro-American). This two-way approach helps to sharpen the ideological boundary between Indian and non-Oglala Indians, and even "mixed bloods" and "full bloods."

Foods have the capacity to stand as symbols of social groups and, among the Oglalas and other Lakota-speakers, even parts of the group. Foods and preparations, in fact, serve as a model for social organization of the entire Seven Fireplaces. At the highest level of sociopolitical organization, the term *oceti* (hearth, fireplace, stove) is translated as "nation" (or perhaps during an earlier period as "lineage"). Thus, the earliest allegiances of those social groups popularly known as "Sioux" were to members of the same hearth or fireplace (rather than "council fire," as has been suggested by earlier writers, for example, Hyde 1937). The idea of confederations rallying around a single or multiple "fire" is common in many regions of native North America (Powers 1977, pp. 3–4).

The next level of organization is termed *oyate* (tribe) and is somewhat problematic. The *o* and *ya* signify the act of placing something in the mouth. There is a strong resemblance between *oyate* and the terms for eating, *wote* and *yute,* as well as the generic term for food, *woyute.* Given that other levels of Lakota organization are predicated on metaphors for food and food preparation, it is worth considering that this term is similar even though linguistic evidence is less firm.

Ošpe is the word for piece or morsel and is an element found in *tiyošpaye* (band). *Tiyošpaye* signifies different kinds of people who dwell together as well as different species of animals that share a similar environment, for example, buffalo, antelope, and, say, prairie dogs. *Ošpaye* is the common word for flock or herd.

The radical element *han* (juice, liquid), which under some conditions changes to *he,* is found in a number of gastronomic terms, including *wohan* (a cooking); *Oohenunpa* (Two Boilings), the name of an *oyate* related to the Oglala; *wohanpi* (feast); *wahanpi* (soup); *canhanpi* (sugar, literally tree juice; that is, maple sugar); and any variety of fruit juice, for example, *canpahanpi* (chokecherry juice). *Han (he)* is also found in *tiwahe* (family); *omahetun* (in-law, literally another cooking), and *owahecun* (kinship term).*

Dog as Ritual Food

The Oglala practice of eating dog on special occasions illustrates how every phase, from procurement to disposal, carries profound metaphysical meanings.

Although dog may be man's best friend, the relationship is not entirely reciprocal. Archeologists and prehistorians tell us that over the past 10,000 years of canine domestication humans have depended a great deal on the dog as hunter, herder, beast of burden, and source of food, particularly when other food supplies are scarce. Although today people generally believe that dogs depend on humans, over the long evolutionary periods in which humans and dogs evolved in a somewhat skewed symbiotic relationship, it is probably equally valid to say that humans have depended on dogs. In historic times we have acknowledged the special status of dogs—a privileged one afforded to the first natural animals permitted to share their lives with the first cultural ones. In the past, societies have erected shrines

---

*Let a few more examples suffice to show how much the Oglala use food metaphors for social relations. Although the Oglala terminologically differentiate between males and females by employing the adjectives *bloka* and *win,* respectively, to humans and animals, three species require special terms for sexual distinction. These three species are regarded as the "oldest" animals hunted by the Oglala: buffalo *(tatanka,* bull; *pte,* cow); deer *(tahca,* buck, *tawinyela,* doe); and elk *(hehaka,* bull; *unpan,* cow). They also represent symbols of sexuality, and parts of these animals are often used as love potions. Additionally, verbal abuse and vulgarisms, as Leach (1964) has noted, take the form of references to animal behavior; for example, *wiiyuhaya* (rape) is derived from *kiyuha* (the manner in which animals copulate).

to dogs, imitated them, and, most of all, anthropomorphized them, transforming these mediating creatures into what Lévi-Strauss terms "metonymical human being" (1966, p. 207).

In America, dogs have been humanized in a particular way: not only are they part of the family, but they are childlike. We force dependency upon them, and we stand, in a manner of speaking, as watchdogs over their humane rights. There are societies for the prevention of cruelty to them, veterinarians who cure them, and organizations that legislate against their abuse, abandonment, and vivisection. From the Western point of view, however, no matter how much humans exploit dogs, they do not eat them. This was not always the case. Early travelers ate dog, although not as a delicacy. Explorers Lewis and Clark, painter George Catlin, and writer Francis Parkman wrote that both the aroma of a stewing dog and its taste were respectable, although lacking the savor of venison. We are also informed that "the flesh of wolf dogs were relished by the employees of the Northwestern and Hudsons Bay Companies, who did not generally eat [dogs] of European descent" (Hodge 1907, p. 398). But today, in obeying our own totemic taboo, we are very different from the Oglala. For the Oglala, eating dog is not only a socially permissible culinary practice, but dog stew, its most common form of preparation, is considered a delicacy.

If we were to compare Euro-American attitudes and behaviors toward dog with those of the Oglala, we would find a great number of similarities, but some notable differences: among the Oglala there is no particular value placed on pure-bred dogs; the large majority of their canine population is made up of mongrels. In English, the Oglala often refer to their dogs as "Indian" dogs, and only a few relocated Oglala actually own pure-bred dogs and occasionally bring them home to the reservation, much to the amusement of their relations. As in Euro-American culture, dogs are considered to be a kind of human. Nevertheless, Oglala dogs are not childlike; they are adults. They are not house dogs: they spend their lives outdoors, even through the severest winters. They are not fed packaged dog foods and survive exclusively on table scraps and whatever they can scavenge from refuse heaps or steal from their dog neighbors.

The average Oglala owns more dogs than the average Euro-American, and six to ten are not uncommon. Dogs are considered useful for protecting one's house from the incursions of strangers, as well as for announcing the presence of friends, although frequently the behavior of the dogs indicates that they do not noticeably distinguish between the two. Like humans, dogs are imbued with a wide range of personalities, often reflecting those of their masters. For example, if horses have wandered from their pasture, the *vicious dogs* belonging to the *unfriendly neighbors* are often accused of being the culprits. Similarly, children are cautioned to beware of packs of wild, cavorting dogs that roam the towns at night. The Lakota expression *sungwapa* (dog barking) is a metaphor for any general commotion, including the place of a celebration where unattached dogs dart from one tent to the next begging for handouts. Anyone living on the reservation soon becomes accustomed to the fact that dogs bark all night long, and the reason for their nocturnal howling is frequently discussed the next morning since dogs not only herald the presence of humans, but that of ghosts as well.

Although veterinary medicine has reached the reservation, and a public health program succeeded in eradicating rabies some thirty years ago, dogs are not customarily treated by vets. Mad dogs and mean dogs, and those perceved to be terminally ill, are disposed of. Even a favorite pet who has lost a momentous battle to an itinerant porcupine and whose snout is irrevocably riddled with quills is not considered worthy of medical attention. Dogs who are losers in nature's battles, like the terminally ill, are removed from the social system: they are most frequently shot and dispatched to the local dump.

Aside from these differences, some of which are perceived by whites to be inhumane, the manner in which the Oglala classify their dogs is similar to the Euro-American's. They recognize the taxonomic relationship between the various members of the family *Canidae*. The dog *(šunka)* is kin to the wolf *(šungmanitu tanka,* large wild dog; or *šungmahetu,* underground dog), the coyote *(šungmanitu),* and the red fox *(šungila)*. When the Oglala first came in contact with the horse, they considered it a kind of dog, a sacred one *(šunkawakan)*. And they, along with anthropologists, recognize the similarities between humans and monkeys, calling the latter *šunka wicaša* (dog men).

The Oglala name their pet dogs much as the American, British, and French do. Some of the dogs we have known bear names which perhaps reflect the Oglala's sense of an expanding social universe, one inhabited by white men of various sorts. Although many dogs are still given Lakota names such at Mato (Bear), Pispiza (Prairie

Dog), Šunka (Dog), or Ite Hanska (Long Face), likening them to animal domains or peculiar physical attributes and behavior, others bear
such appellations, as Blackie, Butch, Sparky, Crawford, and Moho-
met, names similar to those chosen for whatever fanciful reasons by
their non-Indian neighbors.

For a dog to be given a name means much to its master and, one
might say from a humanitarian Western perspective, even more to
the dog, because named dogs are not eaten. Or put the Oglala way,
one simply does not name a dog that is likely to become a candidate
for the stewpot. This designation is made early in the dog's life, because the preferred eating dog is a small puppy, between seven and
ten weeks of age. An older dog is regarded as too tough and stringy
to chew.

The person who owns a named or unnamed dog that has managed
to survive to give birth to a litter achieves a certain status among
Oglalas, for eating dogs are always in demand for an important ritual.
Some Oglalas actually raise dogs for eating purposes, and the puppies
are often treated more like a herd than a litter.

In living out their lives, Oglala dogs are the ultimate symbol of
human frailty: they, like humans, existing in an unpredictable profane world, are *unšike* (pitiable). Historically, their lives have been
similar to those of humans; they have hunted and gathered precisely
the same foods that humans have; and they have been noted for their
sagacity and bravery, their ability to survive. Because of this similari-
ty, Oglalas in the past have deemed them worthy of imitation. For
example, Wissler reports on a society called the Dogs in which members customarily painted their mouths with a horizontal red band,
said to represent the bloody mouth of a feeding coyote. They were
said to be particularly good warriors and horse-stealers; and during
their lodge rituals, they imitated the ferocity of dogs. This was the
only sodality recorded in which members had special names referring to dog behaviors, and the one taboo rigorously enforced by the
lodge was that against the eating of dogs (Wissler 1912; pp. 52–54).
Thus, we may infer that positive and negative rules are reciprocal;
Oglalas who maintain their human-like status refrain from eating
dogs that are named, while Oglalas who perceive themselves to be
named dogs refrain from eating that which is permissible food for
humans.

The Dog Society is now defunct, and today dogs, like humans, are
simply unfortunate beings: they are whipped, beaten, shunned, and

starved, yet they both persist, often against formidable odds. The reasons that humans persist as Oglalas is partly contingent on their eating of dog. And at the point at which dogs become the subject of culinary considerations, they are rescued from their profane status. As the focal point of a ritual feast, dogs are reified: they are ranked even above the more usual creatures of symbolic import—the buffalo, bear, horse, deer, elk, and eagle. At the very moment in which a dog is chosen to transcend its worldliness, it becomes the subject of increasing ceremoniousness. For example, when an Oglala feasts on common meat, he anticipates that the cooks will prepare more than can be consumed, that the participants will eat beyond satiety, and, finally, that they will carry whatever is left over back to their homes for future consumption. But to feast on dog means that very little will be prepared relative to the number of guests present; only the oldest men and perhaps women will be served, and each will consume only a few morsels. Nothing will be left over except the skin and bones, which will be burned or buried. For the Oglala, meat is a gastronomic delicacy, but dog meat is a spiritual one.

The importance of dog ceremoniousness becomes clear only after we understand the way in which the dog is prominent in Oglala cosmology. In the emergence myth, Iktomi (spider), the culture hero, transforms himself into a *šungmahetu* (underground dog) in order to locate humans living in a primordial subterranean world and lead them to the surface of the earth. The culture hero then in a series of episodes encounters his older brother Iya (the glutton), who has a preference for eating humans. In a number of myths, humans who have been devoured by Iya are rescued by the culture hero, who instructs the tribe to build a fire under the cannibal, thus causing him to regurgitate his human meal. If the culture hero, the spider, and the dog are symbolic transformations of the same mythological catalyst, then the ritual eating of dog is part of a significant reenactment of the cosmological order; that is, just as Iya mediates between life and death, the dog mediates between death and rebirth. Here we find a coherent system in which at the cosmological level Iya eats humans in order to live, and at the empirical level humans eat dogs to live. At both levels, the dog emerges as the primary symbol of survival and continuity of the Oglala.

The cosmological importance of the dog and its relationship to humans is further enunciated in the sacrifice of the young puppy. Once the dog is selected, a process that may take several days, the ritual killing is presided over by a medicine man and two female assistants. The medicine man annoints the puppy with *wase luta* (red paint), by drawing a line from the tip of the puppy's nose to its tail. The red line is symbolic of the red road, the Oglala equivalent of the straight and narrow, which itself represents all that is beneficent in the world. Once the dog is annointed, the medicine man extolls its virtues, calling it *mitakola* (my friend), and expresses to those assembled how difficult it is to sacrifice this worthy and faithful creature. He then faces the dog west, while the two women take their places on the north and south side of the dog; here they each place a short rope, at the end of which is fashioned a noose, over the dog's neck and secure it. The medicine man, armed with a blunt instrument, takes his place behind the dog—that is, at the east—and at his signal the women pull the noose tightly while simultaneously the medicine man strikes the dog over the head. The act of killing the dog is likened to being struck by lightning and guarantees that the spirit of the dog will be released in order to go to the west where it will join the thunder people, those spirits who have the power over life and death, and who themselves are symbolized by lightning.

From the cosmological perspective, the principals involved in the sacrifice actually delineate sacred space, by standing in the place of three of the four winds, while the fourth direction, the west, is left open to permit the passing of the dog's spirit. Once the spirit of the dog reaches the west, the sacred circle is joined. It is believed that the dog is the exemplary *wahoši* (messenger) of the people and that its spirit will convey the wishes of the people to the spirits of the west. The dog is choked so that it will utter no cry because the howl of a dog is associated with death. At the same time, it is spiritually alive because its breath *ni* (the same term for life) has not left it.

The metaphor of death by lightning underscores the symbolic relationship between the dog and the spider. For example, if an Oglala accidentally kills a spider, he quickly says *Ho Tunkašla, wakinyan niktepelo* (Ho, Grandfather, the lightning has killed you). In both cases, the dog and spider by being killed by lightning will seek no retribution against humans because both are related to the thunder people, who themselves have the right to take a life.

Once sacrificed, the body of the dog is thrown on an open pit fire to singe off its hair. Once singed, the rest of the hair is wiped off by the women and the body is washed in cold water. The dog is then butchered in such a way that the head remains intact, and the remainder of the animal is cut into three-inch squares. The innards, with the exception of the liver, are burned in the fire. (At one time the head, spine, and tail were left intact, but this is no longer practiced.) Importantly, the skin is left on the meat. Practically this will ensure that the meat remains intact during the cooking, but the Oglala say that this is done so that the *total* dog may be consumed. Although the act of butchering the detotalized individual animal, in the final act of consuming its part, it will be retotalized by the collectivity of festive participants, thus strengthening social as well as spiritual solidarity.

When the women have completed butchering the dog, it is placed in a kettle and boiled for several hours. No spices are added.

As is true of many Oglala institutions, the origin of the dog feast was inspired by a famine. Hunters somewhere in the mythical past pledged that if they could locate food, they would provide a great feast for their dogs. Upon discovering a heard of buffalo, the hunters kept their vow, quickly killing the animals, butchering them, and placing the meat in a great pile. They led their dogs to it and the dogs devoured it. Thus, in myth human food is consumed by dogs so that in reality dogs may be consumed by humans. As mediators between the sacred and profane, both the subject and object of sacrifice are one.

Historically, there have three occasions in which dogs have been eaten: (1) a special feast for prominent men; (2) as a ritual of a society called *Heyoka kaga* (clowns), men who had dreamed of the thunder or lightning and thus were required to live out their lives in an antinatural manner; and (3) as part of the *Yuwipi* ritual, a curing ceremony conducted in a darkened room for a patient suffering from "Indian sickness," one perceived to be prevalent before Euro-American conquest.

What all three have in common is that a ritual dance, the kettle dance, is performed prior to the consummation of the dog. They differ in that humans perform the dance on the first two occasions and the spirits of the thunder people (those to whom the sacrifice is made) perform it during the *Yuwipi* ritual. With minor variations the choreography and significance of all three are the same. Today the first two situations do not obtain except in an occasional reenactment of the kettle dance and then normally without using a dog. The spiritual variation—the kettle dance as it is performed in the *Yuwipi* ritual—persists.

Metaphysical Aspects of an Oglala Food System

During the course of the *Yuwipi* ritual, the medicine man invokes the spirits of birds, animals, and the thunder people to join the common people in the meeting house. These spirits will instruct the medicine man as to the proper methods for curing the patient in whose behalf the meeting has been arranged. Unlike other foods that will be served at the conclusion of the *Yuwipi,* dog stew is placed in the sacred space for the duration of the meeting.

Although the room is pitch black, it is believed that the medicine man can see everyone, including the spirits, clearly. If the medicine man is successful in coaxing the spirits into the meeting, and part of this inducement lies in the fact that they will be given dog stew and tobacco, they will commune with him and instruct him in the proper curing procedures. At this point, the spirits demand the dog stew and the medicine man instructs the singers to sing the kettle dance songs. In the following three songs, the texts are important on two cosmological planes. The texts are a recitation of what the medicine man has himself seen in a vision outside the *Yuwipi,* and they "report" what the thunder people are doing during the course of the kettle dance. At one level, the ritual enactment by the spirits lies in a timeless plane, while at another it is temporal.

As the first song begins, the thunder people, perceived to be about three feet tall, wearing moccasins and breechcloths, their bodies daubed with clay, salute the kettle by raising first their right hand, then left hand, then both hands. The singers begin:

> *Wakantanka uňšimala ye*
> *wani kta ca lecamun welo*
> Wakantanka, pity me
> I want to live, that is why I do this.

During the second song, the thunder spirits dance around the kettle holding forked spears *(caniyuze),* which are symbolic of lightning, stabbing the choicest morsels of dog stew.

The singers continue:

> *Mahp̌iya mimeya kinajinpe*
> *Henake wakinyan oyate ca kinanjinpe*
> They stand in place in the sky
> These, the thunder people stand in place.

And, finally, the spirits eat, while the singers conclude:

55

> *Leciya šunka wan yutape*
> *Wiyohp̌eyata wakinyan oyate wan šunka wan yutape*
> *Wakan yutape*
> Over here they are eating dog.
> In the west, the thunder people are eating dog
> Sacredly, they are eating.

Here the sky, the west, and the thunder people are also at once temporal and atemporal referents because what the thunder people are doing at the ritual is what they are doing in their homes in the west with the sacrificial puppy. At the conclusion of the kettle dance, the spirits go home. The lights are turned on and the participants partake of the substance of the dog stew in the same manner that the spirits have partaken of its essence. The people have eaten, as the Oglala say, not meat, but *pejuta* (medicine), and their eating of the dog stew is perceived to be a ritual that will guarantee health and long life. I do this, says the song, so that I may live.

We would like to conclude with an observation: the ceremoniousness of the dog feast is likely to increase as the years wear on. We have noticed over the past twenty years that in its ritual form it has become more prevalent. At one time only the elderly people ate dog stew, but today men, women, and children of all ages freely participate in the feast. There are no *Heyoka kaga* on the reservation, but one can never say that any Oglala institution is completely defunct because over the years those very rituals which anthropologists have reported as becoming obsolete have flourished again.

The Oglala recognize and bemoan the fact that their once proud horse herds are diminishing and that the buffalo, even though of ritual importance, is no longer free. Even the herd that roams over the northern part of the reservation does not do so without constraint: it is fenced, restricted, controlled. It is also clear to the Oglala that the values they once cherished have come to an end because the white man has decreed it. Only the Indian and the dog survive, spectators to a drama of social change, a drama in which they do not fully participate.

The ritual of the dog feast becomes the *sine qua non* of tribal identity. The positive sanction afforded to the eating of dog, one established as part of the cosmological order, is reenforced by the white man's negative sanction of it. Whites do not kill dogs except under humane circumstances, and they certainly do not eat them. The dog emerges as a total symbol of Oglala culture into which all of the beliefs and values that are Indian have been condensed.

56

The meal is simple: the flesh of dog and water are the only ingredients. But as Douglas has stated, "Perhaps gastronomy flourishes best where food carries the lightest load of spiritual meanings" (Douglas 1977, p. 1). And it is, of course, in the metaphysical aspects that the dog is significant. Dog is a gift to the gods; it is a sacrifice and, like any sacrifice, requires relinquishing something for oneself. But the suffering and hardship beg a return, and for the Oglala the dog's death is reciprocated with a promise of a human's life. I do this so that I may live.

Dog is both a vertical and a horizontal boundary marker; it mediates between the empirical and spiritual, and between that which lies inside Oglala culture and that which lies outside. In consuming the dog the past and present coalesce so as to ensure continuity. Spiritually, the eating of dog removed them from their syntagmatic relationship with humans and transforms them into a paradigmatic one. But all such symbolic transformations are temporary, and the sacrificial eating of the dog must be repeated over and over lest the continuity between the past and present, and implicitly the future, be broken.

For the Oglala, dog is man's best friend because it is man's best sacrifice. Like Humans, dogs are sagacious and brave, and they cling dearly to their lives. But both are also clever. What better strategic choice could there be for a symbol that underscores cultural continuity and at the same time social and individual identity?

For the Oglala, eating dog is decidedly what Lévi-Strauss calls "endo-cuisine" and as such serves as a metaphor for tribal endogamy. The feast is analogous to the totemic prescription: the act of assimilating the dog flesh is at once an act of differentiation, because the "meat of [just] *any* animal species . . . must not be assimilated by [just] *any* group of men" (1966, p. 108). Today, the white man eats buffalo, deer, and elk, sometimes even horse meat. But as long as the white man does not consume dog, he does not consume those who do.

Buffalo as Ritual Food

Like all symbols, food can be manipulated. It can be exchanged, bartered, sold, or given away; it can serve as a medium of exploitation, used for or against people to bring them to a point of capitulation. It can be disguised as an inducement, as entreaty, or a trade-off. Food exists as an ingredient of imperialism, and it can be used profitably against a population as if it were a weapon—paradoxically, one as lethal as starvation.

The annihilation of the bison—the buffalo—and the substitution of cattle by the United States government stands as an instructive case in point. The slaughter of this magnificent beast began in 1870 when it was discovered that buffalo hides were ideally suited to replace leather heretofore obtained from Argentine cattle, the latter becoming nearly obsolete because of overkill. In order to satisfy the needs of eastern and European markets for not only the hides but a newly acquired preference for the taste of its meat, buffalo hunters raged over the western plains for the next fifteen years killing, skinning, butchering, packing, and shipping their products to the commercial markets back east. By 1885, so thoroughly was their job done, that eastern tanneries found the need to seek out another source for their hides and meat. The buffalo was no more (Dary 1974, pp. 93–120).

Before their near extinction, vast herds of buffalo roamed many parts of North America. Population estimates range as high as 75 million at the time of European contact. For the Oglala and other Plains tribes, buffaloes were the single richest source not only of food, clothing, and shelter, but of culture itself. It is not difficult to understand why, given the context in which the buffalo and Indian coexisted, even today young men and women who have spent most if not all their lives in some urban community speak about the buffalo as if they crave its meat. Nor is it difficult to understand why old men or women, seeing a majestic, lone buffalo seated on its haunches away from the rest of the threadbare herd in the Black Hills, would hold their withered hands over their faces and sob, as if they had just received news of a dying relative.

Despite the symbiotic relationship between buffalo and Indian, in 1873 the Secretary of the Interior made this statement:

I would not seriously regret the total disappearance of the buffalo from our western prairies, in its effect upon the Indians. I would regard it rather as a means of hastening their sense of dependence upon the products of the soil and their own labors. [Columbus Delano, cited in Dary 1974, p. 127].

This was the very agency that was to become the overseer and guardian of the Indians' health and prosperity.

To enumerate the multitudinous uses of the buffalo—edible and nonedible, materialistic and symbolic, Indian and non-Indian—is to recite an almost endless litany. Most anthropological students of the buffalo argue over the appropriate number of its material uses: food, clothing, shelter, and that evasive and mystical category, *ceremonial objects* (see particularly, Dary 1974; Ewers 1955; Roe 1970; and Wissler 1940). However, if one takes into consideration the manner in which the buffalo appears in Indian cosmology, as symbol and metaphor, then the list is never complete; the nature of the buffalo is polysemous and generative, constantly reproducing new and meaningful ideas for the people who not only consume it, but revere it.

Buffaloes as men, as women, as children, and as animals flicker and fade in and out of the cosmology, now lowing, now stampeding, sometimes frozen still against the landscape, sometimes uncontrollably angry and dangerous to a band of hunters. Always the buffalo appears tempting humans with its savory meat: raw tongue, and kidneys, and liver, or roast tenderloin and soup boiled in its own paunch. Sometimes it enters dancing, singing, speaking, often defying the same mortals with a promise of hunger, starvation, or even famine, if humans do not propitiate it with the appropriate rituals.

Even in that most sacred myth, in which a woman brings to the Lakota people the seven sacred rites, she turns into a buffalo calf before disappearing over the hill, thus enunciating the relationship between the Indian people and the Buffalo Nation, both of which are in Lakota cosmology, the same.

And in each of the seven sacred rites, the *wicoh'an wakan šakowin,* the buffalo plays a preeminent role. In the now (but temporarily?) defunct sacred ball game *(tapa wankayeya),* a ball made from buffalo hide and stuffed with its hair, is thrown by a child to groups of eager receivers waiting at the four directions, the one catching it being ensured of auspiciousness and longevity. In the ghost-keeping ritual *(wicanagi wicagluhapi),* to coax the spirit of the deceased to linger around the camp near the place of its death for a year, a lock of its hair is wrapped in a buffalo robe, which is wrapped neatly and placed on a spirit post outside the tipi door where it may bask in the sun and sway lightly in benevolent breezes. Once, in the vision quest *(hanbleceya),* a man covered himself in a buffalo robe waiting to commune with visitors from the earth and sky and underground. Even now he often places his sacred pipe on a buffalo skull whose outstretched horns beckon like the embrace of Mother Earth herself. When a female reaches her first menses *(awicalowanpi),* she is instructed to accompany the medicine man in a movement imitative of buffalo bulls and cows, finally lowering her head to drink from a bowl of sacred chokecherry juice in a manner akin to the buffalo drinking from a favorite watering hole (M. N. Powers, 1980).

In the making of relatives *(Hunka),* a bond between two persons is established partially by waving wands tipped with buffalo tails signifying their unity in the oneness of the buffalo nation. In the sweat lodge *(Oinikagapi),* the salutory and spirtual ceremony, the participants pray and sing around the life-cleansing and renewing steam, encouraging the circulation of their blood by slapping themselves with buffalo tail switches.

But it is perhaps in the sun dance *(wiwanyang wacipi),* the annual rite of intensification in which the needs and wishes of the whole tribe are prayed for by individuals who sacrifice themselves through the mortification of the flesh, that the buffalo emerges as the key symbol of identity, health, longevity, and solidarity. High above the dance arena, suspended from the sacred sun dance pole, the living tree, hang suspended the rawhide effigies of a man and a buffalo. At one time, the effigies were characterized by exaggerated genitalia, now missing perhaps because of criticism by the missionaries and government workers, symbolic of cultural castration.

Here in the sun dance the countable, quantitative material aspects of the buffalo coalesce with its uncountable, qualitative immaterial aspects. And perhaps it is the relative absence of the buffalo that makes it such a highly charged symbol of Oglala culture. It is not so much its impingement as a viable object on Oglala reality but its removal from it that makes it so powerful—not operative function but dysfunction, not material appearance but disappearance that allows it to maintain its lofty position in the cosmology.

Below the rawhide effigies, humans dance gazing at the sun, and some offer up their flesh to *Wakantanka*, allowing the medicine men to insert skewers of wood and bone through their flesh, by means of which they will be tied to the sun dance pole, dancing with jerking motions backwards until the flesh is broken and they are freed from ignorance. Encircling the pinned dancers are others whose flesh covering their scapular muscles have been similarly skewered and to the ends of rawhide ropes buffalo skulls—one, two, even as many as five—have been attached. The dancers move slowly clockwise, sun-wise, around the dance arbor dragging the skulls until their very weight causes the flesh to break.

Once the wars between the Oglala and other Lakota and the United States government had ended with the signing of the Treaty of Fort Laramie in 1868, the Oglala were at the mercy of the government's annuity program, designed to outfit the reservation Indians with daily food requirements. Such foods as beef, salt pork, coffee, rice, beans, flour, sugar, and dried corn became, or were soon to become, the staple diet of the Oglala. There are two important points to consider about government annuities, or "rations" as they were called.

First, the food itself was new and strange to the Oglala: it was from the Oglala point of view inedible for both natural and cultural reasons. A staple like coffee was bitter, very much like some kinds of herbal medicines. The salt pork was often rancid. But worst of all, because the Oglala were essentially meat eaters, government beef was regarded as offensive to the palate on a number of counts, as the following attests:

> The first cattle came to us looking thin and gaunt from the long drive across the plains and were then penned in corrals that could be smelled for miles. I remember when my father came home and reported to us that the white men had brought some "spotted buffalo" for us to eat. We all got on our ponies and rode over to see the strange new animals and as we drew near there came to us a peculiar and disagreeable odor. So we stayed off some distance looking at these long-horned "spotted buffalo" and wondering how the white people could eat them for food. [Standing Bear 1978, p. 57]

Second, once the reservation was established, rations were distributed every five days to Indian families, when they received a "pound and a half of beef *(or in lieu thereof one half pound of bacon)*, one half pound of flour, and one half pound of corn: and for every one hundred rations, four pounds of coffee, eight pounds of sugar, and three pounds of beans" (Anonymous n.d., p. 115; italics added).

The frequency of distribution tended to keep the Oglala in a chronic state of hunger inasmuch as the five-day ration was normally consumed in two days (Hyde 1937, p. 229). Between 1871 and 1878, the Oglala were able to live fairly well from the annuities even though children 6 to 14 years of age were exempted from the distribution, as were those Oglala not working on agricultural plots. An already inadequate diet was exacerbated by the fact that the Oglala had not yet learned, nor did they really care, to farm. During this period of time, it was still possible to sneak away to hunt for the now near-extinct buffalo, even though the hunters were ultimately punished for leaving the reservation in pursuit of gamier meat.

Those who did not hunt buffalo anymore of course were forced to adopt beef. To overcome beef's offensive attributes, the Oglala were encouraged *to hunt cattle in the same manner that they hunted buffalo.* (Hyde 1937, p. 207) reports that during the summer and fall of 1871:

> The beef cattle were turned out of the corral, and the young men hunted and killed them like buffalo. The butchering was quickly accomplished, and then there was feasting. The small boys went through the camps carrying messages to come and eat, for now everyone could give feasts to their friends.

This custom was to continue for some time. Even as late as 1934 "an old Indian with his bow and arrows took after [the steer] to kill him in the traditional manner that his father before him had used to kill buffalo" (Spindler 1972, p. 120).

It was partly through this process of transforming a "spotted buffalo" into a real buffalo through the age-old hunting ritual and feast that cattle became not only respectable but an integral part of the Oglala diet. But this transformation did not annul the symbolism of the real buffalo, even though 1875 marked the last buffalo hunt in which the Oglala participated. Of course, the conversion from buffalo to beef was not easy for the Oglala, but as Standing Bear (1978) states: "Our buffalo had perished and we were a meat eating people, so we succumbed to the habit which at first seemed so distasteful to us."

Of course, it was not only the beef that was offensive or unusable to the Oglala. Other rations were regarded with equal disgust. Again Hyde tells us: "The mess-pork was good for white men, who had queer tastes, but the Oglalas could not stomach it. They left it on the ground. Even the dogs, with plenty of beef pickings, would not eat it" (1937, p. 207).

Flour, at first distribution, had been unknown to the Oglala, and for that reason unusable. Sacks of flour were either sold or exchanged for other commodities with local traders, or the contents of the flour sacks were thrown away and the sacks themselves used for shirts and dresses. At some point during the early reservation period, however, Indian women learned to render grease from bacon and add it to the flour, thus inventing one of the most popular of all Oglala foods today: *wigli un kagapi* (fried bread; literally they make it with grease).

Bacon, although eaten frequently today, was unusable because it was usually spoiled. It was regarded simply as *wašin* (fat). Interestingly, the Oglala, who normally still do not eat pork other than bacon, adopted the French term *couchon* as their own word for pig *(kukuši)*, and it stands as the only loan word in Lakota for a foreign food, implying that only foods worthy of classification are worthy of consuming.

Coffee for the Oglala as well as for whites was sold or traded in its raw state, and green coffee beans had to be roasted before being boiled. The original word for coffee underscored the analogy between it and herbal medicine both in its general description "black medicine" and in the manner in which coffee was prepared, which replicated the usual process of stirring herbal medicine. The Oglala regarded the coffee as too bitter to drink and consequently developed the habit of adding several spoons of sugar to each cup, still a practice today. The term "black medicine," however, is no longer used by the Oglala; the word *wakalyapi* (to heat something) is the modern term.

What is ironic about the foods issued to the Oglala by the federal government—food that was repugnant, spoiled, rotten, inedible, and unknowable—is that all of the foods within perhaps a ten-year period became acceptable not only as an integral (if not exclusive) part of their diet, but became regarded as "Indian" foods.

Not all of the ration foods were new. The rice, beans, corn, and sugar (in the original form of maple sugar) were all known to the Oglala long before the reservation period. These, along with the newly adopted "Indian" foods, became the substitute diet of hunters and gatherers which has persisted with little change up through modern times.

Here we are particularly interested in the process by which foreign foods became nativized. Obviously, the Oglala were suffering from hunger and starvation at the time the government began to issue rations. But they did not immediately accept those foods which were offensive to them even though the alternative was to starve. They did not even regulate their own commensal patterns in order to ensure that there would be an adequate amount of food to last them for the five-day ration period.

Based on historical evidence, it is certain that the process of accepting the foreign foods occurred during the 1870s. And the process is marked by two stages of what we call metaphorical extension. In the first stage, the Oglala applied Lakota terms to the new foods in a systematic way: the new food was analogized to an existing form, thus making the raw food or animals a metaphorical extension of a traditional concept. Cattle became *ptegleška* (spotted cow) and cattle were sexually divided into *tabloka* (male ruminant, that is, bull) and *ptewinyela* (female cow [sic]). Cows were to the Oglala a kind of buffalo and, like the buffalo, were distinguished sexually, a classifying process reserved for only buffalo, deer, and elk—that is, traditional Indian game food.

The second stage required performing a ritual, or activity, which helped qualify the new food as Indian. In the case of the cattle, a "spotted buffalo" was hunted as if it were a buffalo. It would have been much more economical to have slaughtered the cattle in their pens the way the white men did it. But the chasing of the cow and killing it with either bow and arrow or rifle was another way of separating it from the offensively odoriferous corral.

Thus, in this double process of classifying and ritualizing, a cow became a kind of buffalo, coffee became a kind of medicine, bacon became a kind of fat, and granulated sugar became a kind of maple sugar (the term *cahanpi,* tree sap, is used for both varieties).

Viewed another way, beef, coffee, flour, and sugar were part of a total new system of food, introduced to the Oglala as a set of relationships, one dependent upon the other. The transformation of foreign foods into traditional Oglala foods was at least partly successful because they were all transformed at the same time as a system, rather than as separate commodities. Beef was treated as a subsystem in itself. Not only was it classified according to Oglala tradition, but cattle were hunted, skinned, butchered, and cooked in the same manner that buffalo were in the past. The same obtains for coffee, which in a sense was totally "herbalized." While the acceptance of flour and bacon were contingent upon each other, they could not be used separately but only collectively, being rendered into a new form of "bread." Later, variations on this theme, that is, store-bought bread and crackers, became ultimately usable and edible because they were subsets of the same systematic mixing of flour and fat.

But despite their status as traditional foods, foods served at sacred as well as secular events and homely meals, the white man's rations never achieved the same symbolic status as buffalo. Buffalo alone was reserved as the major ritual food of the sun dance because of the close relationship historically between the sun dance and the summer buffalo hunt.

Today, despite their near extinction, buffalo herds are on the rise. And perhaps the same commercial greed that served to annihilate most of the herds in the latter nineteenth century is responsible for rejuvenating the herds. The federal government that once condoned the outright destruction of the buffalo herds as a means of controlling the Indian, now guards them carefully in its national parks, such as those in the Black Hills of South Dakota. It is partly due to the need of government rangers to thin the herds regularly that the Oglala and other tribes receive small portions of the herd for consumption at the sun dance.* Additionally, white ranchers raise buffaloes for their tasty meat, a delicacy sold in markets as far east as New York City. At Mount Rushmore, where the carved faces of four presidents deface the Sioux's sacred shrine, tourists are tempted with "buffalo burgers," products of overreproductive herds nearby.

Wasna as Ritual Food

If the symbolic content of food depends little on its gustatory measure, then the least elaborate of Oglala traditional foods, *wasna*—better known by its Cree name, pemmican—is appropriately the most ceremonious. As a ritual food, *wasna* transcends all others in its simplicity; the recipe is stark judging by the following gastronomical requirements: "Dry beef roast in oven for several hours. Remove meat

---

*In 1978, the Oglala Sioux tribe took over the management of a buffalo herd located on the reservation near the town of Allen.

from oven and pound very fine; to this add bone grease (from marrow of bones) or suet, sugar, and dried choke cherries which have been pounded fine. Mix this well. Pack into pan to harden. It can then be taken from the pan and sliced" (Anonymous 1978; p. 120).

This method of preparation does not differ from one reported by Mooney (1965), who states that jerked beef or some other kind of meat was toasted over an open fire until crisp and then pounded into a hash with a stone hammer *(wicaškin)*. A small, shallow hole was dug, over which was thrown the hide from the neck of a buffalo, thus forming a dish. The toasted meat was placed in the dish and pounded to the proper consistency. Marrow bones were split and boiled in water until the grease rose to the top, and it was then skimmed off and poured over the meat. If it was to be eaten immediately, it was usually sweetened with sugar and some wild fruit beaten into the mixture. According to Mooney: "It is extremely nourishing, and has a very agreeable taste to one accustomed to it. On the march it was to the prairie Indian what parched corn was to the hunter of the timber tribes, and has been found so valuable as a condensed nutriment that it is extensively used by arctic travelers and explorers" (1965, p. 302).

Whereas the ingredients of *wasna* are few, its strictures are many. It is the only food in Oglala culture that carries with it a negative sanction; that is, people are more concerned with when it cannot be eaten than when it can, and it can never be eaten at nighttime.

This serious proscription is predicated on the Oglala belief that not only humans but ghosts *(wanagi)* savor *wasna.* Ghosts, in the Oglala cosmology, are the spirits of specific departed persons who for one reason or another linger after death near the homes of loved ones.

Occasionally, ghosts and humans traveling the same roads and paths at night are perceived to collide. When this happens, the human is likely to have a stroke, and it is said that he or she has been killed by a ghost *(wanagi ktepi).* So it is under these nocturnal conditions that humans refrain from preparing, eating, or even carrying *wasna* because of the strong attraction ghosts have for it.

There is one positive prescription for *wasna:* it must be served at a ritual called *wokiksuye wohanpi* (memorial feast), held roughly one year after a person has died. The memorial feast is a functional equivalent of the ghost-keeping ritual mentioned above, and as such represents the culmination of a year-long period of mourning. It is during this feast that close kin, usually the immediate family, invite members from the deceased's *tiyošpaye,* approximately 300 persons. If one views the memorial feast as the culminating ritual of a year-long series of rituals, beginning with the death of an individual, the wake, and funeral, and continuing through the period of mourning, the total range of Oglala traditional commensality manifests itself in a striking way. For example, the manner in which food is selected and prepared, distributed and redistributed, who attends, and prescriptions and proscriptions associated with food coalesce in a manner definitive of Oglala social and cultural values.

After living on the reservation for a long period of time, one gets the feeling of being in a retirement community: there seems to be a preoccupation with going to funerals. This is because the average Oglala's network of knowable kin is much larger than the average American's, and it is his responsibility to attend, or "help out," at a kinsman's funeral. This entails not only attending the funeral, but bringing some food to the feast that will take place during the course of the two- or three-day wake, as well as the feast following the funeral.

There is a great variation in the types of foods served at wakes and funerals. We have witnessed large feasts which included a half beef roasted outside over a pit fire; an assortment of prepared foods such as soups, fried bread, desserts; and an array of fruits, both wild and canned. However, most wakes offer a less formidable variety of foods: sandwiches, coffee, and packaged buns and rolls, all rather tentative and contingent, all appropriate for the occasion.

But the memorial feast is always elaborate; members of the entire *tiyošpaye* have the year, or nearly a year, to plan and prepare the foods they will bring to the feast. And the immediate family will go to great trouble to provide a feast of magnificent proportions. In the interim between the funeral and memorial feast, simple foods will be prepared and eaten by the individual or individuals electing to partake in the ritual of *wašigla* (mourning). It is during this ensuing period that the Oglala believe that the spirit of the deceased lingers around the place where it died. This is a particularly arduous time for the mourner because he or she will not be permitted to partake of a normal social life until the spirit is freed at the concluding memorial feast.

Although by prescription, the period of mourning should last one year, often the memorial feast is hosted at any time within the year. This is because of unpredictable weather in the winter months and the fact that ritual is always held outdoors. During the mourning period, the mourner wears black, cannot attend powwows or any other festive occasions, and has as an extreme hardship the task of ritually feeding the spirit of the departed every day of the mourning period. At each meal, the mourner sets a place for the spirit at the dining table and places a bit of meat or fried bread on the plate and fills a cup with water or coffee. After the mourner and family have completed the meal, the food offered the spirit is buried or burned, the spirit having partaken of the essence of the proffered food.

During this period, the mourner is regarded as *unšike* (pitiable), and all of his or her relatives and friends will try to help out as much as possible by doing errands, buying groceries, and collecting and making things that will be given away on the day of the memorial feast to those who were close to the deceased. The give-away *(wi-iȟpeyapi)*, which also occurs when the person dies, partially fulfills the Oglala precept that one should never own anything more than one needs.

Memorial feasts normally begin at noon, and are thus colloquially called "dinners." To say that so-and-so is having a dinner is tantamount to announcing this important food event. The feasts are quite impressive in their luxurious array of food varieties, as well as a host of things such as star quilts, embroidered pillow cases, yard goods, articles of clothing, and store-bought shawls and blankets that will be given away, particularly to those kinsmen who assisted during the time of mourning.

The main foods, beef soup and *taniga* (tripe), are prepared outdoors over pit fires by the family of the deceased. Other food staples such as *wasna, wojapi* (a thickened soup made from wild fruits, sugar, and flour), fried bread, cakes and pies, and coffee are usually prepared indoors, either at a church facility, which is often the locus of the memorial feast, or at the homes of kinsmen who bring the foods to the feast. Other store-bought items include crackers, bread, stewed tomatoes, sweet rolls, and canned fruit. Because of the anticipated leftovers (more is always prepared than can possibly be consumed), the visitors to the feast carry with them empty lard containers, cans, and even cardboard boxes for *wateca* (leftovers).

Once the visitors have been seated, usually in a large circle outdoors, the members of the family begin to distribute the food, ladling out the soups and meats into plates and bowls which the visitors have provided for their own use. The distribution committee moves in a clockwise direction as many times as are required to distribute all the food. This may require two or three circuits of the guests seated on blankets on the ground or in folding chairs which they have brought from home. While the committee distributes the food, speeches are made by prominent Oglalas who know the deceased of the family, each exhortation being directed to the assembled people using the attributive *mitakuyepi* (my relatives) usually followed by the term *mitahanši* (my cousins). The virtues of the deceased are extolled, and if he was Christian, a clergyman will recite or read appropriate scriptures. While the speeches are being made, it is customary for one member of the family to pass around the circle carrying a picture of the deceased for all to remember.

When all of the visitors have finished eating, and have packed the uneaten food into their *wateca* buckets, a medicine man, or someone of high status who is known for his familiarity with Oglala ways, will take a few morsels of food, meat, *wasna,* fried bread, or *taniga* and bury it in the ground. This is symbolic of feeding the spirit of the deceased for the last time after which time it is free to continue along the spirit path *(Wanagi Tacanku)* to the hereafter. The family of the deceased then distributes the give-away items from a table located in the center of the circle, the announcer calling by name those persons most deserving of the material goods which have been collected over the past year.

The completion of the give-away marks a period of extreme emotional stress for the family, particularly the mother of the deceased who begins to sob profusely and ultimately must be carried away bodily from the feast grounds by her family.

Here we would like to return to the symbolic importance of *wasna* as a ritual food. Although the total inventory of Oglala traditional foods is likely to be prepared by the deceased's family, and other foods will be brought by relatives, *wasna* is the only food that is required at a memorial feast. The actual preparation may be done by the family or close relatives. In either case, it requires that the cooks have on hand chokecherries, usually collected the previous August and dried; and a supply of dried meat, usually beef, although buffalo or venison can be used. An additional supply of marrow is extracted from bones (although today lard may be used as a substitute).

In its ideal form, *wasna* becomes the perfect edible example of the culinary triangle. It is composed of raw food (marrow), cooked (meat), and rotten (dried cherries) (Lévi-Strauss 1969).

The consistency of *wasna* is such that it is easily cut or broken apart into individual helpings when served. The term *wasna* is based on the radical element *sna* meaning to pick apart or unravel, and is thus related to the Lakota concept for ringing, as a bell, which is perceived as a part coming loose from its whole. *Wasna* is thus not picked apart from the whole serving as much as it is unraveled.

Although not as rich as dog or buffalo in its mythological allusions, there is at least one reference to *wasna* in Oglala cosmology. The following story was told by Joseph Eagle Hawk to Martha Warren Beckwith in 1926 and is instructive:

> Mincemeat and Pemmican went on a Journey. Mincemeat said, "Twin, you and I are good friends and we shall always remain such. Let us stand by one another because this is a dangerous journey." On the other side of the ridge they met Ikto (Inktomi). He was feeling very hungry when right in front of him he saw Mincemeat and Pemmican side by side. He quickly contrived a plan. He said, "Brothers, you look very tired. Sit down and I will give you a smoke and we will rest." Soon Ikto said, "Just excuse me a moment!" and he went over a little hill and then came back. Mincemeat said, "Just excuse me a moment!" and when Mincemeat came back Ikto said, "While you were away Pemmican said bad things about you; he said he would kick you. Why don't you kick him?" Then the two started to kick each other until they broke each other up. Ikto laid down his pipe and had a good feast. To this day, two good friends might get along nicely but there's always some one who gets them to kick at each other. [1930, p. 431]

We are fortunate in having this myth for two reasons. First, not only is there a typical trickster intervention but the last line represents a native exegesis. Mincemeat (*wakapapi*, literally meat cut thin and pounded together with marrow fat) and Pemmican (*wasna*; pemmican is the more common Algonquian Indian term for the same meal) call each other Twin *(cekpa)*, which is a reciprocal term used by close friends whose behaviors are similar, therefore establishing their social as well as amicable unity. They commit, in the myth, the most egregious of social transgressions: they fight with each other until "they broke each other up." In real life, the solidarity perceived to be the last hope of the Oglala is underscored by the conflict between two people who should be by all Oglala standards friendly. The act of consuming *wasna* then is the mirror image of the myth: the anthropomorphized delicacies of the myth behave in a way contrary to real social life.

Second, Beckwith's collection is the first mythical reference to *wasna*. The most important collection (Walker 1917) contains myths in which there are numerous references to food, but all of them reflect the culinary habits of an earlier age, one in which the Oglala or their antecedents were living in a semisedentary condition, consuming foods from their original habitat, the Great Lakes region: wild rice, corn, beans, squash, pumpkin, duck, and duck eggs, foods that have been eliminated empirically and mythically from the Oglala diet since the middle of the eighteenth century. If *wasna* enters into Oglala mythology in 1926 we must conclude that it is there for a reason. Its new-found status—that is, the fact that the Oglala in 1926 anthropomorphize *wasna*—seems to be indicative of a symbolic statement which we have caught in the act of transformation.

This transformation is rather easy to retrodict. *Wasna* as a food staple worthy of reification simply does not exist in an earlier period. There are no historical references to *wasna* as a sacred food. In fact, what is exemplary about *wasna* is that it is quite characteristic of a practical food: it is a food prepared for hunters and warriors who must be away from their village for considerable lengths of time. *Wasna* emerges in the historical literature as an ideal field ration: it is light and nutritious, and it can be carried easily by hunters and warriors. According to all reporters of Lakota culture, cakes of *wasna* were prepared by the warriors' and hunters' female kin and placed into bags made from the stomach of a buffalo.

It is primarily this association with now defunct institutions such as hunting and warfare which makes *wasna* such a singularly strong vehicle of symbolic import. The sacred food has achieved its status simply because it is identified with an ancient, unrepeatable way of life, one made extinct by the intervention of the white man and the reservation style of life to which all Oglala and other Lakota peoples must now sacrifice their lifestyle.

Here we see that the sacred and profane need not only be employed as functional typologies spread over space, but also over time. Whether the sacred and profane are regarded as categories standing in complementary opposition or as aspects of the same phenomenon, sacred and profane may be viewed diachronically: today's sacred among the Oglala can be seen as a historical as well as symbolic transformation of the past. Put simply, one generation's concept of the profane is another's envisionment of the sacred. Like other aspects of Oglala culture, the secular activities of the good old days exist in a spectrum of religiosity. Here religion takes on the characteristics of an antique: it is simply oldness that makes sense out of the new.

It is likely that the historical and symbolic transformation of *wasna* from a secular food of hunters and warriors to the sacred meal of mourners and ghosts can be assigned to a specific time period. Once the Great Sioux Reservation was established as a result of the Treaty of Fort Laramie in 1868, the lifestyle of the Oglala and other cognate tribes slowly began to change. The buffalo was gone, and hunters and warriors were soon to be confined to the reservation. The Oglala continued to make *wasna,* but absent was the thrill of the chase, replaced by sedentary boredom. It was only twenty years after the establishment of the reservation that the prophet Wovoka was to inspire numerous tribes on the Plains to participate in the well-known ghost dance movement. During the course of the prophet's teachings, the various tribes were to adopt its exhortations and rituals into a uniquely Lakota variant. Those rituals and symbols which might have succumbed to the new life were invigorated through the prophet's message: dance the ghost dance and in time the white man will disappear.

The Oglala, under the direction of medicine men who had traveled to the prophet and returned with his teachings, began to dance. During the course of the ghost dancing, men and women fell into trances, just as the prophet himself had done, and during their travels to the other world they talked with the spirits of the deceased. When they returned to the corporeal world, they reiterated their visionary experiences in songs newly composed. And among those songs which have been collected we find food one the major subjects of musical discourse. In 1890, the Oglala at Pine Ridge sang:

> Give me my knife
> Give me my knife
> I shall hang up the meat to dry—Ye'ye'!
> I shall hang up the meat to dry—Ye'ye'!
> Says grandmother—yo'yo'!
> Says grandmother—yo'yo'!
> When it is dry I shall make pemmican
> When it is dry I shall make pemmican
> Says grandmother—yo'yo'!
> Says grandmother—yo'yo'!
> I shall eat pemmican—E'yeye'yeye'!

> I shall eat pemmican—E'ye'ye'yeye'!
> They say so, they say so,
> The father says so, the father says so.

Mooney, an eyewitness to the event and collector of the songs, states that these songs conjured up "a vivid picture of the old Indian life . . . the cutting up of the meat after a buffalo hunt was a scene of the most joyous activity" (Mooney 1965, pp. 300–304).

It is perhaps logical that the ritual food which carries with it the highest form of symbolic load is one assigned to life crises, particularly to the memorial feast, where it must be finally decided whether the spirits of the Oglala are assigned to an Indian hereafter or to the white man's. The choice of food, preparation, and distribution—the whole food event—suggests that the ambiguous, multicultural way of the living is unequivocally laid to rest in a tradition which is distinctly Oglala.

Units of Analysis

In order to elicit the systematic ordering of Oglala food events, we focus on types of commensal units and types of menu. The commensal unit is composed of (1) the total number of persons in attendance; (2) the manner in which the attendants are or perceive themselves to be ranked along principles of kinship, friendship, or other relationships based on economic, political, or religious lines; and (3) the location of the kitchen, that is, inside or outside the household (hereafter referred to as internal or external kitchens). The configuration of these components allows one to predict the manner in which food will be distributed (and redistributed), that is, whether or not people are served or serve themselves. The manner of distribution, in turn, affects the ways of preparing food (cooked on a stove or over an open fire) but not necessarily the type of food.

For example, if the average number of persons in attendance at an Oglala event is nine (these numerical averages will be explained below), if they are known to be related along kinship lines, and if the kitchen is internal, we can predict that during the food event the manner of distribution will be such that each serves himself. In contrast, if the average is 30, the rank order is along kinship lines, and the kitchen is external, we can predict with fair accuracy that the persons will be served and, furthermore, that the food event will be associated with a ritual curing ceremony such as *Yuwipi.*

Oglala protocol also determines whether or not food should be set aside for incorporeal visitors: spirits, ghosts, and gods, and the manner in which they should be fed. Thus, these intrusive elements, all of which serve as rationales for the other constituents of the food event, often take on a metaphysical nature. And like the other constituents, the metaphysical components help distinguish one kind of food event from another.

Despite the fact that some food events seem innocuous, the rules are rigorous. In a traditional food event, the participants are served by the host. Males eat before females; the old eat before the young. Participants carry their own utensils, usually a bowl, knife, and spoon, and perhaps a tin cup for coffee. They also carry containers for taking home "leftovers." More food than can possibly be eaten will be prepared and guests are expected to eat beyond satiety, that is, until they are *ipi* (stuffed). The food will be boiled over a fire in an external kitchen, and on some occasions medicine men will bury food and spill water or coffee onto the ground as an offering to deceased kin.

Certain varieties of foods will emerge as superior to all others: buffalo, dog, *wasna,* tripe, soup, fried bread, *wojapi, kabubu* (baking powder biscuit bread), dried corn, and wild turnips. These varieties are typically Oglala because they are the foods of their ancestors. But also, they are foods which white people do not eat.

The Pine Ridge reservation was originally organized into seven "ration" districts, demarcated by natural boundaries (mainly creeks), as a means of distributing government annuities. Each of the districts was originally settled by corresponding exogamous bands *(tiyošpayes).* As the population grew within the fixed boundaries of the districts and reservation, the original bands began to separate into smaller units which today are called *oti* (communities). The number of ration districts was later increased to eight. Pine Ridge Village was, and is, the center for distribution and this fact is reflected in the Lakota name for the village and the district within which it is located, *wakpamni* (place of distribution).

In 1970 the number of communities reached 89 (Maynard and Twiss 1970), but in 1979 the records of the Oglala Sioux Housing Authority showed that the number had decreased to 50, reflecting an attempt by the federal government working through the tribal council to consolidate a number of the smaller communities.

Because of the exogamous principle, members of the original *tiyošpayes* and their descendants are scattered widely throughout each of the communities. However, ideological and kinship ties are still strong and serve as a basis for a number of food events.

The population of each community varies considerably, from a half dozen households (30–50 persons) to nearly 3,000 persons in the largest reservation town, Pine Ridge Village. Whether large or small, each community maintains relationships through intermarriage with members of other communities within the same district, or across district boundaries. Furthermore, members of all communities are related by virtue of the fact that they regard themselves primarily as Oglalas. When investigating the locus of food events, it is necessary to distinguish between communities, districts, and the reservation at large on the one hand and families and extended families on the other because of the significant numbers of people composing each category.

If one examines the spatial relationships between family households in each community, it soon becomes apparent that they are systematically arranged in clusters. Some clusters may contain as many as five or six households, separated from each other by several to a hundred yards. Clustering is reflective of kinship ties, mainly extended families, and duplicates the manner of arranging households during buffalo-hunting days. The clusters of households in each community on the average are separated from each other by a half mile to several miles in some of the remote areas of the reservation. What is important about the cluster is that not all of the households contain kitchens, and in some cases when kitchens are present, they are not functional. Thus, we may distinguish immediately between houses used exclusively as domiciles and houses used as domiciles but which also contain functioning kitchens.

The internal kitchen is usually located in a separate room, although there are still some one-room houses in which families cook as well as sleep (sometimes augmented by a wall tent for sleeping, particularly in the summer).

There are a number of variations in external kitchens. At large celebrations such as the sun dance, families often construct outdoor shades next to their tents or tipis. Tables, chairs, and portable cooking equipment are transported from home, and those meals not provided by the sponsoring committee are taken inside the shade. Constructed from small pine trees and locally called "squaw coolers," the shades offer welcome relief from the sun on an otherwise desolate prairie.

Where there are permanent dance grounds, there are also one or two large pits in which fires are laid and pots of soup or stew cooked on top of an iron grill placed across the pit. Often there is a small shed located near the pits where some of the butchering is done.

Events such as wakes and memorial feasts often require a large amount of space for eating and consequently they are frequently held in church meeting houses. Some of these meeting houses are equipped with modern kitchens and therefore some of the cooking may be done inside as well as outside the area.

During the latter part of July and all of August, families often go cherry picking (for chokecherries). Some of the cherries are eaten on the spot while others are collected for drying. Methodologically, it is convenient to regard external sources of raw foods which are eaten off the tree or bush as external kitchens.

By analyzing the constituents of the commensal unit (attendance, rank, and location of kitchen) within the larger framework of the reservation (community, district), we are able to generate typologies of commensal units:

A. HOUSEHOLD COMMENSAL UNIT

This unit is composed of members of separate domiciles in the same cluster who share a common kitchen, and who are related along kinship lines. The kitchen is normally internal.

Figures 1–4 provide examples of four commensal "families" with whom we have worked and indicate the location of the kitchen and total number of persons in the household, or household cluster.

In these figures, the dotted lines indicate separate households, and the letter K locates the kitchen. We have also included abandoned or unoccupied houses in the figures because they frequently serve as the focus of a food event—for example, ritual curing ceremonies and sometimes wakes. Obviously, these four commensal units exhibit a wide range of variation from the perspective of attendants and kitchen. However, only Figure 2 is unusual in that normally we do not find so many children and grandchildren occupying the same house. In Figure 1 even though there are three kitchens, in practice,

owing to kinship ties between members of these separate households, meals are frequently exchanged—that is, each kitchen alter-
nately serves as the host for the other households in the cluster.

In the community in which we worked, as well as in three other
communities where surveys were taken, the average number of persons composing the household commensal unit is nine.

B. EXTRA-HOUSEHOLD COMMENSAL UNIT

This unit is composed of members of one or more domiciles who
together take one or more meals away from their respective internal
kitchens. In effect, the composition of this unit is the same as for the
household commensal unit with the exception that the kitchen is external—that is, located on one's land; as the primary example we include chokecherry picking in the late summer. The average number
of persons in this unit is ideally nine, but it is less predictable than
other commensal units.

C. EXTENDED HOUSEHOLD COMMENSAL UNIT

This unit is composed of members of two or more clusters of households which make up a segment of a community and who take their
meals in a single kitchen. Figures 1, 2, and 3 are members of this unit
by virtue of close kinship ties. The kitchen is most frequently external, and the average number in attendance is 30.

D. COMMUNITY COMMENSAL UNIT

This unit is composed of multiple clusters of households located
within the boundaries of a single reservation community, as well as
visitors who are normally related by kinship ties from other communities. Community affiliation here is synonymous with *tiyošpaye*
membership. Kitchens are external, sometimes including auxiliary
facilities such as church kitchens, and the average number is 300.

E. DISTRICT COMMENSAL UNIT

This unit is rather artificial, having been developed as a result of
federal policy rather than any intrinsic characteristic of Oglala social
organization. The district is an administrative segment of the reservation. Frequently, several communities within the same district
sponsor food events usually associated with secular activities such as
powwows. The kitchen is external, and the average number in attendance is 1,000. There is an absence of strong kinship ties.

Key to symbols:

△ = male

○ = female

⧍ ∅ = dead or moved away

———— (under symbol) = relationship by marriage

———— (over symbol) = sibling relationship

_ _ _ _ _ = separate households

Ⓚ = kitchen

| = lineal relations

For example, 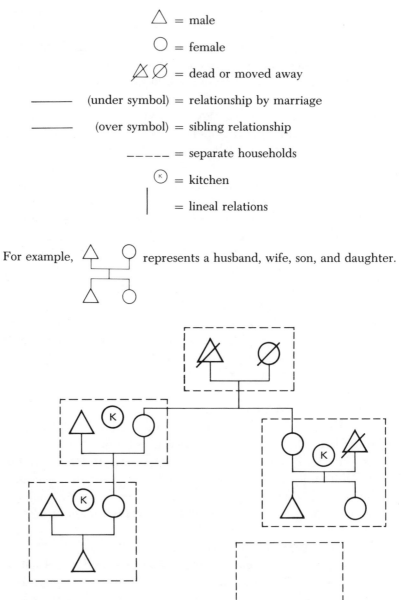 represents a husband, wife, son, and daughter.

Figure 1. A cluster of households in which all residents are related to each other. There are kitchens in only three of the five households; one house is used exclusively as a dormitory; the abandoned house is used occasionally for rituals such as Yuwipi.

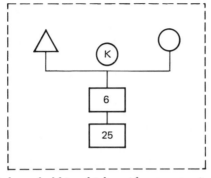

Figure 2.   A single household in which reside parents, six children and their spouses, and twenty-five grandchildren. An unusual case.

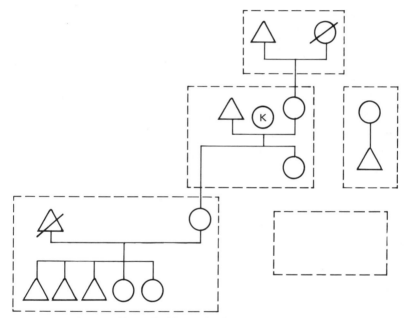

Figure 3.   A cluster of households in which one kitchen serves one extended family living in three houses, and one household of unrelated persons. Again, there is an abandoned house used for rituals.

F. TRIBAL COMMENSAL UNIT

This unit in theory is composed of all households in all communities of all districts on the reservation, as well as occasional visitors from other reservations. The kitchen is external, and the attendance may reach as many as 10,000. There is an absence of strong kinship ties.

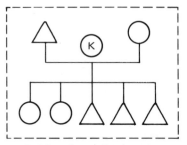

Figure 4. A single household with one kitchen serving a single family comprising parents and their unmarried sons and daughters.

Oglala Meals and Feasts

Food events not only differ from each other on the basis of attendance, rank, and location of kitchen, but on the varieties of foods and their preparations deemed appropriate for each occasion. The menu type indicates the appropriate quantity and quality of food, whether it is classified traditional or modern, the time designated for eating the food (whether it is scheduled or unscheduled), and the length of time required for the entire food event. As we shall see, there is a relationship between menu types and commensal units.

We distinguish between two types of menu: the meal, which may be subdivided into a primary meal and a secondary meal, and the feast, which may be subdivided into a low feast and a high feast.

The Oglala meal corresponds to the usual English sense of the word: it is a combination of food varieties, traditional or modern, served on a daily basis, at regular intervals. The meal is composed of a relatively constant measure of food, and the length of time required to eat a meal is similarly fixed, although some flexibility is permitted.

It is expected that there will be a correlation between food varieties and the daily interval; thus, certain types of food are appropriate during specific parts of the day or night. It is also expected that the selection of appropriate foods as well as the intervals during which they are eaten will vary from one society to the next, and less so within any given society. There also may be a great deal of individual preferences for kinds of food and times to eat them. However, statistically there will be some agreement that certain foods and intervals are more appropriate than others despite one's individual taste.

Some people may be stimulated by sounds of sizzling bacon, the gurgle of a boiling stewpot, or the whistle of a teapot. Similarly, in the preparation of food people may be stimulated by the process of kneading bread or testing the freshness of baked bread with a squeeze; a pinch of salt may be more than a metaphor.

Some Oglala linguistic examples demonstrate a "tactile" classification system for some modern foods:

English	Lakota	Gloss
peach	*taspanhinšma*	hairy apple
pear	*taspan yupestola*	sharp apple
pepper	*yamnumnugapi*	crunched
haw	*taspanslosloya*	mushy apple
sliced bread	*aguyapi tacangu*	lung bread
cracker	*aguyapi psaka*	brittle bread
flour	*aguyapi blu*	bread dust
celery	*wicahiyutapi*	crunchy tooth

In the Oglala food classification system, two points should be made. First, whether classified as traditional or modern, all foods have Lakota terms: the traditional foods are known by their prereservation terms; all modern foods are identified by modifications of terms for traditional foods; for example, *tinpsila* (wild turnip) forms the base for *tinpsila ša* (carrot, that is, a red wild turnip). The Lakota term for apple *(taspan)* serves as the base for lemon *(taspanziskuya,* yellow sour apple), banana *(taspan škopa,* curved apple), orange *(taspanzi,* yellow apple), and so forth.

Second, the classification system itself is amenable to reclassifying Euro-American foods under traditional Oglala categories. Beef, for example, is a kind of buffalo; in fact, the sexual distinctions reserved for some of the older animals are retained for beef—for example, *tabloka* (bull, that is, male ruminant) and *ptegleška* (cow, that is, spotted buffalo cow). Coffee is now called *wakalyapi* (something made hot), but originally it was termed *pejuta sapa* (black medicine), and the process of making coffee was regarded as analogous to concocting herbal brews. Today, black coffee (as opposed to coffee with cream and sugar) is still called *paza* (bitter) rather than *sapa* (black).

The ubiquitous fried bread, variations of which are found in nearly all Native American tribes, is, according to the traditional classification neither fried (for which there is no term) nor bread. It is *wigli un kagapi* (made with grease), the latter being a staple diet long before the white man. Baking powder biscuit bread, another staple also considered traditional, is called *kabubu,* which refers to the sound made when patting the pancake-like biscuit between the hands. Like fried bread it is "cooked" in grease.

As a final illustration of menu in terms of food preparation, the Oglala distinguish between only two types of cooking in the traditional classification system: *lolobya* (boiling, literally, to render something soft and fleshy) and *ceunpa* (roasting, perhaps relating to preparing food on an open fire). The term for roasting is the same one used for "frying" in an open pan.

Like the commensal unit, the menu permits us to predict the nature of the food event, based on the variety of food and how it is classified and prepared.

Primary meals are here defined as those food varieties and daily intervals which correspond to the American notion of three meals a day: breakfast, lunch, and dinner. On the Pine Ridge reservation, as well as other midwestern communities, the same meals are terminologically distinguished as breakfast, dinner, and supper. The intervals at which they are eaten and the duration of each meal correspond with the work or school day. Thus, breakfast is eaten immediately before work, dinner at the assigned work break, midday, and supper immediately after the work day has ended. There is a great deal of conformity of intervals at Pine Ridge owing to the synchronization of the work and school day, as well as the fact that most workers are employed near their own homes and can return there even for dinner. Most people eat breakfast between 7:00 and 8:00 A.M.; dinner between noon and 1:00 P.M., and supper between 5:00 and 6:00 P.M. Even those who are not employed subscribe consistently to this pattern. Most primary meals are thus scheduled and occur in the household commensal unit. The types of food served are most frequently classified as modern, although some traditional foods are served at dinner and supper.

Secondary meal is useful as a classification although it is somewhat problematic. It frequently corresponds to the American notion of snack, or in-between meal, and is usually not scheduled. The secondary meal is highly individualistic therefore less predictable with respect to food variety, frequency, and duration. Nevertheless, the category is particularly useful in differentiating primary meals from, say, ad hoc chokecherry picking, eating a quick meal in one's car or even on horseback, as might be the case at Pine Ridge. The location of the secondary meal is either the household commensal unit or the extra-household commensal unit.

The next type of menu, the *feast,* also carries with it the American notion of a food event which is somehow commemorative or celebratory of perhaps a historical or religious occasion. Where meals are predicated on a need to respond to biological hunger in some culturally defined way, feasts need not be. Feasts may in fact satisfy hunger, but they are seen as having some intrinsic social value which transcends the nutritive function of eating. Feasts have social goals achieved by cultural means.

The feast is partly differentiated from the meal on the basis of frequency and attendance: it is periodic, perhaps on a calendrical basis, such as the sun dance, but not always. Feasts tend to be held for commensal units larger than the household commensal unit. The varieties of foods served at a feast, as well as the manner in which they are prepared, is often correlated with the specific objectives of the feast, and therefore feasts tend to be highly structured relative to the meal. In Western society the nature and function of the feast is often predictable solely on the basis of the varieties of foods served: a wedding cake, a birthday cake, and a turkey dinner all carry symbolic significance of the occasion to be celebrated. Similarly, in Oglala society the ritual foods buffalo, dog, and *wasna* serve the same symbolic purpose. Feasts last longer than meals, and the measure of food apportioned to each of the celebrants is likely to be relatively more than that offered at the meal.

Low feasts are secular: they take the form of parties, picnics, school graduations, birthdays, and some types of powwows. High feasts are sacred: they take the form of the sun dance, memorial feast (and wakes), and ritual curing ceremonies. The varieties of foods served and their manner or preparation are mainly traditional at both low and high feasts, but only high feasts *require* ritual foods.

The rules for distributing food are strictly prescribed according to the kind of feast. At low feasts, the participants usually serve themselves from a centrally located table. At high feasts, however, participants are always served by members of the sponsoring family or committee. At high feasts, participants will be expected to eat beyond satiety. At high feasts in particular participants arrive with their own eating utensils and *wateca* buckets.

By combining the variables discussed heretofore, it is possible to construct a typology of food events that will account for all possible variations of food procurement, preparation, distribution, consumption, and redistribution or disposal at Pine Ridge.

Type 1   Secondary meal. Extra-household commensal unit. External kitchen. Kin based. Average number = 9. Menu: traditional/modern foods.

Type 2   Primary meal. Household commensal unit. Internal kitchen. Kin based. Average number = 9. Menu: traditional/modern foods.

Type 3   Low feast. Extended household commensal unit. Internal kitchen. Kin based. Average number = 30. Menu: traditional/modern foods.

Type 4   Low feast. Community commensal unit. External kitchen. Kin based. Average number = 300. Menu: traditional/modern foods.

Type 5   Low feast. District commensal unit. External kitchen. Mixed kin and nonkin. Average number = 1,000. Menu: traditional/modern foods.

Type 6   High feast. Extended household commensal unit. External kitchen. Kin based. Average number = 30. Menu: ritual food required.

Type 7   High feast. Community commensal unit. External kitchen. Kin based. Average number = 300. Menu: ritual food required.

Type 8   High feast. Tribal commensal unit. External kitchen. Mixed kin and nonkin. Average number = 10,000. Menu: ritual food required.

The largest clustering of traditional food events is between May and September. There are some logical reasons as to why this should be so. First, the period between late spring and early fall is more predictable with respect to the weather, and many of these events are held outdoors. Second, during the September–May period, normal commensal units are disrupted owing to the fact that children are in school. Children, as well as adults who are employed by the school, take all their meals in the school facilities, at least during the school week. School meals are of the primary meal type and correspond in terms of food variety and preparation to those served in the household commensal unit. It should be noted that district food events cluster in the same manner as household food events, because schools located in the districts often provide facilities for various food events, some being frequently more Indian than white in function, for example, powwows.

Metaphysical Aspects of an Oglala Food System

A closer examination of the typologies of food events indicates that all events are kin-based with the exception of type 5 (district food event) and type 8 (tribal food event), which are composed of mixed kin and nonkin. These food events are of particular interest to us because we hold that these events have provided historically a means by which new foods have been introduced into the traditional system. The district was originally established as a center for distributing annuities, the so-called ration district. It is at the district level that traditional foods and modern foods commingled; it became the point of intersection between the old and the new.

The tribal food event also has much in common with the district. Despite its religious overtones, and its prescription for ritual food, historically the sun dance was associated with a time in which the various *tiyošpayes* gathered for the communal buffalo hunt. The worship of the sun dance proper was always conjoined with intrusive celebrations: sodality dances, trade, and, most importantly, the selection of spouses. The Oglala joke that children are born nine months after the sun dance is not without some empirical base. But aside from the intrusive secular activities, once the reservation was established, the sun dance became the event in which food sellers, both Oglala and white, introduced a number of modern foods to the traditional system. The sun dance was often accompanied by a fair, rodeo, or carnival. Foodstands were set up, and while the participants in the sacred part of the sun dance feasted on buffalo, those in the secular part of the sun dance arbor satisfied their hunger on hamburgers, hot dogs, cold pop, coffee, and, in recent times, Navajo tacos, imported from the Southwest.

Despite the secular and sacred nature of the district and tribal food events, they have one thing in common: they both depend on participants who bear no kinship ties, and they serve as loci where new foods are introduced into Oglala society. In the past two years, as threats to Oglala identity have manifested themselves in arguments over an individual's "blood quantum," it has also been decreed that the sun dance shall remain sacred, and that all secular aspects, such as powwow dancing (once a favorite pasttime after the sun dance had ended), are no longer to be permitted on sacred grounds. In 1979, there were no powwows following the sun dance; they had been postponed until another dance arbor could be located. Although never articulated in the master plan to make the sun dance exclusively a sacred food event, there were also no foodstands selling modern foods on the sun dance grounds.

Meanings in the Oglala Food System

Food is capable of symbolizing the manner in which people view themselves with respect to insiders and outsiders of society. Here, gastronomic categories and culinary practices have meanings far beyond their biological and historical contexts. Food systems may be treated as codes, bearing messages relative to everyday social interactions:

> If food is treated as a code, the message it encodes will be found in the pattern of social relations being expressed. The message is about different degrees of hierarchy, inclusion and exclusion, boundaries and transactions across the boundaries. Like sex, the taking of food has a social component, as well as a biological one. [Douglas 1971, p. 61].

These patterns of expression are often complex and highly structured. And the structure of even the simplest meal is subject to decoding. But it is not only the order of food which is decipherable according to changes from hot to cold, soft to hard, or savory to sweet. In the same manner, societies change with regard to what they consider appropriate culinary symbols of their own place in history.

Preferences for specific foods, methods of distribution, occasions for feasting, and even the manner of disposing of uneaten foods are often perceived to be ordained by the gods. Thus, even the most casual proffering of food is likely to be highly charged with cosmological significance. For example, conservative Oglala believe that all people before birth exist in a spiritual state *(tun)* located in the north. There, before being born into the physical world, they are instructed by the *Tunkašila* (Grandfather(s)) who tell(s) them that they are about to embark upon a journey. They will pass through four stages of life before they die whereupon they will return again to the south to report on their experiences. Before they leave, the Tunkasila advise(s) them: *Ho, iya po! Tka takuni akab yuha šni po!* (Go now. But never own more than you need!)

At a certain age a child learns that of the four Oglala virtues—generosity, bravery, patience, and wisdom—the first *(wacan-tognaka)* is the most important. The act of being generous reinforces the cosmological prescription to own nothing more than is required, and it is manifested in the continuous act of food sharing. Whites are often surprised to find even a three-year-old offering a stranger some of its bottled milk or soda pop.

The child later learns that the cardinal virtue generosity is countered by the cardinal fear starvation *(akih̆'anpi)*, which always needs to be reconciled, kept in harmony with the social and cosmological order. But this reconciliation does not simply take the form of staying alive or satisfying biological hunger or fear. Attitudes toward food and starvation manifest themselves in specific behaviors fraught with rules, proscriptions, and taboos, all of which are irrefutably distinct from those of the white man. These rules, then, do not simply distinguish between that which people eat; they serve to classify through ritual observances and preferences that which people are or perceive themselves to be. The social and cultural components of Oglala food taking and sharing do not so much rekindle the fires of the past, as they guarantee a sense of tribal and individual identity for the future.

Since the establishment of the Pine Ridge Reservation in 1879, the question of just who is an Oglala has been in the forefront of social, political, and economic debates. The need for distinguishing one's tribal identity came about as a result of intermarriages between white men, mainly French traders, and Indian women at the beginning of the nineteenth century. Prior to this time, as well as subsequent to it, Oglalas occasionally intermarried with the Cheyennes and Arapahos, as well as other Siouan tribes, but there is no record of any stigma being attached to intertribal marriages.

The offspring of Indian and white marriages became known as *iyeska,* a term signifying a person who spoke "white," that is, metaphorically, intelligibly (as contrasted with *šaiyela,* to speak red, that is, unintelligibly; also, the name for the Cheyennes). *Iyeska* therefore came to connote both bilingual persons and products of mixed marriages. In vulgar English the term is translated as "mixed blood" or "half breed." It is also frequently glossed as "interpreter" and, in ritual language, "medium," that is, medicine men who commune with supernaturals.

The prevailing (and then militarily enforced) myth of white superiority, as well as the fact that bilingual persons were capable of simultaneously communicating with both monolingual Lakota-speakers and federal administrators, gave the *iyeska* an overwhelming advantage in the politics of the early reservation period. They became the first cadre of official interpreters and thus were able to influence tribal chiefs and reservation agents through the spoken and written word. As the federal bureaucracy grew on the reservation, the *iyeska* became the most eligible to assume government jobs, and consequently many of them could afford better homes and chose to live in a manner akin to whites. Opting for a modern way of life, however, alienated many *iyeska* from more conservative Oglalas who preferred to maintain what they perceived to be *Lakol wicoȟ'an* (the Indian way), a lifestyle distinct from both whites and *iyeska.* The tension between full bloods and *iyeska* manifested itself in a number of dramatic ways and still continues to do so.

For example, full bloods are considered to be darker complected, to bear an Indian sounding surname, to be more competent in the native language, to adhere to native religion and other cultural ways, and generally to be uneducated. In terms of modern programs, they are perceived to be among the first on welfare, and generally maintain a lower standard of living, a standard delineated by the dominant society.

Against this stereotype, the *iyeska* profile contrasts predictably: some can pass for white (and for this reason some became the first generation of bootleggers); bear a surname of French, Spanish, English, or Irish origin (Spanish surnames elicit the comment "he's really a Mexican!"); are losing their native language; and have been raised or converted to Christianity. They are the first to be offered jobs, and, ultimately, local control of the reservation. They are included in such key positions as the tribal council, judicial system, police force, and agencies controlling annuities, welfare, aid to dependent children, and housing. In other words, the *iyeska* are viewed as potentially controlling the total range of activities and program affecting the everyday lives of the full bloods.

Since 1978, the tension has increased because of bills reintroduced by members of the Oglala Sioux tribal council which would redefine the amount of "blood quantum" required by a bona fide member of the tribe as one-half instead of one-quarter. The *iyeska* regard this legislation as particularly threatening since their children and grandchildren may be technically classified as white and thus lose not only membership in the tribe but rights to inherit land on the reservation.

Furthermore, in 1979 the Oglala and other Sioux were asked by the federal government to again reconsider settling a claim for the Black Hills. Upon settlement, over 100 million dollars would be distributed among only those persons who are bona fide members of numerous Sioux populations. Although it is anticipated that the claim will be litigated for some years, once settled, the majority of *iyeska* would not be entitled to any part of the claim. Hence, debates over tribal membership and degrees of Indianness rage even more strongly today than they did during the early reservation period. At the moment, being Oglala is primarily determined by birth and residence on the reservation.

Statistically, the distinction between *iyeska* and full blood does not obtain very well, as might be expected. Some *iyeska* speak Lakota more fluently than full bloods; there is an equal representation of Indian and non-Indian sounding surnames on the tribal council, and so forth. And although it is often difficult to see wherein lies the basis for *de facto* discrimination, it exists with enough frequency that the myth of mixed blood favoritism can be said to rise periodically with the occurrence of white threats to Oglala solidarity, both from the perspective of ideology and economics.

In distinguishing between patterns of social relations and their various modes of expression, we see here in the political and economic arena a recognized distinction between persons inside the Oglala tribal boundary, the full bloods; those completely outside, whites; and a mediating social group, the *iyeska*, which shows characteristics of both groups. In many respects, this latter group has evolved into what has elsewhere been described as an anomalous category (Douglas 1966; particularly chapter 3).

If all facets of the food system—procurement, preparation, distribution, consumption, and disposal—are indeed part of a code, then the message found in the pattern of gastronomic relations among the Oglala is analogous to the structural relations between the full bloods, whites, and mediating *iyeska*. The message is also about endogamy (a priority is placed on intermarriage between Oglalas, even among *iyeska*, who are admonished to "marry back into blood") and exogamy (marriage between Oglalas and whites or, recently, between Oglalas and members of other tribes).

The Treaty of Fort Laramie between the federal government and Sioux tribes, and subsequent ratifications of this treaty, established firmly the annuity program on the Pine Ridge Reservation. This was followed by the construction of trading posts and general stores by entrepreneurs, and eventually supplemented by grocery stores, supermarkets, cafes, restaurants, and fast-food chains, all within a sixty-mile radius of the reservation. Therefore, today foods and preparations of Euro-American origin are readily accessible by the Oglala. Most meals eaten in the household and in the schools reflect newly introduced foods, though not exclusively. Under certain conditions perceived to be *ehanni Lakota* (old-time Indian) or *ikce Lakota* (originally Indian) there is a decided preference, if not prescription, for traditional foods, that is, those foods that were eaten by the Oglala before the arrival of the white man. In the sacred rituals, special traditional foods—that is, ritual foods—underscore the relationship between food and cosmology. Buffalo meat is required for the sun dance; dog meat for ritual curing ceremonies such as *Yuwipi;* and *wasna* for the memorial feast. Furthermore, all foods are classified as *ehank'ehan* (traditional) or *lehanl* (modern). Some foods such as beef, coffee, and fry bread, although newly-introduced by Euro-Americans, are today regarded as traditional foods and are consumed as an integral part of both sacred and secular events.

Food as a Code

By way of conclusion, we should like to emphasize some of the points made above with respect not only to the Oglala case, but to future cross-cultural studies of the relationship between food and culture, and to raise some more questions.

It is useful in the analysis of food events to consider a distributive component which focuses on the relationship between attendants from the perspective of kinship, friendship, or other forms of status and upon the location of the kitchen within a larger geopolitical boundary. Another set of general questions would ask whether some societies prepare more food than can possibly be eaten by the participants; whether participants are expected to eat "just enough" or beyond satiety. Perhaps in some societies so little food is offered that hunger is not satisfied, for example, partial fasting required by some participants in the sun dance. The question begged is whether or not the amount of food served lives up to cultural expectations. These expectations take the form of conscious or unconscious rules about portions of foods, whether second or third "helpings" are permitted (or required), or whether one simply tastes a morsel no matter how elaborate the preparation time.

If more or less food must be offered relative to actual nutritional requirements or satisfaction of hunger, then the practice conveys a message that is decodable to the members of the society in question (or to the anthropologist who investigates them). At either end of the pole—too much or too little food—a statement of values is being conveyed through the medium of food. In Oglala society, overindulgence at a feast is a statement about generosity from the host's point of view, generosity ordained by the Grandfathers. But the statement does not rest simply on the relationships between anticipated quantities of food, number of commensal participants, or whether the meal or the feast is held in a dining room or rented hall. We must also consider gastronomic criteria for varieties of foods and preparations, and how they are classified. We must study the expected effects on the sensory modalities and the sensory ordering of the meal: hot to cold, savory to sweet, or perhaps mushy to jagged, if it is the tactile modality which serves as the basis for classification. We must also employ visual, olfactory, and gustatory criteria. We must not simply seek to quantify the number of food varieties, but to understand their structural relationships within the consumption unit.

There is a relationship between gastronomic considerations and the commensal setting, whether the meal is served indoors or outdoors, on a table or on the ground, whether special service is required, or whether food is eaten with the fingers. In American society, sitting on the ground, perhaps on a picnic blanket, and helping oneself to an assortment of cold cuts "says" casual social relationships. In Oglala society, sitting on the ground and eating with one's fingers "says" formal social relationships.

As nutritionists know, gastronomic preferences are difficult to change, even at the expense of starvation. The process associated with those circumstances under which peoples accept newly introduced foods must be viewed with respect to other aspects that we have suggested here. In the Oglala case, perhaps the process of understanding foods in terms of their position in the classificatory system, as well as the ambience in which they are prepared and eaten, plays a bigger role in determining what foods will be accepted or rejected than simple attraction to the sensory modalities. Modern foods that have undergone such transformations such as beef, coffee, and types of bread were once rejected by the Oglala on sensory grounds, but later accepted when they could be assigned what was perceived to be an appropriate Oglala cultural setting.

The metaphysical aspects identify the nature of the food event with respect to the cosmological order as it is perceived by members of the social group and rationalize ideas of protocol, propriety, etiquette, and convention. We need to account for why candles are placed on a cake, why glasses are clinked at a toast, or how much food satisfies the gastronomic requirements of a ghost. This will usually be a metaphysical explanation of the relationships between food and exhortation, song, prayer, dance, costumes, masks, or icons appropriate to the feast.

Food itself may be capable of conveying the message of social relations: its shape, color, taste, odor, or special preparation. Thus, in American society, a cookie decorated with a red and green pine tree "says" something about the Christmas holidays, while Oreo cookies say nothing beyond themselves. Among the Oglala, buffalo meat and dog soup require a religious context—a sun dance or a ritual curing ceremony—but the foods are always symbolic of tribal identity, not simply because they are tasty, but because whites rarely eat buffalo and never eat dog. On the other hand, *wasna* is required at memorial feasts and may be served only during the daytime. *Wasna,* like other ritual foods, is symbolic of the traditional way of life because it was the food of hunters and warriors of another generation. It represents the cosmological order: the spirits of the ancestors prefer it over all foods, hence it is served in the day time when mischievous spirits are not likely to be attracted to it.

Given that statements about the structure and content of food events correspond to statements about human relations, then the process of internalizing Euro-American foods by the Oglala are simultaneous expressions of internalizing Euro-American peoples and their cultural values. The reluctance with which Oglalas admitted whites into their society as affines and the subsequent problem of the status of the *iyeska* are expressed analogously in the values assigned by the Oglalas to various foods and food preparations where the proposition is:

Oglala culture: Euro-American culture:
traditional food events: modern food events

and where there is an ambiguous or anomalous category created out of the point at which the dominant and subordinate societies intersect. Where we find such a point of intersection expressed in terms related to social relations both within and across the boundaries, we should expect to find similar expression in the food systems. That is, a traditional and modern food system should be mediated by foods somehow selected from both systems. In the Oglala case, the mediating foods are relatively few, and they are constantly in the process of becoming "nativized,"* just as the *iyeska* are being admonished to "marry back into blood."

By examining the types of food events, we see that specific foods and culinary customs are highly correlated with kinship behavior—at least in theory, because they provide a meeting place for unrelated people. It is at the district and tribal events that individuals are permitted to seek a mate, and it is precisely at these food events that exotic foods have been and continue to be introduced to Oglala society. (The same of course can be said of the school setting.) It is at these events that both insiders and outsiders and their respective food systems commingle.

It is anticipated that the relationship between food and identity will differ from one culture to the next, but these differences will only be a matter of degree. The degree of differentiation between people (and food) will likely continue to be found where social, cultural, and

---

*This process of "nativization," a theme which has been more fully developed elsewhere for the Oglala (Powers 1977) is contrary to most acculturation theory which sees Native Americans as exclusive recipients of Euro-American culture. In this theory it is implied that the process of acculturation is one-sided, and that Indians not only adopt the institutions of Euro-Americans, but they also subscribe to the full set of values which are assigned by the donors to these institutions.

Thus, because an Oglala has traded in his warbonnet, hair roach, and *wapegnaka* for a broad-brimmed Stetson, Bailey, or Resistol; his moccasins for a pair of Laramie, Tony Lama, or Acme boots; his horse and travois for a Chevrolet or Ford pickup; and his tipi for a split-level house, he has become, or is in the process of becoming, "typically" American. Although the idea of complete transformation from one technological state to another is quite compatible with some forms of cultural evolutionary theory, as well as with theological and philosophical notions of progress, from a social scientific point of view there is simply no empirical evidence which adequately supports a theory that explains the total acculturation or assimilation of an entire society, although the idea of individuals becoming acculturated or deculturated is perfectly tenable.

individual identity is threatened from the outside. The distinctions need not be sought in exotic cultures, as our own American culture attests—where we constantly seek to refine and reestablish the relationships between tamale, spaghetti, sauerkraut, bagels, curry, chitlins, fried rice, and sukiyaki, a smorgasbord of messages which we peculiarly decode as apple pie.

Acknowledgments

We would like to thank Zona Fills the Pipe, Clarence and Sadie Janis, Bill and Nancy Horncloud, Pugh and Etta Youngman, Everett and Hildegarde Catches, Darlene Short Bull, Oliver and Helena Red Cloud, and the Cornelius family, all of the Pine Ridge reservation, South Dakota, for their hospitality and continuing participation in our food project. Without them the research would have been impossible. But more importantly, we will treasure their warmth, love, and hospitality. We would like to thank the Russell Sage Foundation for its generous support, and our colleagues in the Food and Culture Program for endless hours of fruitful dialogue. In particular, we would like to acknowledge our great intellectual debt to Mary Douglas, who set very high standards and maintained them throughout the research.

Bibliography

Anonymous. *Pute Tiyospaye (Lip's Camp): The History and Culture of a Sioux Indian Village.* Wanblee, S.D.: Crazy Horse School, 1978.

Anonymous. *Treaties and Agreements and Proceedings of the Treaties and Agreements of the Tribes and Bands of the Sioux*

Nation. Washington, D.C.: Institute for the Development of Indian Law, n.d.

Bean, S.; Catches, H.; Fills the Pipe, E.; Makes Him First, E.; Powers, M.; and Powers, W. K. *Lakota Wicozanni— Ehank'ehan na Lehanl* (Indian Health—Traditional and Modern). Pine Ridge, S.D.: Oglala Sioux Community College, 1976.

Beckwith, M. W. "Mythology of the Oglala Dakota." *Journal of American Folk-Lore* 43 (1930): 339–442.

Buechel, S. J., Eugene. *Lakota-English Dictionary*. Pine Ridge, S.D.: Red Cloud Indian School, 1970.

Cohen, E. "After Wounded Knee: the Feeding of the American Indian." *Food Magazine* 9 (April 1974): 28–43.

Dary, D. A. *The Buffalo Book*. New York: Avon Books, 1974.

Densmore, F. *A Collection of Specimens from the Teton Sioux*. Indian Notes and Monographs, vol. 11 New York: Heye Foundation, 1948.

Douglas, M. *Purity and Danger*. London: Routledge & Kegan Paul, 1966.

———. "Deciphering a Meal." In *Myth, Symbol and Culture*, edited by Clifford Geertz. New York: Norton, 1971.

———. "Introduction." In *The Anthropologist's Cookbook*, edited by Jessica Kuper. New York: Universe Books, 1977.

Dubos, R. *Man Adapting*. New Haven: Yale University Press, 1965.

Ewers, J. C. *The Horse in Blackfoot Indian Culture*. Bureau of American Ethnology, Bulletin No. 159. Washington, D.C.: Government Printing Office, 1955.

Gilmore, M. R. *Uses of Plants by the Indians of the Missouri River Region*. Bureau of American Ethnology, Thirty-third Annual Report. Washington, D.C.: Government Printing Office, 1919.

Hanson, J. A. *Metal Weapons, Tools and Ornaments of the Teton Dakota Indians*. Lincoln: University of Nebraska Press, 1975.

Hassrick, R. B. *The Sioux: Life and Customs of a Warrior Society*. Norman: University of Oklahoma Press, 1964.

Hodge, F. Webb, ed. *Handbook of American Indians North of Mexico*, vol. 1. Bureau of American Ethnology, Bulletin No. 30. Washington, D.C.: Government Printing Office, 1907.

Hyde, G. E. *Red Cloud's Folk*. Norman: University of Oklahoma Press, 1937.

———. *A Sioux Chronicle*. Norman: University of Oklahoma Press, 1956.

Kemnitzer, L. "White Man's Medicine, Indian Medicine and Indian Identity on the Pine Ridge Reservation." *Pine Ridge Research Bulletin*, no. 8 (1969): 12–22.

Leach, E. "Anthropological Aspects of Language: Animal Categories and Verbal Abuse." In *New Directions in the Study of Language*, edited by Eric H. Lenneberg. Cambridge, Mass.: MIT Press, 1964.

Lévi-Strauss, C. *The Elementary Structures of Kinship*. Boston: Beacon Press, 1949.

———. *The Savage Mind*. Chicago: University of Chicago Press, 1966.

———. *The Raw and the Cooked*. New York: Harper & Row, 1969.

Maynard, E., and Twiss, G. *That These People May Live*. Pine Ridge, S.D.: U.S. Public Health Hospital, 1970.

Mooney, J. *The Ghost-dance Religion and the Sioux Outbreak of 1890*. 1896. Bureau of American Ethnology, Fourteenth Annual Report, pt. 2. Washington, D.C.: Government Printing Office, 1965.

Nurge, E. "Dakota Diet." In *The Modern Sioux: Social Systems* and Reservation Culture, edited by Ethel Nurge. Lincoln: University of Nebraska Press, 1970.

Olson, J. C. Red Cloud and the Sioux Problem. Lincoln: University of Nebraska Press, 1965.

One Feather, V., and Little Thunder, J. Tiyospayes. Pine Ridge, S.D.: Red Cloud Indian School, 1972.

Ortiz, R. D., ed. The Great Sioux Nation. Berkeley: Moon Books, 1977.

Powers, M. M. N. "Menstruation and Reproduction: An Oglala Case." Signs 6, No. 1, (1980): 54–65.

Powers, W. K. "Contemporary Oglala Music and Dance: Pan-Indianism Versus Pan-Tetonism." Ethnomusicology 12 (1968): 352–72.

———. Oglala Religion. Lincoln: University of Nebraska Press, 1977.

———. "The Art of Courtship Among the Oglala." American Indian Art Magazine 5 (1980a): 40–47.

———. "Plains Indian Music and Dance." In Anthropology on the Great Plains, edited by Raymond Wood and Margot Libert. Lincoln: University of Nebraska Press, 1980b.

———. Yuwipi: Vision and Experience in Oglala Ritual. Lincoln: University of Nebraska Press, 1982.

Roe, F. G. The North American Buffalo. Toronto: University of Toronto Press, 1970.

Spindler, W. H. Tragedy Strikes at Wounded Knee. Vermillion: University of South Dakota Press, 1972.

Standing Bear, L. Land of the Spotted Eagle. Lincoln: University of Nebraska Press, 1978.

Tambiah, S. J. "Animals Are Good to Think and Good to Prohibit." Ethnology 7 (1969): 423–59.

Utley, R. M. The Last Days of the Sioux Nation. New Haven: Yale University Press, 1963.

Walker, J. R. "The Sun Dance and Other Ceremonies of the Oglala Division of the Teton Dakota." Anthropological Papers, vol. 16, pt. 2. New York: American Museum of Natural History, 1917.

Wallace, A. F. C. Religion: An Anthropological View. New York: Random House, 1966.

Wissler, C. "Societies and Ceremonial Associations in the Oglala Division of Teton Dakota." Anthropological Papers, vol. 2, pt. 1. New York: American Museum of Natural History, 1912.

———. Indians of the United States. Garden City: Doubleday, 1940.

———. Red Man Reservations. New York: Collier Books, 1971. (Originally published as Indian Calvacade, or Life on the Old-Time Indian Reservations, 1938.)

3

Sociocultural Dynamics and Food Habits in a Southern Community

Tony Larry Whitehead

Introduction and Methods

Traditionally, the methodological orientation of anthropologists is to study cultures as whole systems. I agree with Leach (1976, p. 4) however, that all too often we end up studying a culture's social relationships, or its economic system, or its system of ideas. Others emphasize the role of the environment in cultural patterns (for example, see Harris 1977 and Rappaport 1968), while still others debate the importance of history in determining cultural factors (for example, see Herskovits 1960). I am of the opinion that all of the above have to be considered in trying, as Sahlins (1976) put it, to discover the system in culture.

I consider food behavior to be part of a cultural system because it is influenced by all of the above-mentioned factors. But like other aspects of culture, these various sociocultural categories are not usually studied together as related components. As an applied anthropologist–health educator, I believe that understanding such systemic relationships will be of great value in the development of nutrition education programs for health promotion and disease prevention. Thus, ethnographic data from eight study households in a North Carolina community are presented here to suggest possible relationships between food behavior and other aspects of the cultural system.*

SELECTING THE STUDY HOUSEHOLDS

One of the most frequently documented correlates or determinants of food behavior is socioeconomic status. Thus, in selecting the study households, I wanted some households of lower socioeconomic status (SES) and some of higher SES. The three indicators of SES that are most frequently used and that I used in sample selection are median household income, occupational status, and educational background of the heads.†

Another factor which has been found to influence dietary patterns is ethnicity or culture (for example, see Anderson and Anderson, 1977; Back 1976, Cussler and DeGive 1953; Goode 1977, and Shack 1976). Since there are two major permanent ethnic groups in Bakers County (a fictitious name)—black and white—I wanted to study both black and white households. I also wanted to keep the total number of households small enough to be able to study them intensively for twelve months. Therefore, I chose eight households—four lower SES and four middle SES.‡ These households are further di-

---

*This report represents only the first phase of a three-phase research project. This first phase was carried out as an intensive ethnography to generate valid suggestions as to the culturally systemic nature of dietary behavior and to present these suggestions in a (theoretical) model format. However, additional phases are being carried out to evaluate the relationships suggested in the model by testing them on larger, more randomly selected samples. The author was awarded a three-year Young Investigators Award from the National Heart, Lung, and Blood Institute to carry out the second phase of this research, which is now under way.

†The U. S. Department of the Census has recently switched from the use of "household head" to "householder" as the primary reference person for household census data. I am continuing the use of the word "head" here; in the case of an intact conjugal union I refer to both members of the union as heads. My rationale for this usage is to indicate that household decisions may be made by someone other than the primary money earner or the homeowner or renter—particularly decisions regarding what foods to purchase and prepare.

‡Lower SES households in this study are those that have an annual household per capita income of $2,000 or less; the householders have twelve years of school or less; and are unemployed, irregularly employed, or employed in menial, unskilled, or semiskilled jobs. Middle SES households are those in which the household per capita income is at least $4,000; the householders have twelve years of school or more; and are employed or have professional or skilled jobs. The household per capita figure for

vided into two black and two white households in each category.

Two other factors that are thought to influence food behavior are *household size* (in terms of number of members) and *conjugal status* (single parent versus a conjugal pair). Thus, within my sample of eight households, I wanted to include large as well as small households, and households headed by single females as well as by conjugal pairs.

DATA COLLECTION

When we began the research we had expected to live with the study households for thirty days to share and observe their meals. This method has been suggested by Nicod (1974). However, this method was possible with only one of our eight study households for a number of reasons.* Our data collection in the other households included sleeping in the home on some nights and visiting and sharing meals on other days. To supplement our observations, we recruited the female "key kitchen person" (KKP) from each household to maintain a thirty-day food diary of total household and individual food behavior. The validity of the data was checked through the observations made while participating in household meals. In addition, a household composition questionnaire was filled out by either the male or the female household head, eliciting information on the size of the house; the size of the household; the relationship of the members of the household; their ages, sex, number of years of school completed; their occupations and incomes; and the amount of property and number of cars owned by household members. Finally, a lengthy questionnaire was administered to everyone in the household ten years of age and above, eliciting information about their food practices and preferences, the various meanings that food and food

lower SES households is based on the 1979 United States Census designation of $7,412 (median household income) as the poverty threshhold for a nonfarm family of four (double that of 1970). Thus, a poverty household per capita income of $1,853 is slightly below the $2,000 figure. Assuming that the influence of income would be minimal for those immediately below the poverty threshhold and those immediately above it, I arbitrarily selected a household per capita income of $4,000 to designate middle income and excluded amounts between $2,000 and $4,000 so as to indicate real income differences.

*The reasons included overcrowded housing conditions for even regular family members, let alone an outside ethnographer; (2) some families not being receptive to anyone staying in their home; (3) the potential for conflicts occurring between fieldworker and same-sex household head because of suspicions of his or her mate being attracted to the ethnographer; and (4) the frequency of family crises that require privacy.

events (events in which food is consumed) had for them, and the level of network involvement and types of network reciprocity they practiced. Network involvement was also observed when we participated in domestic and network feasts, such as holiday dinners, family reunions, funerals, "homecomings,"* banquets, and church suppers.

The Conceptual Framework: Food Behavior as Part of a Cultural System

In order to study food behavior as part of a cultural system we must first understand what is meant by food behavior; how such behavior could be conceptualized as part of a cultural system; and what is a cultural system. I will discuss these three conceptual areas in reverse order, presenting the more general concept of a cultural system first.

A. THE HUMAN ECOSYSTEM

Figure 1 represents my notion of a cultural system (B) as part of a larger human *ecosystem* (A), which also includes the physical environment (C) and basic human needs necessary to physical and psychological survival (D), which are repeated over time (E). The development of this conceptual framework was highly influenced by the work of deGarine (1972) concerning the range and complexity of sociocultural determinants of food behavior, and Jerome, Kandel, and Pelto's suggestion of an ecosystems approach to the study of the sociocultural determinants of food behavior (1980). My paradigm combines concepts from both of these works, which I call a cultural systems paradigm because culture is a central part of it. The term "paradigm" rather than "model" is used because the concept has not yet been empirically tested as a model. The cultural systems paradigm is *structural functional* in that it focuses on what a cultural system is (structure) and what it does (function). Structurally, the notion of culture as a suprasystem consisting of systemic relationships between social systems, ideational systems, and behavioral systems is an old one in cultural anthropology. So is the idea that, from a func-

*"Homecoming" is a church-sponsored event held in honor of old members, most of whom have moved out of the area. These members are invited back for the event, at which a feast is the primary component.

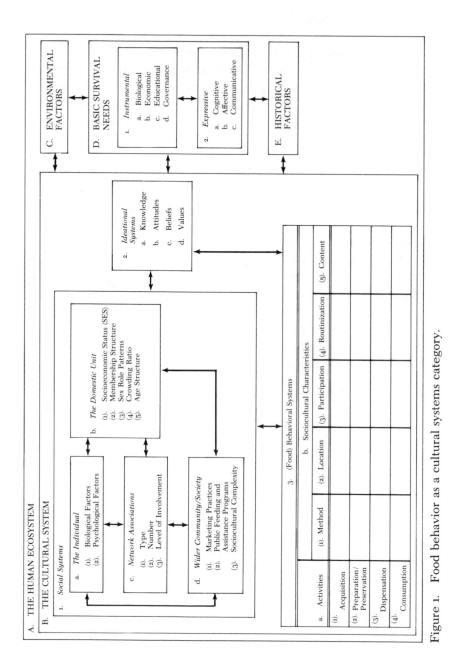

Figure 1. Food behavior as a cultural systems category.

tional perspective, culture is humans' primary means of environmental adaptation through the successful response to basic survival needs. The success of needs fulfillment over time provides the cultural entrenchment of a cultural system.

The systemic quality of the paradigm is indicated by the feedback loops (arrows) between the paradigm's components. The implication here is that relationships among components are not unidirectional but, rather, that the effect of one component on another results also in an effect in the opposite direction (Braden and Herban 1976).

B. THE CULTURAL SYSTEM

1. *Social systems.* The relationship between social systems, ideational systems, and behavioral systems suggests the place of food behavior within a cultural system, as social and ideational systems are viewed as determinants of behavior. It is suggested that three general categories of social systems exist in all human societies. They are *domestic groups, extraresidential networks and associations,* and *institutions of the wider community/society.* The individual is at the center of each of these social organizational levels. Individual determinants of behavior include biological predispositions (such as health status) and psychocultural preferences. Biological predispositions to food behavior are beyond the scope of my research, while individual preferences are viewed as being highly influenced by the social systems of which the individual is a part.

Domestically related influences on food behavior that have been suggested by my research in Bakers County include the *socioeconomic status* of householders, household *membership structure* (dyadic, nuclear, and extended), *age and sex roles, crowding ratio* (number of rooms per person), and *age structure.*

Extraresidential influences include the types of networks or associations (for example, kinship and friendship networks, fraternal organizations, church and other religious institutions) and the level of network involvement. Wider community and societal influences include *marketing practices* which facilitate the *advertising* and *availability* of certain foods (Jerome 1975; Popkin et al. 1979); public feeding and assistance programs; and sociocultural complexity, such as characteristics associated with *ruralism* (Bennet 1943, 1946; Cussler and DeGive 1953) and *urbanism* (Goode 1977; Harrison 1975; Jerome 1967, 1969, and 1975), and the level of cultural heterogeneity which leads to food-related social, ideational, and behavioral diffusion (Passin and Bennet 1943; Simons 1961).

2. *Ideational systems.* Ideational factors are what Leach (1976, p. 4) refers to as a people's system of ideas which structure their view of the world. In this category, I include *knowledge, attitudes, beliefs,* and *values.* Ideational factors associated with food behavior include knowledge and beliefs about what and how often one should eat; the association of certain foods with racial, class, or ethnic status (Bennet 1943; Cussler and DeGive 1953; deGarine 1972; Khare 1976); the association of certain foods with physical attributes such as health, strength or sexual potency (Ballentine 1978; Chang 1977; Gonzalez 1969; Kandel 1975); and ideas regarding sex role functioning (Konovitz 1975).

3. *(Food) behavioral systems.* In most nutritional research, food behavior is usually studied in terms of how food is acquired or prepared, or what is actually consumed. However, as a number of social science studies of food behavior have shown, there is more to food behavior than these three factors. The paradigm which is presented here addresses this complexity by identifying two general categories of food behavior and a number of subcategories in each. The two general categories are labeled food activities (a) and sociocultural characteristics (b). Included as food activities are (1) *acquisition;* (2) *preparation/preservation;* (3) *dispensation;* and (4) *consumption.* Sociocultural characteristics are those particular characteristics that help us answer inquiries of how, where, who, when, and what. Thus, I have termed these characteristics *method* (how the activity is carried out); *location* (where the activity is carried out); *participation* (who is carrying the activity out); *routinization* (when the activity is carried out and if there is a routine pattern of implementation); and *content* (what the substance is of the activity). Each of the four activities can be analyzed in terms of each of the five sociocultural characteristics, suggesting twenty possible analytical categories of food behavior.

C. THE PHYSICAL ENVIRONMENT

The physical environment is very important in societies and communities in which hunting, foraging, gathering, gardening, or animal husbandry contributes substantially to household subsistence; the physical environment in such societies determines what foods are available and when they are available. These factors also influence the social and ideational factors which contribute to particular (food) behavioral patterns. In most American communities, physical environment has less influence on food behavior than the wider community/societal influences that are discussed in this paper. Most foods are bought from retail outlets, and a small percentage of the population in certain parts of the country produce the bulk of the foods that are distributed throughout the nation. However, rural communities in the Southeast, like Bakers County, still have a number of families who garden and keep animals to supplement household diets. Such practices continue to influence food behavior for these families, as we shall see later.

D. BASIC SURVIVAL NEEDS

Because of the functional quality of culture, the paradigm also suggests that need fulfillment should be analyzed as a determinant of behavior. Elaborating on the work of Bennet and Tumin (1948), I have categorized basic adaptive needs as *biological, economic, governance, communicative, affective,* and *cognitive. Biological needs* must be met in order to survive. They include shelter, space, clothing, food, water, waste elimination, prevention and treatment of illness, control of harmful environmental factors (for example, insects and parasites), and reproduction. *Economic needs* are met through the production, distribution, and consumption of goods and services. *Governance* (political and legal) needs are concerned with maintaining order, resolving conflicts, making decisions for group purposes, and selecting and developing group leadership. *Affective needs* include social acceptance, social status, being liked or loved by others, having self-esteem, personal identity, and group identity. *Cognitive needs* are concerned with having an orderly view of the world, both natural and supernatural, and a sense of one's place in it. Finally, *communicative needs* include those for socialization or enculturation through formal and informal means of information transmission, and those for self and group expression through language, music, dance, art, folklore, dress, symbols, and so on.

As part of a cultural system, food behavior frequently meets needs other than simply the obvious nutritional (biological) ones. Food is used to meet health needs (Cussler and DeGive 1953; Gonzalez 1969; Hill and Matthews 1982) and economic needs (as when food is used as an item of trade or reciprocity). The timing, seating arrangements, and dispensing protocol of a meal reflect ideas regarding role allocations, gender orientations, social order, status, and control (Bott 1971; Budsall 1972; Burt and Hertzler 1978; deGarine 1972; Douglas 1978; Montgomery 1977). Other governance and affective needs that are met through food behavior can be seen when food is used as an ethnic, racial, or class marker (Bennet 1943; Cussler and DeGive 1953); as a marker of self-image, adequate sex role functioning (deGarine 1972; Lévi-Strauss 1964); or as a marker of group identity (Konovitz 1975; Regelson 1976; Shack 1976; Williams 1974). The location of a food event can be considered sacred by a group of people (Khare 1976), and the seating arrangement, dispensing protocol, and arrangement of the food can reflect their world view (cognitive needs) and act as a means of communicating that reality within the social group (Douglas 1978).

E. HISTORICAL FACTORS

When specific food behaviors exist in the apparent absence of any cultural, environmental, or functional reasons for their existence, one might look for historical reasons for the behavior. Though the factors that gave rise to the behavior or maintained it may cease to exist, the pattern may have become so entrenched that it continues simply as a matter of habit.

The remainder of this paper will further clarify the paradigm presented in Figure 1. The paradigm at this point is only tentative, however; the relationships between categories and the strength of such relationships are presently being tested on a larger sample.

Demographics of the Social System

THE SETTING: BAKERS COUNTY, NORTH CAROLINA

Bakers County (a fictitious name) is a community of 80,000 inhabitants, 79 percent of whom are white and 21 percent black. It is a typical rural southern community in terms of its history of agrarian economics, low educational levels, poverty, and racial segregation.* There is only one city with a population as large as 7000 inhabitants—the county seat of Bakersfield. The county has experienced rapid industrial growth in the last three decades, with eighteen firms

---

*The reader should keep in mind that the figures presented here are 1970 census figures; as of this writing, the 1980 census data have not yet been released and, as is the case with a number of rural counties, we have very little data between census periods with which to report. In 1970, the poverty line was $3,317 for a male-headed (conjugally intact) family of four.

employing over 25 percent of its labor force. However, 14 percent of its male labor force are still employed as farm laborers, and almost half of its land area of nearly 200,000 acres is still harvested or is idle farmland. Bakers County also annually receives hundreds of migrant workers, mostly black, who come from other parts of the country to work on farms from around May to October or November. The median education for men over 25 is a little less than nine years and for women almost ten years. For blacks, these figures are about seven years for men over 25 and almost nine years for women. Only 28 percent of the men and 33 percent of the women have a high school education. For blacks, these percentages are 16 percent and 22 percent, respectively.

There are other socioeconomic differences between whites and blacks, who make up 21 percent of the 80,000 county population. The median family income is only about $6000 for whites, and a little over $4000 for blacks. About 25 percent of all families are considered to be below the poverty line, but this figure rises to almost 50 percent for black households.

Income figures are, of course, related to employment opportunities. While almost 60 percent of both blacks and whites are in the labor force in Bakers County, blacks are more likely to hold nonprofessional and lower income jobs. The unemployment rate for blacks is 11 percent, while that of whites is 2.5 percent. The recent trend in Bakers County toward industrialization and mechanization has also displaced a number of unskilled and uneducated workers.

Twenty-one percent of the housing in Bakers County is considered to be substandard, but this percentage rises to 54 percent for black families. Seventy-nine percent of the housing in the country has plumbing, but only 46 percent of black housing has plumbing. Black households are also a little larger than white in terms of membership.

Retail grocery and fast-food chains are present in Bakers County as they are in other parts of the United States. However, there are also numerous farm stands in the towns and along highways that sell fresh fruits and vegetables. There are also "truck farms," which produce fruits and vegetables for sale to the retail chains, but also allow individuals to buy at the wholesale price. A number of people in the county have gardens and/or raise pigs, chickens, and, in rarer cases, cattle. The produce from such small-scale production is used primarily for home consumption, although people also sometimes sell some produce at the farm stands, from their trucks, or to members of their networks. Food is also sometimes given to intimate network members as gifts in exchange for services (for example, babysitting, or simply as a show of "southern hospitality" to a new acquaintance).

Some families that raise pigs carry them to the slaughterhouse to be killed and dressed. Other families still have traditional "hog killings," in which network members assist. In return, they may be paid as well as receive gifts of such produce as "chitterlings" (intestines), "maw" (stomach), "crackerlings" (fat), lard (fat used for frying), feet, snouts, tails, and ears. Sometimes pigs are killed for a "pig picking" (barbecue); network members are invited, and if there is food left after the feast, it is sold or given to network members.

While only 10 percent of the total housing units in Bakers County have more than one person per room, 28 percent of the black households have more than one person per room (as compared with only 7 percent for whites).

Although legal mandates have forced public integration, the remnants of the racially segregated past are dying slowly, if at all. Only recently have the welcoming signs in Bakersfield inviting old inhabitants, newcomers, and visitors to join the United Klans of America (KKK) to fight integration and communism been removed. A number of whites in Bakersfield expressed shame at the signs and seemed to genuinely feel that they did not truly reflect race relations in the county. Blacks, on the other hand, still feel that the Klan is a force in the county. They say that while the Klan does not resort to traditional threats and acts of physical violence toward blacks, it continues to hinder the advancement of blacks through its influence on local political, economic, legal, and educational systems. Within the last two years, the Klan in the area has joined forces with the local American Nazi party to carry out such activities as celebrating the birthday of Adolph Hitler and providing training for members and sympathizers in paramilitary activities.

THE STUDY HOUSEHOLDS

1. *Lower SES Black: James* The James family (all household names are fictitious) is a large three-generational household headed by a 52-year-old nonconjugal female. The family lives in a housing project in Bakersfield. But Mrs. Gertrude James, the household head, was born and reared in a rural part of the county, which she considers home and where a number of her relatives still reside. When our research first began three years ago, Mrs. James's household included

a 21-year-old daughter, Helen; a 19-year-old daughter, Jenny; an 18-year-old daughter, Celeste; an 11-year-old daughter, Joyce; a 16-year-old son, Andrew; a 15-year-old son, Michael; a 14-year-old son, Henry; a 5-year-old granddaughter, Deidrus (daughter of Helen); an 18-month-old granddaughter, Jennifer (daughter of Celeste); and a 4-month-old grandson, Askew (son of Jenny). Mrs. James's house has only three small bedrooms, a kitchen, and a living-dining area. There are back and front yard areas and a small front porch.

All of Mrs. James's adult children have finished high school, and the young ones are still in school. The employment opportunities in the area have provided this family with reasonable residential stability; they have lived in the present house for about thirteen years. Mrs. James, Helen, Jenny, and Celeste work as laborers in local industries, while the three boys work on farms in the area during the summer. Nevertheless, in 1978, the wages for all of the income earners of the household were minimal. The total net household income (after deductions) ranges between $1000 and $1200 a month (all from earned income). They spend about $350 a month for food. Their rent is $120 a month, they own no cars or real estate, and they do not have a telephone. The James household does not produce any foods, but it belongs to kinship networks in which some home production is done. The members of the James household are active networkers. Mrs. James is very active in the church and has a large network of family and friends in the area. Helen is very active socially, and Jenny and the three older boys are participants on various school and community athletic teams.

2. *Lower SES Black:* The Hart household is headed by Richard, 38, and Martha, 36. When we began our research in 1978, they had six children: James, 15, Mary 14, Boyce, 11, Jimmy, 5, and 4-year-old twins, Barry and Garry. However, during the spring of 1979, Jimmy died of a brain tumor. Martha's mother also lived with them until she died nine years ago.

The Harts lived in Circle, a small town bordering Bakersfield, in a small three-bedroom house they had built in the early 1970s. Both Martha and Richard are employed outside of the home. However, Martha's employment as a skilled blue-collar worker is more regular than Richard's work as a construction laborer. Richard's work is mostly outside, and there are periods when he is without work because of inclement weather, particularly during the winter and rainy days. Richard has only ten years of schooling, while Martha has a high school diploma and some technical training. All of their children are still in school. The total net household income ranges between $800 and $1000 a month (all from earned income). They own two cars, both are paid for: a late 1960s model and an early 1970s model. Their biggest expense is their mortgage, which is $130 a month. They spend only about $150 a month on food because they maintain their own garden and keep a few chickens and, sometimes, a few hogs. The only real estate the Harts own is the house in which they live. This house is on an acre of land, a quarter of which is used by Richard for gardening. Richard is an avid gardener who is very proud of what he is able to produce. Even when Richard does not have hogs of his own, he is able to get pork from relatives, and in return provides them with produce from his garden. The Harts are also active networkers. Mrs. Hart and the three older children sing in their church choir and with a gospel group that sings in churches in Bakers County and adjacent communities.

3. *Lower SES White: Clarks.* The Clark household has six members: Clarence, 23; his wife, Sadie, 23; and their children, Johnny, 6; Teresa, 5; Katy, 3; and Woodrow, 6 months. When we first contacted this family, they lived in a damp two-bedroom wood-framed house. The foundation of this house consisted of piles of unmortared bricks and stones. The family was also without water and toilet facilities. The primary means of heating their home was a small wood-burning stove in their living room. However, they stayed in this house for only six months after we met them. In fact, they moved three times within a twelve-month period. This high mobility seems to be related to where Clarence can find work as a skilled construction laborer. Sadie does not work, and the only employment outside of the home that she has ever had was part-time work in a tobacco factory during the summer of 1972 when she was a school girl. Neither she nor Clarence has a high school education. Their two older children are in school, and Sadie takes care of the younger ones during the day. The total net household income from public assistance and Clarence's pay is about $600 a month. They spend almost $200 a month on food. They paid only $65 a month for rent in the first house mentioned above. They do not have a car or a telephone. This family does not do any home food production and did not seem to do much networking. Clarence appeared to have a group of male peers that he spent time with, but Sadie tended to spend most of her time at home with the children.

4. *Lower SES White: Vincents.*

The Vincent family has three members: Betty Vincent, 23; her common-law husband, Herman Jones, 36; and their 3-year-old daughter, Lydia. The Vincents rent a two-bedroom mobile home in Bakersfield. Betty has never held a job outside the home, and Herman works irregularly as a construction worker. Betty has about nine years of schooling, and Herman has eleven. They have been together for about seven years, having met in a nearby large city and moved to Bakersfield about three years ago. Their total net household earned income (including public assistance) ranges between $500 and $600 a month. They own a late 1960s model car, but have no real estate or telephone. They do not home produce any foods, and, similar to the Clarks, spend very little time networking. Also like the Clarks, Herman spends time with his male peers, but Sadie does not have family in Bakers County and has not attempted or been able to make friends.

5. *Middle SES Black: Joneses.* The Jones family lives in Eaton, a town about ten miles outside of Bakersfield. James and Sally are both 30, and their sons Andrew and Jackie are 9 and 3, respectively. James has a college degree and a technical diploma. He works full time as a professional and part time as a special education teacher in a government-funded technical training program. Sally, with only a high school diploma, has worked for ten years as a skilled laborer. The Joneses own their seven-room home. James has used his technical skills to build an additional room. He also owns a large console television set that he partly assembled himself and a sophisticated stereo system that he loves to play and show off as a symbol of his skill and status. They have a telephone and two early 1980s model cars. They own no real estate except their house and the half acre on which it sits. Their total net household income is about $1800 a month. Their mortgage payment is $295 a month, and they spend another $200 a month for food. Both James and Sally grew up in Bakers County, and they both came from large families (four siblings for James and five for Sally). They are not food producers, but James's father produces vegetables, and Sally's parents produce vegetables and pork. James is very skilled in electronics and carpentry work. While the produce that he receives from his father is a gift, his skills are also frequently called upon. Sally is the "baby" in her family and she continues to get various gifts, including food, from parents and siblings.

6. *Middle SES Black: Smiths.* Kenneth and Joyce Smith are both

college graduates and Joyce has a master's degree. They live on the outskirts of Bakersfield. Joyce, 36, works as a professional, while Kenneth, 39, is self-employed in a small business that allows him to be home only on weekends. They have two children: Jean, 17; and Kenneth, Jr., 7. They own their seven-room house, on an acre of land, and two cars, one an early 1970s model and the other a late 1970s model. Both are fully paid for. They have a telephone and have no other real estate except the house. Their monthly net household income is about $1700. Their mortgage is $285 a month. Their food bill is about $220 a month. They do not produce any food. Both Kennedy and Joyce grew up in Bakers County and have an extensive network of kin and friends. There is some food production in these networks, but the Smiths receive very little of it. Yet the members of both of their families are very close and spend a lot of time together. They are also both very active in local civic and social groups.

7. *Middle SES White: Browns.* Albert and Karen Brown, both in their late twenties, have been married and living in their own home, a seven-room ranch-style brick house, for seven years. They have two children: Melvin, 5, and Jessie, 2. They are both high school graduates. Albert is part owner of a small business with his father, and Karen, who hadn't worked since early in her marriage, recently returned to work as a clerk. They have a telephone and own two cars, both late 1970s models, which are fully paid for. On their acre lot, they also have another house, which they use as rental property. Their monthly net household income is about $1500. Their monthly mortgage is $320. Their food bill is about $200 a month. Both Albert and Karen grew up in Bakers County and have extensive networks of kin and friends. They do not home produce any food, but have relatives who do raise some cattle and from whom they get some beef products.

8. *Middle SES White: Millers.* Harold, 58, and Molly, 56, and their 13-year-old daughter, Carol, live in their own six-room house on half an acre. Harold is a retired state official, while Molly has her own small business. Molly is a high school graduate, but Harold finished only ninth grade. They have a telephone as well as two cars, both late 1970s models that are fully paid for. Their house is a duplex, one half of which is used as the residential area for the family, and the other half for Molly's business. They own no other real estate. Their net household income is about $1400 a month. Their biggest expense is for food, on which they spend about $200 a month. Harold and

Molly both grew up in Bakers County and actually belong to the same kin network as do the Browns. They do not produce any food, but are recipients of beef products from beef-producing network members.

Food Acquisition

METHODS AND LOCATION

Three methods of food acquisition are used by the study households: *purchasing, home production,* and *informal exchanges.* Most of the foods that are consumed by all of the households except the Harts are purchased from grocery stores. Prepared foods are also purchased from the fast-food outlets that are now very popular throughout the United States. Fresh vegetables and fruits are sometimes purchased from the farm stands in town and along highways and from the various truck farms in the area. Fresh foods are also purchased from relatives, friends, and others who produce foods and sell some of the surplus. Snack-type foods (candies, cookies, carbonated beverages, popcorn, chips, ice cream, and so on) are also purchased from the mobile vendors that sometimes sell their wares in the streets of Bakersfield. Nonfood items that are purchased (and in some cases, home-produced) are alcoholic beverages. Beer and wine are sold in grocery outlets, but the "harder" liquors are sold in state-controlled alcoholic beverage stores and in private homes.

The Harts do not purchase most of their food because they have gardens and belong to networks in which some members are involved in food production. Mr. Hart maintains gardens on both sides of their house. The Harts' house also sits at the end of a housing development, adjacent to some idle forested land. This land belongs to a white patron of the Hart family, on whose farm Mr. Hart and members of his family have labored off and on for years and who allows Mr. Hart to keep pigs in these woods. Mr. Hart and his children also frequently keep chickens, which provide eggs and meat for the family, in a pen in their backyard. Thus, food production not only provides food for the Hart family, but surplus is sometimes sold for cash and used as a medium of informal exchange with network members.

However, the Harts are also food recipients. For example, Mr. Hart usually receives his pigs from his stepfather as a gift or at a lower price than they are sold on the market.

While none of the other study households are food producers, five of them (the Millers, the Browns, the Smiths, the Jameses, and the Joneses) belong to networks in which they get some of their food. Both the Millers and Browns belong to networks in which they sometimes get garden produce and beef products as gifts or in exchange for services. Similarly, the Jones household obtains vegetables and such pork products as hams, shoulder, ribs, tails, ears, snouts, fatback (less salty form of salt pork), and lard as gift items and in exchange for helping with harvesting the vegetables, slaughtering the pigs, and preserving. Similarly, Mrs. Smith and Mrs. James belong to kinship networks in which some gardening and raising of chickens are done.

These food acquisition practices continue to support preferences for fresh foods among much of the adult population in Bakers County. But again, the ready availability of prepackaged, snack-type, and fast foods, their high content of sugar, salt, and other spices, and their convenience have resulted in a growing popularity of such foods, especially among the young and those who can afford such foods.

In addition, such factors as economic status, conjugal status, age structure, role allocations, and the levels of internal household extension help determine food acquisition practices. Moreover, these determinants seem to be interrelated. For example, economic status can be related to the other factors because it is equivalent to purchasing power. A single-female-headed household may have different types of foods from a nuclear one because of less purchasing power, particularly if both the male and the female in the nuclear family are employed outside the home. On the other hand, an internally extended household may have more purchasing power if it has several adults employed. Thus, the Clark household, which is sometimes a single-female-headed household, has a lower household income than the nuclear Vincent household; but the Vincent household has lower household income than the nuclear households of the Harts, Joneses, Smiths, and Millers. The latter are all households in which both wife and husband work outside the home. The Vincent and Hart households have less income than the internally extended James household, which, although female-headed, has four adults working outside the home.

PARTICIPATION AND ROUTINIZATION

Usually the household KKP purchases the food from grocery outlets and farm stands. Food purchased from fast-food outlets, mobile vendors, and alcoholic beverage outlets is usually purchased by individuals. In home production and informal exchanges of food, any family member may become involved. Again, household composition factors are very important. For example, Mr. Hart is primarily responsible for the home production in his family. Of course, in single-parent homes producing food, it is that parent who produces food, unless there are children old enough in the home to be given this responsibility. In informal exchanges and purchases, either husband or wife may be involved. Whether it is the husband or the wife will be highly dependent on the degree of the husband's or wife's involvement in networks in which some food production takes place.

The routinization or regularity of food acquisition is influenced by the market availability of foods and the family's financial status at the time that the family purchases most of its foods. For the family that produces its food, the availability of land is important to routinization, as well as the development of the idea of routinizing production. Ideas of routinization and abilities regarding food preservation also contribute to the routinization of food acquisition. Routinization of informal network exchanges is dependent on the productive capabilities of food-producing network members, a sharing of ideas regarding exchange, and a willingness to become involved in such exchange patterns.

CONTENT

Tables 1 and 2 show the food items that were consumed at evening meals of the study households during thirty-day observation periods. From the tables, one can see that what has been acquired for evening meals may be a function of the method and location of acquisition. The Clarks and Vincents, who are most dependent on the purchasing of foods from grocery outlets, also tend to have more canned products and prepackaged foods than did any of the other study families. The four black families, on the other hand, had more pork products and fresh vegetables than the white families, which is related to more instances of food production and to higher levels of involvement in gardening and pork producing networks. The middle SES white families tended to have more "high-status beef" (discussed in more detail later) than the other families, except the Vincent family, because they can afford high-status beef and they belong to beef-producing networks.

In addition to these social system factors, ideational factors also seem to contribute to the difference in the foods acquired and eventually consumed by the households, particularly ideas around ethnic, racial, class, and personal attributes. For example, the lower SES black and middle SES white KKPs referred to such pork products as neck bones, "fatback," feet, ears, and tails; chicken necks, feet, giblets, and backs; black-eyed peas, and dried beans as "poor people's food." Lower SES whites and middle SES blacks, however, consider the same items "black people's food."

For both middle SES blacks and lower SES whites, the reference to such food as black is an indicator of dietary content as an ethnic marker. However, for the former, it indicates "ethnic inclusion"; while for the latter, it indicates "ethnic exclusion." For the middle

TABLE 1

Meats and Vegetables Served at Thirty Evening Meals

				Frequency Distribution of Meats Consumed				
Meat Types	Harts (Black)	Jameses (Black)	Vincents (White)	Clarks (White)	Joneses (Black)	Smiths (Black)	Browns (White)	Millers (White)
Total Pork	14	12	6	11	16	8	5	13
Pigs' tail	5	—	—	—	—	—	—	—
Shoulder	3	1	—	—	3	—	—	3
Hotdogs	2	—	—	2	—	—	—	2
Neck bones	2	1	—	—	2	2	—	—
Hogshead	1	1	—	—	2	—	—	—
Spareribs	1	1	—	3	3	—	1	—
Pork chops	—	2	6	6	—	3	3	3
Chitterlings	—	2	—	—	1	1	—	—
Sausage	—	1	—	—	1	—	—	2
Liver	—	1	—	—	—	—	—	—
Pigs' feet	—	1	—	—	1	—	—	—
Ham hocks	—	1	—	—	—	1	—	—
Ham	—	—	—	—	2	1	1	2
Backbones	—	—	—	—	1	—	—	1
Total Beef	9	7	23	10	7	12	17	14
Hamburger	3	4	23	1	3	4	5	2
Meat loaf	5	1	—	1	2	3	4	—
Beef stew	1	2	—	—	1	3	2	2
Liver	—	—	—	—	—	—	2	1
Roast beef	—	—	—	4	1	2	2	5
Steak	—	—	—	4	—	—	2	4
Total Chicken	7	10	1	6	7	6	7	4
Total Fish	3	3	—	3	3	3	1	1

TABLE 1, *continued*

Vegetable Types	*Frequency Distribution of Vegetables Consumed*							
	Harts (Black)	Jameses (Black)	Vincents (White)	Clarks (White)	Joneses (Black)	Smiths (Black)	Browns (White)	Millers (White)
Total Leaf Vegetables	22	20	11	2	14	6	5	8
Cabbages	8	6	—	2	5	—	2	8
Turnip greens	7	2	—	—	5	6	—	—
Collards	4	6	11	—	3	—	1	—
Chow chow	2	—	—	—	—	—	—	—
Mustard greens	1	—	—	—	—	—	—	—
Lettuce	—	6	—	—	1	—	2	—
Total Legumes	9	6	13	15	9	9	15	7
Field peas	—	—	—	—	3	—	—	—
Lima/butter beans	—	—	2	2	2	—	9	3
Garden peas	4	—	1	6	—	4	1	2
Blackeye peas	2	2	—	—	—	—	—	—
Navy beans	—	1	9	—	—	—	—	—
Baked beans	—	—	1	1	—	—	—	—
Pinto beans	—	—	—	—	—	1	—	—
Green beans	3	3	—	6	4	4	5	2
Total Starch Vegetables	29	22	28	9	25	19	21	12
White potatoes	11	9	22	6	12	4	12	7
Pasta	8	3	2	2	5	3	3	1
Sweet potatoes	4	3	—	—	—	—	2	1
Rice	6	7	4	1	8	12	4	2
Grits	—	—	—	—	—	—	—	1
Others								
Corn	7	—	9	8	3	1	8	11
Tomatoes	2	6	—	—	1	15	—	—
Squash	2	1	—	—	—	—	1	3
Cole slaw	—	4	—	—	—	—	—	—
Okra	—	—	—	—	1	—	1	1
Broccoli	—	—	—	—	1	—	—	—
Turnips	—	—	—	—	—	—	—	1

NOTE: The study families refer to the starch vegetables (rice, pasta, potatoes) as starches and not vegetables.

Pasta includes macaroni, spaghetti, noodles.

Lettuce and tomato were always consumed together as a tossed salad.

SES black KKPs, the more humble parts of the pig and chicken are a part of the "soul food" menu, a consumption pattern that they perceive themselves to share with lower SES blacks as an indication of their ethnic identity. For lower SES whites, however, the association of such foods with blacks is a negative one, and they refer to such foods as "nigger foods." For them, not to eat such foods is a marker of superiority. (See Bennet 1943, p. 63, and Cussler and DeGive 1953, pp. 132–33, for similar findings among rural poor whites.)

The idea of foods as ethnic, racial, and class markers are reflected in the dietary content of our study families, as illustrated in table 2. During the data collection period, low-status chicken and pork products were eaten most frequently in lower SES black homes, less frequently in middle SES black homes, and almost never in the white homes. The different use of pork products by blacks and whites suggest possibly another ideational trend. Whites frequently had pork products during the data collection period, but they usually had them either at breakfast or—in high-status forms such as chops, ribs, hams, shoulders, and roasts—at the midday and evening meals. Blacks not only had these foods, but they also had pigs' tails, neck bones, chitterlings, hogs heads, and pigs' feet with much greater regularity.

Because of this trend and because our families do distinguish pork by ethnic and racial associations, we have categorized pork products

TABLE 2

Pork and Beef Served at Thirty Evening Meals

Study Households	Distributions of Pork at All Suppers (N=30)			Distributions of Beef at All Suppers (N=30)		
	All Pork	Main-stream	Ethnic	All Beef	High-Status	Low-Status
Harts	14 (46.7%)	6 (20.0%)	8 (26.7%)	9 (30.0%)	0 (0.0%)	9 (30.0%)
Jameses	12 (40.0)	6 (16.7)	6 (20.0)	7 (23.3)	2 (6.7)	5 (16.7)
Vincents	6 (20.0)	6 (20.0)	0 (0.0)	23 (76.7)	0 (0.0)	23 (76.7)
Clarks	11 (36.7)	11 (36.7)	0 (0.0)	10 (33.4)	5 (16.7)	5 (16.7)
Joneses	16 (53.3)	9 (30.3)	7 (23.3)	7 (23.4)	1 (3.3)	5 (20.0)
Smiths	8 (26.6)	4 (13.3)	4 (13.3)	12 (40.0)	2 (6.7)	10 (33.3)
Browns	5 (16.7)	5 (16.7)	0 (0.0)	17 (56.6)	7 (23.3)	10 (33.3)
Millers	13 (43.3)	12 (40.0)	1 (3.3)	14 (43.3)	9 (30.0)	5 (16.7)

NOTE: Mainstream pork includes chops, ham, shoulder, spareribs, hot dogs, and sausage. Ethnic pork includes ham hocks, liver, pigs' feet, neck bones, pigs' tails, pigs' ears, hog heads, and backbones. High-status beef includes primarily steak and roast beef. Low-status beef includes such items as ground beef (hamburger) and beef stew.

as *mainstream* (bacon, sausage, chops, hams, shoulders, ribs) and *ethnic* (chitterlings, neck bones, pigs' tails, pigs' feet, and so on). Table 2 shows the patterns of mainstream and ethnic pork products consumption by our study families during the data collection period. The percentage of evening meals in white homes in which pork was consumed ranged from 17 percent for the Browns to 35.1 percent for the Clarks. There were *no instances* of ethnic pork products consumed in either lower or middle white SES homes.

Similar to the way pork products are separated along lines of ethnicity, beef products seem to be distinguished along class lines. The study families considered steak and roast beef to be food eaten by people who are economically well off. Hamburger, other food items with ground meat, and beef stew were associated with lower incomes.

Table 2 presents a breakdown of the beef consumption patterns of our study families. Note that the consumption patterns of high-status beef by our lower SES families is relatively low (nonexistent for the Vincents). Because 16.7 percent of the Clarks' evening meals contained high-status beef, and 36.7 percent mainstream pork, one might conclude that, since the Clarks are very poor, this is a personal preference or they may buy expensive meats as a symbol of higher social status than this family actually enjoys. Of course, these data may be unreliable since they are based solely on food diaries kept by the Clarks.

Food Preparation

This section will deal only with the preparation of evening meals, since those were the only household meals that all the study households regularly prepared during the observation periods.

LOCATION, METHODS, AND CONTENT

All household meals in the study household were prepared in the kitchen. In all households, the most popular method of preparing meats is frying. Vegetables are usually boiled or stewed (simmered in closed pots with lots of water). All of the families also like their "starches" prepared in a similar style—boiled and fried, rarely baked. Sweet potatoes are fried, baked, and candied. Rice is boiled and eaten with gravy. Cornbread is baked as muffins or fried on top of the stove. Biscuits and rolls are baked, and purchased "loaf bread" is eaten from the package.

When questioned about why certain foods were prepared in certain ways, the study KKPs would respond "that's just the way it is done," "that's the way my mother taught me," or "that's how my family likes it." However, methods of food preparation are related to what is prepared, and it is in content that the study families differed. From table 3, it can be seen that the Vincents fried all of their meats during the data collection period; the Browns and the Millers more frequently fried their meats than prepared them any other way. The differences in the methods of meat preparation by these families is a function of the types of meats prepared. The Vincents eat mostly ground beef dishes, mainstream pork (usually pork chops), and fish, all of which are fried at some stage of the preparation process. All of our study families believe this is the proper way of preparing these foods. Blacks do not score as high on fried foods because they consume a lot of ethnic pork such as neck bones and pigs' feet, which are usually boiled, broiled, or baked. Ribs are a favorite mainstream pork product for blacks and they are also prepared by broiling or baking.

The four black families tend to fry their foods more frequently in pork fat and season their vegetables more frequently with ham hocks, fatback, "streak-of-lean" (pork fat with a streak of lean meat in it), or pork grease than the white families. White KKPs tend to use margarine and butter more frequently than the pork seasoning used by black KKPs, although they too tend to view pork seasoning as the proper way of cooking green, leafy vegetables. This discrepancy suggests a relationship between the methods of acquisition, content, and preparation. The white families tend to purchase most of their vegetables from grocery outlets, rather than produce them or acquire fresh produce from farm markets, truck farms, or networks, as the black study families do. Although grocery outlets do sell some fresh vegetables, canned and frozen ones are more convenient. Because they rely on this method of acquisition, the white study families tend to consume more legumes and canned corn than the black families (see table 1). However, because these products are precooked, they are not as tasty when stewed like fresh vegetables. Salt, pepper, and margarine are best for seasoning prepared produce. And, when the KKPs do cook green, leafy vegetables, they tend to use those ingredients that they have on hand.

Two other ingredients that the study household KKPs seem to use

TABLE 3

Methods of Meat Preparation During Thirty-Day Observation Periods

Study Households	Frequency of Preparation Method by Meat Type																N	Percentage Distribution of Total Preparation Methods			
	Pork				Beef				Chicken				Fish/Seafood								
	Fry	Bake	Boil	Broil	Fry	Bake	Boil	Broil	Fry	Bake	Boil	Broil	Fry	Bake	Boil	Broil		Fry	Bake	Boil	Broil
Harts	0	8	6	0	4	2	2	1	4	1	2	0	2	1	0	0	33	30.3	36.4	30.3	3.0
Jameses	4	3	4	0	5	1	2	0	7	2	1	0	3	0	0	0	31	61.3	19.4	19.4	0.0
Vincents	6	0	0	0	23	0	0	2	1	0	0	0	0	0	0	0	30	100.0	0.0	0.0	0.0
Clarks	7	0	4	0	2	6	0	2	1	5	0	0	0	0	0	0	30	43.3	36.7	13.3	6.7
Jones	7	3	6	0	2	2	2	1	3	2	2	0	3	0	0	0	33	45.5	21.2	30.3	3.0
Smiths	2	1	4	1	0	5	3	4	3	0	3	0	3	0	0	0	29	27.6	20.7	34.5	17.2
Browns	5	0	0	0	11	1	2	3	4	0	3	0	1	0	0	0	30	70.0	3.3	16.7	10.0
Millers	9	1	3	0	5	5	2	2	2	2	0	0	0	0	1	0	32	50.0	25.0	18.8	6.2

NOTE: N does not indicate the number of evening meals (30), but rather the number of times meats were prepared during the 30 day period. For some families (the Clarks, Smiths, Browns, and Millers), there were evening meals without meats, while there were other meals with two or more meats of different preparation types.

120

TABLE 4

Menu Variety in Food Group Menus During the Thirty-Day Observation Periods

Study Households	Menu 1 MSVB	Menu 2 MSV	Menu 3 MVB	Menu 4 MSB	Menu 5 SVB	Menu 6 MS	Menu 7 MV	Menu 8 MB	Menu 9 M	Menu 10 SB	Menu 11 VB	Nontraditional Menu
Harts	23	6	1	—	—	—	—	—	—	—	—	—
Jameses	15	3	8	4	—	—	—	—	—	—	—	—
Vincents	23	7	—	—	—	1	1	2	—	—	—	—
Clarks	1	—	15	3	2	1	1	1	—	1	4	—
Joneses	17	4	5	2	—	—	—	2	—	—	—	—
Smiths	5	10	—	1	—	1	4	2	—	—	—	8
Browns	1	13	1	—	—	7	4	—	2	—	—	4
Millers	2	6	4	2	2	2	7	2	2	—	—	3

NOTE: The letters MSVB represent: *meat, starch* (which includes noodles, potatoes, and rice), *vegetable* (which includes legumes), and *bread*. Letter combinations (for example, MSV) represent the food categories included in each menu. Nontraditional menus are usually "fast foods" such as pizzas, hamburgers, and barbecue (hotly spiced shredded pork) sandwiches, and other items such as soup, sandwiches, varied fruits, or salad).

in great quantities are salt and sugar. We developed an instrument for testing the level of salt use or preference; it consisted of five chicken broth mixtures with exact graded differences in proportions of salt. We then validated the instrument on students of diverse cultural backgrounds at the University of North Carolina by asking them to tell us the mixture which represented the degree of saltiness which they prefer for their foods. The mixture mentioned most frequently was labeled number 3, "the most preferred." The two mixtures with less salt were designated number 2, "too little salt," and number 1, "much too little salt." The two mixtures with more salt were designated number 4, "too much salt," and number 5, "much too much salt." When we administered this test to our study households, number 5 was most frequently selected as the amount of salt preferred.

KKPs also made desserts and beverages that seemed to be very sweet to us. They made cold beverages with powdered mixes, seven cups of water, and one cup of sugar. Ice tea required six and a half cups of water and one and a half cups of sugar. These drinks are very popular, particularly in the summertime. Children and young adults, particularly adolescents, drink six and seven glasses a day, equivalent to drinking a cup of sugar. (Sweet drinks are such a cultural phenomenon in North Carolina that it is a custom in restaurants to serve presweetened tea unless the customer asks for it unsweetened.)

The rationale given by Mrs. Clark, Mrs. Vincent, Mrs. Hart, Mrs. Jones, Mrs. James, and Ms. Brown that they prepare their foods in a certain way because that's how their families like it suggests an association between methods of preparation and their view of themselves as wives, mothers, and good cooks. The possibility of such an association is indicated in the comments from a KKP who is not a member of the study: "Tony, I have a real problem. I know that John [her 14-year-old son] is a candidate for a stroke or a heart attack because his father had a stroke and died from a heart attack and because John is so fat. I know that the way I cook doesn't help the situation, but he loves my fried chicken and pork chops, and my cakes and pies. He refuses to eat other things and I enjoy the fact that he likes the way I cook."

Women's reputations as good cooks are also perpetuated by network involvement. Elderly people who have children who also live in the area with their families usually come for Sunday dinner and for such holiday feasts as Thanksgiving and Christmas dinner; such family ties are one of the reasons for extra care being given to the preparation of these feasts. Sunday is also a day for visiting and receiving visitors. Finally, many of the preachers in Bakers County churches are itinerant; that is, they may not live in the community in which they are pastoring. In such cases, the minister will be fed following the "service" (church program) by one of the active female members of the church. For these women, like Mrs. James and Mrs. Hart, the preacher's comments about how good their food is are highly valued. Mrs. Hart has taken such comments to mean that she is "the best cook in Piney Grove's congregation!"

Women are also the primary food preparers at church dinners, family reunions, and homecomings. Dinners are usually served at special events, such as late Sunday afternoon programs with visiting ministers, choirs, or gospel groups. The leading women in the church are responsible for bringing the food and warming it on the kitchen stove. Again, they receive accolades for their dishes.

There are two types of family reunions in Bakers County: those held by the direct descendants of an ancestral conjugal pair and those held by the direct descendants of siblings. Members of four or five ascending generations from various locations around the country usually attend. These reunions are held during the summer to coincide with vacations. Family members who come from great distance say that the greatest incentive for attending is the "good cooking and good food that one gets down home." Not only are feasts the focal activity of such reunions, but some visiting members carry fresh and prepared foods back home with them. All these activities contribute to the continuation of food preparation methods in Bakers County.

PARTICIPATION AND ROUTINIZATION

In the external settings described above, women are seen as the ideal preparers of food, except in the case of barbecues, or "pig pickings" where men slaughter and clean the pig the evening before the feast. At midnight, the pig is placed on the grill, frequently made from an old oil drum, and is cooked through the night. Sometimes, several men are invited to help with the preparation and bring their favorite spices with which to baste the pig during the night. The most common practice, however, is to invite one man who is known for his ability to barbecue a pig, who brings his own "patented" barbecue sauce. He allows the other men to baste the pig during the night with his sauce. The men usually stay up all night cooking the pig, drinking, and telling stories. The next day, the hostesses bring out the various side dishes (vegetables, starches, breads, and desserts) an hour or so before the feast begins.

Mrs. Clark, Mrs. Vincent, Mrs. Brown, and Mrs. Miller do almost all of their household meal preparation. Mr. Brown and Mr. Miller periodically prepare special meals, such as a big breakfast on Saturday or Sunday morning. Mrs. Clark and Mrs. Vincent are the only two KKPs who are not employed outside the home. Although Mrs. Brown does work outside the home, she and her husband share, with the Clarks, Millers, and Vincents, a strong ideational orientation for a sexual division of labor. Mrs. Brown went back to work following her youngest child's second birthday, which was necessary to maintain her middle-class standard of living; but she frequently complained about not being able to prepare her family decent breakfasts because she had to get to work so early. Mrs. Miller has her own business at home, which allows her the flexibility to carry out the tasks of the KKP.

The four households discussed above are also small nuclear units with very young children, as compared with the Jameses and Harts. The James household is large and internally extended, with a number of adults who share domestic tasks including food preparation. The sharing of domestically related tasks is a major reason for internal domestic extension. It allows for flexibility in work schedules (such as the shift work of the three working James daughters), while at the same time always having someone to prepare meals for the younger household members. Of course, external extensions may play a similar function if network households are nearby and network members have some agreement regarding the sharing of food preparation and child care tasks. The female KKPs in large nuclear households may also receive assistance in preparation if there are adolescent children, particularly daughters, who can cook or are learning to cook, such as in the Hart and Smith households.

However, sex role ideology may be a stronger contributor to differences in preparation participation than household composition factors. The basis for this assumption is the fact that the Jones and the Brown households are similar in terms of size, age of children, nuclear structure, and female KKPs working outside the home; but the Browns have a much stronger orientation for a sexual division of labor than the Joneses. This is manifested in Mr. Jones's assisting in food preparation more frequently than Mr. Brown.

The ideology for a rigid sexual division of labor seems to be strongest among men who are the primary money earners in their homes. This is supported by the fact that this is the point of view of Mr. Clark and Mr. Vincent, whose wives brought in no income; while Mr. Hart's wife, who had more regular employment than he did and brought in more cash income, showed the least ideational support. Mr. Hart's support of a more flexible sex role allocation was manifested in normative behavior as he tended to participate in food preparation more frequently than any other conjugal male in the eight study households.

Three routine meals per day is the ideal among all eight study households: a morning meal, a midday meal, and an evening meal. However, these three meals were routinely prepared only in the Clark and Vincent households. The two primary determinants of routinization seemed to be women not working outside the home and sex role ideology. Mrs. Clark and Mrs. Vincent are the only two KKPs who do not work outside the home, and they share with their husbands the strongest orientation among the eight households for a more rigid sexual division of labor.

Among the other six families, Mrs. Miller is closest to the Clarks and Vincents in terms of the frequency of routinely preparing three household meals a day. Again, running her business from home allows her the flexibility to do so.

Food Dispensation

There were three patterns of food dispensation observed among the study households: the *complexity* of dispensation (the different types of containers used); the *number of courses* served at meals; and the *protocol* used in dispensing food (for example, who should be served first).

The most complex method of dispensation involves the use of different containers for the preparation, serving, and consumption of food. In such instances, food is dispensed from preparation containers (pan, pot, bowl) to service containers (bowl, platter, plate) to consumption containers. The second method eliminates the service containers and dispenses food directly from preparation containers to consumption containers. The third method dispenses food from preparation containers to the mouth. The fourth method uses no containers at all.

A number of factors influenced the method most frequently used by our study households. First of all, snack-type foods as well as many of the fast foods do not require any containers. Thus households with the highest frequency of meal displacement with snacks and fast foods also have the highest frequency of method for dispensation—utilizing no utensils (the Harts, the Jameses, and the Smiths). Some foods, particularly casseroles, and some desserts are simply transferred from the preparation container to the consumption container. Thus, households that consume a lot of casseroles (the Clarks and the Vincents) and desserts (the Joneses, Millers, Browns, and Harts) will frequently use the second method of dispensation.

Income can be a very important determinant of dispensation complexity. I would expect less complicated methods of dispensation to be used by lower SES families simply because of the expense of dispensing utensils. However, household size and age structure can also be a factor. For example, the Clarks and the Vincents—the lowest-income households—utilized method one (inclusion of a service container) at their evening meals more frequently than did the Jameses and the Harts. Because the latter two households had more adolescents and adults with varying individual schedules, their members seldom sat down and ate a meal together; members frequently ate as individuals or subunits of two and three. Thus, they more frequently ate directly from the preparation pot or simply dished the food onto a plate.

Weekday meals were usually one course in all our study households. Sometimes in the higher SES households, a dessert was served as a second course. But usually, this depended on the type of dessert. If it was pudding, jello, ice cream, or some other "runny" dessert, it was served as a second course. But if it was a solid dessert such as pie or cake, it was piled on the plate with the other food or served in a separate dish, but served at the same time. The same was true at feasts. Here, the amount of foods available seemed to be the most important factor. A second course simply consisted of the foods that would not fit on the plate the first time.

In terms of protocol, the presence of the conjugal male seems to be an important factor, since men are served first at meals in the nuclear study households. External extensions are also important, particularly with regard to church involvement. When ministers show up for a meal, they are usually served first. The same is true for guests who have status but are not a part of the "intimate network" (such as the author of this paper). Members of the most intimate network are not treated the same way because they are expected to "make themselves at home."

A similar protocol is observed at feasts. At church dinners and church homecomings, the ministers and officers of the church are served first. At family reunions, participants usually serve themselves buffet style. In such cases, family members either line up by generations (the oldest generation first), or the oldest generation is served by female family members. If a minister is present at the meal, he will be served with the oldest generation or will be allowed to get in line with the elders.

Household size and age structure also influence the location, participation, and routinization of dispensation. For the two larger households, the total dispensation process seems to take place more frequently in the site of preparation—the kitchen—than was the case with the smaller households, where dispensation always started at the site of preparation but usually ended in a dining room or dining area.

The ideal in Bakers County is for the female KKP to be responsible for dispensation. But, in reality, this ideal is followed more closely in church-related food events than at domestic meals. At church dinners, female members prepare the food and serve it to ministers, important guests, and other church leaders (who are usually men). In the smaller households, the female KKPs usually dispensed food from the preparation container to the service container. Dispensation from the service container to the consumption container is usually an individual affair, or the person closest to the particular food item will fill the bowls of other members. In the larger households, individuals more often served themselves, dispensing straight from the preparation container to the consumption container or from the preparation container to the mouth.

Food Consumption

FOOD EVENT CATEGORIES

Three types of food events are discussed in this section: *snacks, meals,* and *feasts.* The differences in the three, as made by the study households, are based primarily on *content* (what food is consumed) *routinization* (when food is consumed) *method* (how food is consumed), *participation* (who is involved in the food event) and *function* (the significance of the event).

Among the study households, snacks can be both snack-type foods and meal-type foods (meats, starches, bread, and vegetables), if the meal-type snack is eaten as a single item, rather than in combination with other meal-type foods. These characteristics reflect additional differences between snacks and meals in Bakers County. Snacks are not consumed at routine times and are usually eaten as single items or in combinations of usually not more than two items (for example, chips and a beverage). Meals, on the other hand, are consumed at routine times (early mornings, midday, and early evening). The early morning meal consists of eggs, bacon, sausage, or ham, bread, grits, and a beverage (coffee or juice as optional). A balanced evening meal consists of a meat, a vegetable, a "starch," and bread. The midday meal can consist of the same items as the evening meals (and in the old days it did),* but it can also simply be a sandwich and a beverage. The meal is also considered to be somewhat of a social event in that it is a time for interaction between household members (and sometimes with a few intimate network members), whereas snacking is not usually considered to be a social event. Domestic rules regarding the differential statuses of household members may also be reflected at mealtime in dispensing protocols and seating arrangements.

Feasts differ from meals primarily in terms of the amount of food and the number of participants involved. In terms of what is eaten, most of the same foods that are served at meals are served at feasts—just larger amounts of them. Feasts may also be categorized in terms of differences in the amount of food dispensed and consumed. A *small feast,* such as Sunday morning breakfast, may be different in content from a weekday meal in that more bacon, sausage, or ham and eggs are eaten than during the week. On some occasions, a special food will be eaten for the Sunday morning feast, such as pork chops, rice, and gravy. Sunday morning breakfast differs in

---

*Because of the heavily agrarian past of Bakers County, most of its older residents have worked as farmers or farmworkers or had parents who had such occupations. Usually, the entire family worked and the adult female(s) would leave the field around 10:00 A.M. and cook a big "dinner" which would be served when the other family members left the field. This would be the main meal during the day, with "supper," or the evening meal, consisting primarily of leftovers from the midday dinner.

terms of participation from weekday breakfasts only in that more of the regular household members will be present (unless they have employment that necessitates their absence).

Sunday afternoon dinner is another small feast. The content consists of pretty much the same foods as are served during weekday meals, simply larger amounts of them. There may be some special foods at the Sunday feast that are not served during the week, such as cokes, pies, and dishes that take some time in preparation (hot rolls and barbecued spareribs). A household might have two meats, and/or two starches, and/or two vegetables, rather than one of each. The amount of food is partially determined by who will be present, which in turn is influenced by the level of network intervention. The Clarks and Vincents do not have as elaborate a Sunday dinner as the rest of the study families because their network involvement is much lower, and they receive fewer guests.

Medium-sized feasts are held during celebrations such as Thanksgiving, Christmas, New Year's Day, Mother's Day, Father's Day, and special birthdays. The content of these feasts differs from Sunday dinner in the amount of food (to respond to more guests) and the presence of certain special foods such as turkeys, ducks, hams, fruit cakes (Christmas), hogs' heads, and black-eyed peas (New Year's Day). Large feasts differ from medium-sized ones only in terms of the amount of foods served and the number of participants. Whereas medium-sized feasts are usually celebrated with immediate extended family members (other primary relatives such as parents, children, or siblings living in different households), large feasts will include more distant extended kin (such as family reunions) and kith* (such as church dinners, homecoming feasts, and pig pickings).

Feasts serve as communicative and interactive events, as well as a mechanism for displaying the different statuses of household and network members, in positional arrangements and dispensing protocols.

METHODS

The methods of consumption that were observed among the study households include precedence (whether hand-washing and the saying of grace or a prayer take place before consumption) and the social

---

*Kith refers to a person's social support network of nonkin. Kith are not only friends and acquaintances, or persons of peer status, but also nonpeers, or patrons and clients as well.

atmosphere of the food event (which includes special utensils, foods [such as wine], objects [such as candles], or music, and the amount of conversation). Whether hand-washing and the saying of a "grace" or a prayer take place depends on whether one is engaged in a snack and consuming snack-type foods or consuming a meal. People usually do not wash their hands and very seldom pray before a snack. Thus, large households which frequently displace meals with snacks, such as the James household, will tend to consume food without washing or praying. In the Hart household praying is usually done at meals in which the meal is a social event.

Network involvement also affects praying and hand-washing before meals in that the presence of guests encourages more of a social meal atmosphere. Grace is said if the minister or a religious member of the church is present. Grace is also usually said at feasts.

The presence of the minister or others of status and/or respect in the home or at an extraresidential feast can influence the social atmosphere of the food event. For example, their presence can promote the playing of gospel music which might not be played if they were not present. At family reunions, we have seen generational conflicts occur because the presence of the minister meant a change from rock music to gospel music.

The presence of church people can also affect consumption content, particularly the consumption of alcoholic beverages. The all-night drinking at pig pickings either subsides or the men move their drinking paraphernalia elsewhere. Some church women such as Mrs. James and Mrs. Jones do not allow the consumption of alcohol in their homes. At a number of the festive occasion feasts, men had to go to secluded places to drink because of the presence of a number of older religious women.

Network involvement is highly influential in other areas of the social atmosphere. The presence of special guests usually influences whether special utensils or items such as candles or wine are part of the food event. (Wine and candles at meals seem to be highly influenced by socioeconomic status. We observed them only in the Smith household, whose members are the most highly educated and have the highest household income of all the study households.)

Income influences whether or not one has special utensils. All four of the middle SES households have a set of special consumption utensils. However, while the James and Hart households are lower income, they also have special utensils that are used for guests. Only the Vincents and Clarks do not have a special set of utensils, possibly because they rarely entertain network members.

Another component of the social atmosphere of the food event is conversation. When the two lower SES black households had meals together, there was much more conversation than was the case with the two lower SES white households. However, there may be more conversation at meals in the two lower SES black households because they have more people of varying ages with varying activities. Yet, the black households also seem to have more of an egalitarian quality than the white households, where the conjugal male is viewed and treated as the primary authority in the household.

LOCATION AND PARTICIPATION

Consumption location among the households includes the location of the event itself and the location, or positional arrangement, of the participants at the event. Snacks can be consumed almost anywhere, but all of the households have an area or two in which ideally household meals are to be consumed. Whether a household has one or two dining areas seems to be influenced mostly by income; the four middle SES households have either a formal dining room or a dining area, as well as a secondary dining area off the kitchen, while the lower SES households have only a single dining area off the kitchen. The middle SES families, either as total units or subunits, consume almost all their evening meals in the secondary dining area, except when they have guests or during the household feast periods (Sunday and holiday dinners).

Within households, a number of factors seem to influence where some family members consume their evening meals. One, of course, is occupation: Mr. Smith's truck driving and the Jones girls' shift work forces them to eat evening meals outside the home. Another factor is household size. In the James household, one or two people may sit down to eat together at the dining table, while others eat in the living area, in the kitchen, on the back porch, in the back yard, on the front porch, or even in a car. In the James household, residential crowding seems to be a factor, prompting members to eat in various locations in the house. The Harts also eat as subunits at the dining table, while Mrs. Hart frequently takes her food to her bedroom and eats while watching television. After working all day, and then cooking or serving other family members, she says that she needs to relax. Mrs. Jones and Mrs. Smith, two other women who work outside the home, follow a similar pattern of serving their families and then going to their own rooms to eat and watch television. Yet Mrs. Brown and Mrs. Miller, who have cash-earning employment, usually eat the evening meal at the table with their families.

Network involvement contributes to domestic meal location. Receiving guests results in a need for more space than is necessary for routine household meals. This is not much of a problem for the middle SES households, since parents and guests use the formal table and the children use the secondary one; if there are a large number of guests, a card table is used by children, or they are fed later. Having only one dining area and one table does not inhibit the guests in the lower SES black households (the Harts and the Joneses) because of their dispersed style of eating. Guests usually eat at the table with the person(s) they are visiting and maybe one or two other household members, while the other members eat elsewhere. Lower SES whites rarely have more than one or two guests, so that eating space is not a problem.

Churches are very important support systems for families in Bakers County. Thus, those families with higher involvement in the church sometimes utilize the church as a location for large kin-related feasts such as family reunions, banquets, and funeral feasts. When a family does not have the facilities to hold the funeral feast, it is frequently held at the church.

ROUTINIZATION AND CONTENT

As stated earlier, the ideal meal pattern of our study households is three "balanced" meals per day. The existence of wider community influences such as public food programs (for example, school and Headstart breakfasts and lunches) and food assistance programs contributes to the maintenance of this ideal for children. However, for adults, there is quite a bit of meal displacement by frequent snacking. Wider community influences also contribute to this phenomenon, such as marketing practices that heavily advertise snack-type foods and the ready availability of such foods.

Domestically related factors also affect when and what people eat. For example, some occupations, such as Mr. Smith's truck driving or Mrs. Hart's shift work, contribute to frequent snacking. Household income can contribute to snacking, since some households can afford more snack-type foods, as was the case with the Browns, Smiths, and

Joneses. Snack-type foods do not necessarily displace meals, but provide something to "nibble on" between meals and while looking at television. Working female KKPs and large household size (the Joneses and Harts) contribute to eating snack-type foods for meals and to between-meal snacking on meal-type foods, since there is a tendency to cook large amounts of food either to serve as two meals or to respond to schedule variations. There are more routine meals and less snacking in the Vincent and Clark households in which the women do not work outside the home.

It seems that women not working outside the home coupled with sex role ideas supporting a traditional division of labor are the greatest contributors to meal routinization. Ideas regarding a sexual division of labor are very important to this relationship, for the Harts have very routinized household meals, although Mrs. Hart works outside the home. But their views in favor of a sexual division of labor are not as strong as those among the Millers, Clarks, and Vincents. Moreover, in all of the study households in which there was a conjugal male present, more men than women insisted on three meals a day prepared at a routinized time, again except Mr. Hart. Mr. Hart is not the primary money earner in his home, which might suggest that the influence of the conjugal male on meal routinization is dictated by his adequacy in carrying out the traditional male role of family provider.

Network involvement, particularly church and extended family obligations, contributes paradoxically to meal routines as well as to snacking and meal displacement. The main program for most churches begins at 11:00 A.M. and ends by 1:00 P.M. For our families that are regular church-goers (the Harts, Mrs. James and her younger children, the Joneses, the Smiths, and the Millers), Sunday morning "breakfast" is usually consumed between 8:00 and 10:00 A.M., and Sunday afternoon dinner is usually consumed between 1:30 and 3:30 P.M. These times also make it possible for some family members to attend additional programs, such as Sunday morning Sunday school (the Hart children) which usually runs between 10:00 and 10:45 A.M., or special programs that might occur on Sunday afternoons and/or evenings (Mrs. James and the Harts).

Both Sunday breakfast and dinner are small feasts, as special items and large amounts are prepared. The large Sunday afternoon dinners obviate the necessity of preparing an evening meal. This frees the household for leisure-time activities such as attending special afternoon and evening church services, going to baseball games, and receiving guests.

IDEATIONAL FACTORS

The ideational association of humble pork products with blacks by lower SES whites is probably related to the fact that the lower SES white families in our study consumed fewer varieties of meats than did lower SES blacks. During the data collection period the two lower SES black households consumer 11 and 15 varieties of meats, while lower SES whites consumed only 3 and 9 (see table 1).

Ideational trends were suggested in other areas in our study. For example, in response to the question of whether certain foods should always be eaten together, middle SES black KKPs had no response, but the other three groups named items frequently eaten in their households. Betty Vincent named hamburgers, potatoes, and vegetables; when we look at table 2, we see that hamburger and potatoes made up two thirds of her evening meal menus. Sadie Clark mentioned bananas and peanut butter, a frequent item in her lunches. She also cited fish and slaw, as did Karen Brown, items that show up in both of these KKPs' lunch and dinner menus. Gertrude James spoke of greens and ham hocks, a frequent item in her Sunday dinners and foods prepared for festive occasions. She also mentioned rice and pork chops, a luxury combination that sometimes showed up in small Sunday morning feasts of some of the study families.

The reasons given for most of these selections were taste ("taste good together") and the natural order of things ("they just go together" or "everyone does it this way"). Martha Hart's selection, however, gives an indication of what is considered a "balanced" meal in this community: a vegetable, a starch, meat, and bread (table 4, menu 1). Acceptable variations within this category of balanced meals are menu 2 (meat, starch, and vegetable, without bread) and menu 3 (meat, vegetable, and bread). The majority of the evening meals fall into one of these categories.

All the families sometimes had two vegetables with their evening meals. This is a reflection of the idea that vegetables are considered a "health" food. Meat (and other high-protein food) is also associated with strength and health and was consumed at almost every evening meal in all the study households; however, all the KKPs considered one meat—pork—as causing ill health, particularly hypertension. Blacks were strongest in their statement of this belief, although they tended to consume more of it than the white households (see tables 1 and 2). Black households also believed that one shouldn't eat two starches at once because it leads to ill health and obesity; yet two or more starches were frequently eaten together during Sunday dinner and festive occasions.

Fatty foods and sweets are also associated with promoting obesity and ill health. While milk is considered a health food, Gertrude James believes that too much milk will cause a baby to have a "thrash." This is one of the reasons that children are fed from the "soft portions" of adult diet in the James household as early as four months of age. "If you wait too long, when they get older, they will be messing with their food and stay sick all the time." There is also an association of "plumpness" in children with health as people speak of children looking so "fat and healthy."

Various seafoods are associated with sexual potency by black and white households of both economic groups. However, the lower SES black pattern of having fish at the evening meal almost every Friday during the observation period seemed to be based on taste and situational factors.

The Functional Significance of Food Behavior

Because food behavior is part of a larger cultural complex, it serves other social and cultural functions than the obviously nutritional. It was suggested that gender-specific ideals are projected through the media and educational materials in food preparation and dispensation. These ideals are carried out in some of the study households in gender-specific activities associated with food production, preparation, dispensation, and consumption protocol. The acting out of ideal gender patterns fulfills basic human needs such as self-identity associated with roles and the maintenance of order and a sense of reality that comes with role portrayal in social interactions. These functional qualities of routinization are achieved not only with role patterns, but also in the meal regularity.

The larger study households, however, do not practice the ideal of role and (dietary) behavorial routinization. For internally extended families like the Jameses, the larger household is functional because it contributes to the sharing of meager economic resources, as well as services. The lack of routinization in the James and the Hart households seems to be a functional or adaptive protection against crowding. It also seems to contribute to household harmony in that individuals with varying schedules are not hampered by unit rules and routines. It seems that a historical tradition of economic marginality has not only contributed to large internally extended households as an adaptive strategy among lower income blacks in Bakers County, but that the lack of domestic routinization has become the cultural norm to accommodate such a domestic situation. In other words, the regularity which is so important to culture is found in the lack of routinization.

The food behavior patterns that contribute to regularity of role portrayal, the assignment of status, the maintenance of order, and the shaping of a group's reality are carried out not only in domestic meals, but also in the feasts held by and for network members. Women usually do the food preparation. Ministers are usually given special seats or preference within the buffet line. The presence of the minister can also result in an informal prohibition against rock music and alcohol.

We have also seen how the passing of food items to network members as gifts or in exchange for services or cash serve economic functions and such social functions as the inclusion of new members in social networks and the reconfirmation of the rights and obligations implied in network ties. As a result of our research, we became aware of the fact that the "southern hospitality" shown new acquaintances is not simply a matter of regional etiquette. It is actually a strategy of network inclusion. This can best be exemplified through the development of our relationship with the Harts.

The Harts are very skillful networkers. As we have already mentioned, Mr. Hart, who is irregularly employed as a construction worker, has used network interactions to help secure the land for his house and gardens, to secure pigs and chickens, and to sell surplus. Mrs. Hart and the three older children not only sing in their own church choir, but also travel with a gospel group that gives concerts in other churches in the area. This participation gives Mrs. Hart the opportunity to meet and recruit new people into her personal network.

When my research assistants and I first met the Harts, they invited us to dinner. Then they wanted to kill one of their pigs and have a pig picking in our honor. When I went to the Hart house, Mrs. Hart frequently gave me either fresh produce from the gardens or some food that she had preserved. We were invited by the Harts (as well as by other study families) to the various festive occasions such as family reunions and Christmas and Thanksgiving dinners, where feasts are principal events. (When we began attending these events, we saw how such occasions were powerful mechanisms for reconfirming and maintaining extensive network ties.) Later when the Harts' son Jimmy became ill with a brain tumor, I found out that the hospitality shown us was also given the neurosurgeon who operated on Jimmy and some of the staff in the pediatric ward in the hospital where Jimmy stayed for three months.

The networking of the Harts was very important in their attempts to deal with Jimmy's death, both economically and psychologically.

Friendship and kinship networks intensified their gifts of food, clothing, and cash, and the ministers and various church leaders who were then a part of Mrs. Hart's network introduced the Harts as a family in need of the money collected for "the sick and shut in" during Sunday morning church services. For this support, the Harts fulfilled their obligations through gifts of food and on the first anniversary of Jimmy's death, they killed three hogs and had a pig picking, inviting friends, relatives, members of the church who had been supportive, and friends from the University (the neurosurgeon and me).

Summary and Conclusions

The findings from an eighteen-month investigation of the family and network dynamics of eight households in a North Carolina community have been presented in support of a proposed model for the study of cultural process and food behavior. It was suggested that food behavior should not be viewed simply as "food habits" or foods consumed, but as part of a paradigm of systemic relationships which include ecohistorical and sociocultural determinants of behavioral patterns which have cultural meaning. The next step in the research is to test these relationships on a larger and more representative study sample. These relationships cannot be tested in bivariate formulas in which ecohistorical and sociocultural determinants are viewed only as independent variables in their relationship to food behavior, and food behavior is viewed as an independent variable in its relationship to cultural meaning. A multivariate design has to be developed to explore the complexity of relationships between the subsystemic categories within the four major categories: (1) historical and environmental factors within ecohistorical determinants; (2) the various structural levels within the social and ideational subsystems; (3) the differentiation between food activity categories and food behavior characteristics; and (4) the cultural meaning of food behavior as determined by its various survival functions.

Acknowledgments

I would like to thank Judit Katona-Apte for her early contributions to our research efforts. We are also most grateful to Julie Morial, Joseph Thomas, Diana Hamilton, and Joanne Taylor for their assistance in the data collection, and Laurie Price, Erma Wright, Jennifer Bass, and Judi Aubel for their assistance with the literature review and proofreading. I would like to thank Vera Bennett for her typing assistance. I am grateful to the Russell Sage Foundation for funding and to Mary Douglas and my colleagues in the Russell Sage Gastronomic Categories Program for their support and intellectual stimulation. Finally, to the study families described herein, I am grateful for their continuing cooperation, receptivity and hospitality.

Bibliography

Anderson, E.N., and Anderson, M. L. "Modern China; South." In *Food in Chinese Culture,* edited by K. C. Chang. New Haven: Yale University Press, 1977.

Apte, L., and Katona-Apte, Judit. "The Left and Right Sides of a Banana Leaf: Ethnography of Food Arrangement in India."

Paper presented at the American Anthropological Association meeting, San Francisco, December 1975.

Back, W. "Food, Sex and Theory." In *Nutrition and Anthropology in Action,* edited by T. K. Fitzgerald. Assem. Amsterdam: Van Gorcum, 1976.

Ballentine, R. *Diet and Nutrition: A Holistic Approach.* Honesdale, Pa.: Himalayan International Institute, 1978.

Bennet, J. W. "Food and Social Status in a Rural Society." *American Sociological Review,* 8 (1943): 561–69.

———. "Subsistence Economy and Food Ways in a Rural Community: A Study of Socio-Economic and Cultural Change." Doctoral dissertation, University of Chicago, 1946.

——— and Tumin, M. M. *Social Life Structure and Function: An Introductory General Sociology.* New York: Knopf, 1948.

Boas, F. "The Social Organization and the Secret Societies of the Kwakiutl Indians." Report of the U S. National Museum, for 1895. Washington, D.C.: National Research Council, National Academy of Sciences, 1897.

Bott, E. *Family and Social Network.* London: Tavistock. 1971.

Braden, C. J., and Herban, N. L. *Community Health: A Systems Approach.* New York: Appleton-Century-Crofts, 1976.

Budsall, M. I. "Factors Related to Vegetable Consumption of Preschool Children in Low Income Families." Doctoral dissertation, University of Chicago, 1972.

Burt, J. V., and Hertzler, A. A., "Parental Influence on the Child's Food Preference." *Journal of Nutrition Education* 10 (1978): 127–28.

Chang, K. C., ed. *Food in Chinese Culture: Anthropological and Historical Perspectives.* New Haven: Yale University Press, 1977.

Codere, H. *Fighting with Property: A Study of Kwakiutl Potlaching and Warfare, 1792–1930.* American Ethnological Society, monograph No. 18, 1950. Seattle: University of Washington Press, 1966.

Cussler, M., and DeGive, M. L. *Twixt the Cup and the Lip.* Washington, D.C.: Consortium Press, 1953.

deGarine, I. "The Sociocultural Aspects of Nutrition." *Ecology of Food and Nutrition* 1 (1972): 143–63.

Douglas, M. "Deciphering a Meal." In *Implicit Meanings: Essays in Anthropology.* London: Routledge & Kegan Paul, 1975.

———. *Structures of Gastronomy.* New York: Russell Sage Foundation, 1978.

Dubois, C. "The Wealth Concept as an Integrative Factor in Tolowa-Tutuni Culture." In *Essays in Anthropology.* Berkeley: University of California Press, 1936.

Firth, R. *Symbols: Public and Private.* Ithaca, N.Y.: Cornell University Press, 1973.

Fomon, S. J., and Anderson, Thomas, eds. *Practices of Low-Income Families in Feeding Infants and Small Children.* Rockville, Md.: U. S. Department of Health, Education and Welfare, 1972.

Gonzalez, N. S. "Beliefs and Practices Concerning Medicine and Nutrition among Lower-Class Urban Guatemalans." In *The Cross-Cultural Approach to Health Behavior,* edited by L. Riddick Lynch. Rutherford, N. J.: Fairleigh Dickinson University Press, 1969.

Goode, J. G. *Foodways as an Ethnic Marker: Assumptions and Reality.* Paper presented at the Northeastern Anthropological Association meeting, Providence, R.I., March 25, 1977.

Grifft, H.; Washbourn, M. and Harrison, G. *Nutrition, Behavior and Change.* Englewood Cliffs, N.J.: Prentice-Hall, 1972.

Gross, D. R., and Underwood, B. A.

"Technological Change and Caloric Costs: Sisal Agriculture in Northeastern Brazil." *American Anthropologist* 73, 1971: 725–40.
Harris, M. *Cows, Pigs, Wars and Witches.* New York: Vintage Books, 1974.
———. *Cannibals and Kings: The Origins of Culture.* New York: Random House, 1977.
———, and Ross, E. B. "How Beef Became King." *Psychology Today,* October 1978.
Harrison, G. "Food Waste Behavior in an Urban Population." *Journal of Nutrition Education* 7 (1975): 13–16.
Henry, J. "The Economics of Pilaga Food Distribution." *American Anthropologist* 53 (1951): 187–219.
Herskovits, M. J. "The Ahistorical Approach to Afro-American Studies." *American Anthropologist* 62 (1960).
Hill, C. E., and Matthews, H. "Traditional Health Beliefs and Practices Among Southern Rural Blacks: A Complement to Biomedicine." In *Social Science Perspectives on the South.* New York: Gordon and Breech, 1982.
Jerome, N. "Food Habits and Acculturation: Dietary Practices and Nutrition of Families Headed by Southern-Born Negroes Residing in a Northern Metropolis." Doctoral dissertation. Ann Arbor, Michigan: University Microfilms, 1967.
———. "Northern Urbanization and Food Consumption Patterns of Southern-Born Negroes." *American Journal of Clinical Nutrition* 22 (1969): 1667–69.
———. "On Determining Food Patterns of Urban Dwellers." In *Gastronomy: The Anthropology of Food Habits,* edited by Margaret Arnott. The Hague: Mouton, 1975.

———, Pelto, G., and Kandel, R. "An Ecological Approach to Nutritional Anthropology." In *Nutritional Anthropology: Contemporary Approaches to Diet and Culture.* Pleasantville, N. Y.: Redgrave Press, 1980.
Johnson, M. B. *Household Behavior: Consumption, Income and Wealth.* London: Penguin, 1971.
Jones, J. "Child Feeding in the Rural Low-Income Family." In *Practices of Low-Income Families in Feeding Infants and Small Children.* Rockville, Md.: U.S. Public Health Service, 1972.
Kandel, R. F. "Rice, Ice Cream and the Guru: Decision-Making and Innovation in a Macrobiotic Community." Doctoral dissertation, City University of New York, 1975.
Khare, R. S. "Food Area-Spatial Categories and Relationships." In *The Hindu Hearth.* Durham: Carolina Academic Press, 1976.
Konovitz, J. "Identity, Self-Expression and the American Cook." *Centennial Review* 13 (1975): 85–95.
Leach, E. "Anthropological Aspects of Language: Animal Categories and Verbal Abuse." In *New Directions in the Study of Language,* edited by E. H. Lenneberg. Cambridge, Mass.: M.I.T. Press, 1964.
———. *Culture and Communication.* Cambridge: Cambridge University Press, 1976.
Lévi-Strauss, C. *The Raw and the Cooked.* New York: Harper & Row, 1964.
———. "The Culinary Triangle." *Partisan Review* 33 (1966): 586–95.
Lewin, K. "Forces Behind Food Habits and Methods of Change." In *The Problems of Changing Food Habits.* National Research Council Bulletin No. 108, 1943.

Mead, M. "Dietary Patterns and Food Habits." *Journal of the American Dietetic Association* 19 (1943): 1–5.

Montgomery, E. "Stratification and Nutrition in a Population in Southern India." Doctoral dissertation, Columbia University, 1972.

———. "Social Structuring of Nutrition in Southern India." In *Malnutrition, Behavior and Social Organization,* edited by L. S. Greene. New York: Academic Press, 1977.

Nicod, M. "A Method of Eliciting the Social Meaning of Food." Master's thesis, University College, London, 1974.

Olson, D. A. "The Perception of Nutrition and Nutritional Labeling in the Buying Among Affluent Consumers." Doctoral dissertation, Michigan State University, 1973.

Parsons, T., and Bales, R. F. *Family Socialization and Interaction Processes.* New York: Free Press, 1955.

Passin, H., and Bennett, J. "Social Process and Dietary Change." In *The Problem of Changing Food Habits.* National Research Councils, Bulletin No. 108, October 1943.

Pelto, G., and Jerome, N. "Intracultural Diversity and Nutritional Anthropology." In *Health and the Human Condition,* edited by M. Logan and E. Hunt. North Scituate, Mass.: Duxbury Press, 1979.

Popkin, B. "Nutrition and Labor Productivity." *Social Science and Medicine* 12c (1978): 117–25.

———, and Solon, F. "Income, Time, the Working Mother and Child Nutrition." *Environmental Child Health,* August, 1976.

Popkin, B. M., et al. "Breast-Feeding Practices in Low In-come Countries: Patterns and Determinants." *Carolina Population Center Papers.* Chapel Hill: University of North Carolina, 1979.

Rappaport, R. A. *Pigs for the Ancestors: Ritual in the Ecology of a New Guinea People.* New Haven: Yale University Press, 1968.

Regelson, S. "The Bagel: Symbol and Ritual at the Breakfast Table." In *The American Dimension: Cultural Myths and Social Realities,* edited by W. Arens and S. P. Montague. Port Washington, N.Y.: Alfred, 1976.

Rosenblum, C. "You Really Are What You Eat." *Salt Lake Tribune,* May 28, 1978.

Sahlins, M. *Culture and Practical Reason.* Chicago: University of Chicago Press, 1976.

Shack, W. "A Taste of Soul." *New Society,* July 15, 1976.

Simons, F. J. *Eat Not This Flesh: Food Avoidance in The Old World.* Madison: University of Wisconsin Press, 1961.

Spiro, M. "The Acculturation of American Ethnic Groups." *American Anthropologist,* 57 (1955): 1240–52.

Suttles, W. "Affinal Ties, Subsistence, and Prestige among the Coast Salish." *American Anthropologist* 62 (1960): 296–305.

Toombs, S. "Soulfood: American Culture, Cuisine and Customs." *Forecast for Home Economics,* 21 (1976): 19.

Valentine, B. L., and Valentine, C. A. "Poor People, Good Food and Fat Babies: Observations on Dietary Behavior and Nutrition Among Low-Income, Urban Afro-American Infants and Children." In *Practices of Low Income Families in Feeding Infants and Small Children with Particular Attention to Cultural*

Subgroups, edited by S. J. Foman and T. A. Anderson. Rockville, Md.: U.S. Department of Health, Education and Welfare, 1972.

Whitehead, T. L. "Industrialization, Social Networks and Food Flow: Survival Techniques in a Jamaican Sugar Town." Paper presented at the Tenth International Congress of Anthropological and Ethnological Sciences, New Delhi, December 1978.

Wilcox, M. E. "Discussion." In *Practices of Low Income Families in Feeding Infants and Small Children, with Particular Attention to Cultural Subgroups,* edited by S. J. Foman and T. A. Anderson. Rockville, Md.: U.S. Department of Health, Education and Welfare, 1972.

Williams, M. *Community in a Black Pentacostal Church.* Pittsburgh: University of Pittsburgh Press, 1974.

Wilson, C. "Nutrition in Two Cultures: Mexican American and Malay Ways with Food." In *Gastronomy,* edited by M. L. Arnott. Chicago: Aldine, 1975.

4

Meal Formats, Meal Cycles, and Menu Negotiation in the Maintenance of an Italian-American Community

Judith G. Goode, Karen Curtis, and Janet Theophano

Introduction

The basic goal of this study is to explore the nature of a food system, or set of rules shared by a group for patterning food intake. The research was primarily concerned with the degree to which food systems are coherent systems with internal logic; the way they relate to other cultural subsystems such as social organization, religious and health beliefs; and the way they are affected by external factors such as resource availability and the scheduling of activities. In selecting an ethnic group, we focused on a historically transmitted cuisine and examine the processes of continuity and change in the system. However, we also wished to explore the relationship between food and ethnicity, a relationship about which many assumptions have been made with little empirical evidence. Thus, the research also addresses significant issues of the processes of ethnic identity, the transmission of ethnic consciousness, the maintenance of ethnic group boundaries, and, most specifically, the role of food—often considered a major marker—in such processes.

The research presented and discussed here forms the core of an ongoing study of the Italian-American food system. The ethnographic phase, made possible by the Russell Sage project, enabled us to undertake intensive research in one of the two enclaves in the Philadelphia metropolitan area which had been studied previously. The ethnography took place in the suburban Philadelphia community of Maryton. However, other phases of the research had taken place in South Philadelphia as well, a center city area that has little contact with Maryton and very different socioeconomic characteristics. We were struck by the similarities in food patterns in both communities. This ethnic group seemed to provide an interesting example of a food system which was flexible and open to change in the American setting and which still maintained some structure and pattern rules over time.

In the rapidly expanding literature on food habits in America, the role of ethnicity is assumed to be either all important or insignificant. Spiro (1955) assumes that ethnic food patterns are conservative; that food is the last aspect of an ethnic culture to be lost. The basic reason implied for such conservatism is that food socialization takes place early and is an intensely affective and sensory experience. Other commentators, interested in exotic folkways, describe America as a series of ethnic enclaves. The wartime National Research Council research on American food habits took ethnic groups as logical units of analysis, assuming that they were the locus of differentiated eating in America.

Other students of ethnic food habits see them as disappearing over time. In most studies of American eating patterns, ethnic food systems are defined in terms of the food items used and the frequency of their use. Continuity is measured in terms of food item use, and change is measured by shifts in items used and their frequency. Recent studies of what Americans eat which focus on items assume that successive generations will continue to lose traditional items. Freedman and Grivetti (1981) come to this conclusion for Greeks in Sacramento. Others find that ethnic identity as a household characteristic does not explain food item frequencies. This, too, suggests assimilation and the loss of ethnic patterns. Thus, Jerome (1975) found that ethnicity was unimportant in her study of a Kansas City population.

Current thought about influences on household food consumption places great emphasis on the significance of structural variables—income, time, education level—rather than cultural variables (Jerome et al. 1980). Focus is frequently on the extraordinary variety and abundance in the American food system and the increase of individualized household or personal choice rather than group-patterned guides for selection. The complexity of American social life—varieties of work and leisure schedules as well as other structural variables—has led to a bias toward external explanations of eating over internal socially transmitted normative systems of which ethnicity is a prime example.

Another reason frequently given for the assumed decline of socially transmitted ethnic food-choice patterns is the impact of advertising and the creation of media models which are supposedly generating a system of national norms. Both the competing national norms and the external pressures inhibiting the maintenance of closed systems of ethnically perpetuated choices are assumed to have led to ethnic dietary patterns that are salient only with regard to holiday feasts and life-cycle celebrations and not to everyday eating.

Thus, American eating habits are thought to be either more homogeneous or more individualized as households are faced with extraordinary choice, high degrees of mobility, and disparate work and leisure schedules. Households are assumed to develop patterns which, except for special occasions, are either highly idiosyncratic or highly uniform (generated by mass media and fast-food outlets), but not socially mediated by peer groups. We questioned this assumption and wished to study socially mediated rules for food use transmitted within a stable community of interacting households.

In other words, we were looking for group-shared food patterns in American society. We wanted to understand the *social* processes which are involved in transmitting, reinforcing, and modifying such group-shared patterns.

We chose a subgroup defined by ethnicity because it was relatively easy to define, had historic continuity, and could be easily analyzed in terms of intergenerational transmission. Moreover, we chose an ethnic enclave which was a relatively closed and stable set of households in order to provide us with a classic case of households which interacted frequently and whose adults and children were close friends throughout life, often intermarried, and rarely left the community after growing up.

However, we assume that most Americans can be similarly located within similar lifestyle groups sharing a food system. These lifestyle groups can be based on occupation, class, region, or ideological movement rather than ethnicity. There may be discontinuity between childhood food patterns and adult lifestyle in households characterized by geographic or occupational/educational mobility. However, there are still social peer pressures from networks of kin or friends which affect food patterning. Food patterning is a socially mediated phenomenon more complex than the models of unfettered individual choice or media-dominated choice.

Italian-Americans were chosen for this study for several reasons. First, there is a significant literature on the food patterns of prewar immigrant Italians. Second, Italian-Americans are considered to be highly food-involved. While it is difficult to compare the concern with food from one group to another, there are frequent references to the importance of food to Italian domestic life. (Advertisements, for example, trumpet the sensory attachment of Italians to the color, texture, and spiciness of spaghetti sauce and the focus on Italian food in family life.) Finally, Italian-Americans provide an opportunity to observe change over two generations since immigration.

Research completed before the ethnographic phase had indicated that existing models of ethnic group food change were inadequate. The emphasis on persistence of an Old World pattern seen in newspaper food features and ethnic folk festivals was oversimplified. Moreover, the model of simple Americanization (acculturation/assimilation) was also inaccurate. In the communities we studied, a widely shared set of community norms operated both for everyday meals and for special events. Also, this community-shared pattern was not necessarily characterized by patterns which were persistent from an Old World tradition. They were not necessarily intergenerationally transmitted; but they *were* shared and thus socially transmitted across households. Such new practices were often perceived by group members to be continuous, persistent aspects of a traditional Italian pattern or at least traceable modifications of an older pattern. Moreover, stability in pattern was not necessarily more significant for major ritual events than for more routine events. In fact, ritual events had changed significantly, too. Finally, there were some indications that many patterns of food-related behavior within the communities were indeed intergenerationally transmitted. However, the locus of continuity of pattern was not necessarily the food item itself or a particular dish, but, for example, notions of periodic patterning of meals as social events and beliefs about correct food attributes and combinations in the construction of a recipe or meal for a particular social event.

LEVELS OF ANALYSIS

Several levels have been used in past research as defining characteristics of a food system: food items, recipes, menus, and meal cycles. We recognized that one reason for the inability to see continuity in the food system derived from an overemphasis on food items as the analytical components of a food system. Our goal was to attempt to use more complex components than food items in our analysis. Jerome (1976), following Bennett (1943), used food-item frequency in her Kansas City study. It was with regard to these frequencies that ethnicity was found not to be significant. She was borrowing a model from Bennett's work in which a food system is viewed as composed of segments: items of high frequency, moderate frequency, and low frequency use. The emphasis on items in the anthropology of food follows from an emphasis on items in all of the food sciences. A concern with nutrient intake and health issues leads to a focus on the smallest culturally defined unit of the diet, the individual foodstuff. The frequent use of twenty-four-hour recall in gaining lists of foods eaten or the use of household consumption data (quantities of foods purchased and household inventories) encourages a concentration on lists of food-item use in describing a dietary system. It takes much more intimate knowledge of preparation and meal structures to deal with more complex levels of food systems. Items may be significant factors in the activities of food production and shopping (food acquisition) but are secondary in the processes of meal planning.

Another level of analysis is the recipe, which provides dishes as a focus of analysis, thus pointing to different types of item complexes as defining a food system. A dish is a culturally defined complex of food items. While the rules for structuring a dish are encoded in "recipes" which may differ in detail from household to household, the basic structure of the dish or recipe is a group-shared, socially transmitted pattern. Significant to the dish are both the food items (which may differentiate one group from other groups if the contents are exotic or unique) and the way the items relate to each other (which derives from the method of preparation). It is mode of preparation rather than food items that often differentiates groups. Methods of preparation include rules for segregating or mixing elements, the medium used for cooking, the type of heat application, the way items are cleaned and cut, and spices or flavoring used. The study of Chinese cuisines (Anderson and Anderson 1969, 1972), for example, includes these elements as essential in differentiating between national and regional Chinese cuisines. Rozin (1973) assumes that cuisines are marked by a distinctive flavor, such as chili peppers for Mexican cooking. Gans (1962) assumes, in his study of Italian-Americans in Boston, that this is the way ethnic cuisines are preserved—in this case, through the Italianization of American food items via spices, cooking media, and methods of preparation. Principles of segregation and combination can be found in the analysis of recipes and provide rules for different classes of items which underline a food system. Such principles themselves can be viewed as the hallmarks of a distinctive cuisine.

Chang (1977) locates the continuity of the structure of Chinese cuisine in the conceptual separation of staple and accompaniments (bits of meat, fish, vegetables, sauces, and spices). Regardless of changes in food-item content or cooking mode from time to time and place to place, staples are prepared one way and accompaniments another, and they are joined at the meal. While recipes thus provide insights into the principles underlying a food system, a problem which exists in the analysis of recipes in several distinctive cuisines is that recipes are more frequently elicited for exotic and special meals rather than for the bulk of the eating events. Again, the system as a whole is missed.

Whether food items or recipes are analyzed, the important characteristics of food should include not only categorization by nutrient content but the analysis of as many attributes of foods as possible: color, temperature, texture, and viscosity, as well as taste (sweet, salty, sour, bitter) and degree of spiciness (mouth irritation).

More complex levels of analysis involve the structures of meals (menus) and the periodicity of different types of meals in a temporal cycle of days, weeks, and seasons. The work of Mary Douglas (Douglas 1972; Douglas and Nicod 1974) first illuminated this level. She was concerned with the way that weekly and calendrical meal cycles contained structural components which were repeated through time. For the British working-class meal system, Sunday dinner was a prototype structure containing elements which were repeated on smaller or larger scales for both mundane weekly meals and feasts. Jerome (1980) also used formats in her study of change in northern black families. We use this level of analysis in our work. It subsumes the other levels (items and recipes) and is most relevant to understanding the relationship between food and the social order, which is of primary concern in this research. We assume that food systems (models and rules) are socially transmitted and that rules are shared across households. One of the reasons for this assumption is the frequency with which food is used to underscore social relationships, to signify different status positions, to symbolize significant exchange relationships, and to express group identity and group boundaries.

Using this level of analysis, we address the following questions:

1. Are ethnic food patterns conservative?

2. Does change occur as a loss of items over time?

3. Are feasts and celebrations most conservative?

4. What is the relative importance of metaphysical beliefs (magical, religious, and health), aesthetic/sensory tradition, and social relationships in continuity and change?

5. What role do group-shared, socially mediated rules for intake play in menu planning?

6. What is the relationship between food, individual ethnic identity, and ethnic group boundary maintenance?

7. How do group-shared rules interact with structural constraints to produce actual menu decisions?

While this study focuses on these issues which the ethnographic phase illuminated, we will also briefly mention some insights developed from the whole study, including the complementarity of different data sets and the way that different community characteristics influence change.

Sociocultural Context

Before we proceed with the analysis of a local food system, we must locate the food pattern and the community which perpetuates it in a larger sociocultural context and in the political economy.

HISTORICAL MACRO-CUISINE

The Italian immigrant groups which migrated to the United States came from different regions in which food patterns varied. They derived from both rural and urban environments in which the nature of production/distribution and activity patterns created differences in the food system. Despite the diversity in Italy, the dominance of migrants from certain regions and the control of food distribution networks by certain regional groups in American cities eventually led to a common pattern in the immigrant population. We use this historically documented pattern for the early immigrant years as a baseline for this study instead of the regional Old World patterns.

The earliest interest in what Italian immigrants ate was developed by dieticians who were ethnocentrically concerned with dietary inadequacy among immigrant groups. They overemphasized carbohydrate consumption and ignored the value of complementary proteins. However, one intensive study of the diet by a dietician in New Haven, Connecticut (King 1935), provides us with menu information pointing to the intriguing cyclical patterning of meals. Later, a study by Nizzardini and Joffe (1942; concerned with wartime needs, as part of Mead's effort for the National Research Council) also found the cyclical patterns through interview data in New York City. The recollections of the women in our study (1974; both communities) again reiterated these weekly cyclical patterns. (See table 1.)

The Italian-American diet described in the literature and by our informants' childhood recollections can be described both in terms of items and in terms of patterns. Items frequently emphasized include macaroni, greens, tomatoes, poultry, fish, fruit, Italian bread, cheese, olive oil, wine, and coffee. Meat and fish were used in small quantities—simmered with tomato sauce or fried. Shellfish were sautéed in oil and garlic or steamed in a tomato sauce. Roast chicken could be served as a main dish. A "one-pot" meal was characteristic of this dietary pattern. Combinations of vegetables and macaroni, legumes and macaroni, sauce and macaroni, and soups which stressed vegetables were prevalent.

As striking as the items emphasized was the patterned periodicity of meal types. A weekly cycle of meals was shared in which Sunday (the prototype) was stressed; Mondays were soup nights—an easy dish to follow Sunday's major production. Fast days were observed on Wednesday and Friday, and macaroni was eaten three times a week.

TABLE 1

The First Generation Dietary Pattern: Weekly Schedules of Food Consumption

	Sunday	Monday	Tuesday	Wednesday	Thursday	Friday	Saturday
1935 (King pp. 179–90)	Macaroni with sauce; or soup, macaroni with sauce, and roast chicken	Soup or stew	Meat or vegetable combination	Meatless meal, vegetable combination, or macaroni with shellfish	Macaroni with sauce	Meatless meal; fish, fried or in sauce; or omelet	Soup or stew
1942 (Nizzardini and Joffe p. 13)	Spaghetti, soup, meat, vegetable, salad, and fruit	Soup	Spaghetti	Fish	Spaghetti	Fish	
1974 (Maryton: interviews about mothers of informants)	Macaroni with sauce; or soup, macaroni, and roast chicken	Escarole soup (with chicken and meatballs)	Macaroni	Vegetable combination	Macaroni	Fish, fried or in sauce or omelet	Fried steak with potatoes

The most detailed information exists for the New Haven community. Their meal repertory, based on an analysis of the weekly and holiday menus of twenty families, consisted of a series of formats which differed in content and structure. Sunday emerged as the prototype from which the meal formats of the daily and weekly cycle were drawn; while calendrical holidays and life-cycle rituals were celebrated with an elaborated version of the Sunday meal format.

On Sunday the first meal was breakfast, taken early in the morning. It was a simple meal composed of a hot beverage (coffee or tea), bread or toast, and fruit. Dinner, the main meal, was consumed in the middle of the day. It was an elaborate meal, and its expanded form included four courses: soup; a gravy dish; roast meat or fowl, with accompanying vegetable, salad, bread, and wine; and coffee and a dessert of fruit or baked goods. The third meal on Sunday, supper, was eaten in the early evening. Its format was chosen from the main meal (dinner), omitting the first course and including either gravy or roast meat or fowl.

On ordinary days, the first meal, breakfast, was identical in format to the first meal on Sunday. Dinner, the main meal, was served in the middle of the day. Two variations of the Sunday main meal format were observed. Both were two courses: one focused on a meat, fish, or egg dish with side dishes; the other consisted of a gravy or other one-pot dish.

The daily round concluded with supper, eaten in the early evening. Suppers included a reduced number of courses and a reduced quantity. The format was the opposite of that of the main meal of the day. (If the main meal included meat, fish, or eggs, then supper included a gravy or other one-pot, and vice versa.) This opposition was frequently maintained between supper on one day and dinner on the next day. Within this context, Friday was observed as a meatless fast day.

The expanded "Sunday" menu for feast occasions was a five-course format which includes appetizer (preserved meat or fish, fresh and pickled vegetables); soup; a one-pot dish (often baked macaroni); roast fowl with accompanying vegetable, salad, bread, and wine; and coffee with pastries, liqueurs, and nuts.

Each localized Italian-American population entered a different social context. In the United States the significant differences for food are related to the other ethnic groups present, and whether relationships with these groups were symmetrical, dominant, or subordinate. An important factor was the nature of competition with other groups for jobs and housing in the new community. As we will see, such differences affected the rate of change in the two communities we studied, but not the direction and process of change.

In the process of settlement, the Italians brought with them a food pattern and established their own systems of food production, importation, and marketing to help maintain it. For example, for Philadelphia, truck gardening enterprises in southern New Jersey were linked to wholesaling networks in South Philadelphia producing and distributing traditional greens. Local processors provided sausages and lunch meats. Italian breads were baked. Cheeses and olive oil were imported. However, existing local food institutions also exerted influence. At this time, food production and distribution were largely organized locally in the United States. Thus, the presence of other groups greatly increased the variety of food available. Meat, particularly beef, was consumed more frequently. Unfamiliar vegetables and potatoes were generally used. In Philadelphia, the baked goods, especially cakes, of other groups were frequently consumed.

However, after World War II and up to the present, the development of national level mass food processing and distribution and the attendant development of media communication about food and food use contributed significantly to the processes of modification and incorporation in the system. Thus, the local intergroup context is no longer as important to food item and meal model variety as the national system is today.

THE AMERICAN SYSTEM, THE ITALIAN-AMERICAN ENCLAVE, AND THE HOUSEHOLD

When we look at the impact of the nationally generated systems of food availability and the communications of models for food use, we are looking at factors which impact only indirectly on the household. In our view, such influences must be socially mediated either within the household or within the network before they become operative in food decisions. National food availability and models of food usage are external factors. The degree to which they are perceived, approved, or disapproved is the outcome of social processes—teaching, imitation, evaluative discussion, and so forth. Thus, the traditional foods, recipes, and meal formats available and the national foods, recipes, and meal formats afford possibilities for the dietary repertory. It is the social mediation process within households and between households clustered in social networks which creates the actual patterns.

We were looking for a community-wide pattern. It soon became apparent that the social network rather than any geographically defined community was the major social unit for the interhousehold transmission and reinforcement of food norms. Patterns of appropriate eating had been taught by mother to daughter (and after marriage by mother-in-law to daughter-in-law), and ideas about food were strongly influenced by female networks of friends and acquaintances. In Maryton (a fictitious name), such peer groups originate in childhood and are stable over time. The networks are extremely sociable, meeting frequently throughout the week. Food is an important focus of social interaction. The following information about the historical development of Maryton, migration patterns, and changing residential, occupational, and social configurations of the Italian-American community will help explain the degree to which the community is a relatively closed and bounded sociocultural unit.

Migration to northern cities of the United States from southern Italy in the early part of this century occurred largely by chain migration—the movement of linked families in a continuous stream to a single new community (MacDonald and MacDonald 1964, p. 84). Therefore, immigrants from many towns and villages in southern Italy settled together in certain localities and job markets in the United States. The destination of southern Italian (and other southern and eastern European) chain migrants was often a "company town." Allen (1966, p. 102) explains the attraction of company towns for southern and eastern immigrants: "Since the immigrant usually arrived almost penniless, the paternalistic situation in the company town immediately gave him a home as well as credit in the company store." In many of these immigrant communities, this migratory pattern fostered the development of "ethnic brokers," who, in addition to providing employment information, functioned as bankers, landlords, foremen, scribes, interpreters, and legal advisers (MacDonald and MacDonald 1964, p. 86). Since the adoption of the quota system (in 1925) in this country, which requires sponsorship by close relatives as a necessary but not sufficient condition, chain migration is the only type of immigration permitted.

While this phase of our research emphasizes Maryton, the total research focuses on comparing changes in food systems in both Maryton and South Philadelphia. A major concern is the examination of the effect of different migration patterns, occupational experience, and community contexts on changing food behavior and the use of food as a group marker. While South Philadelphia was an entry point for migration from all over Europe (thus ethnically heterogeneous), Maryton was a white Anglo-Saxon Protestant community. While Italians from several regions in southern Italy came to South Philadelphia, Maryton was populated by chain migration from one town in Calabria. While migrants to South Philadelphia moved into many kinds of economic activities, migrants to Maryton came specifically as construction labor, and their employment opportunities were restricted by a company-controlled town.

The borough of Maryton is located north of Philadelphia, in southeastern Montgomery County. As a borough, it is more urban than surrounding formerly agricultural townships. Its mixed land use includes residential, institutional, light industrial, and commercial. The borough is divided into three sections known locally as Maryton, West Maryton, and South Maryton.

Maryton's early history is typical of the region. Originally sold as a land tract by William Penn in 1682, the land was subsequently resold and subdivided. The area became an early mill center which stimulated growth. As part of the level route from Philadelphia to the Lehigh Valley, the North Penn Railroad reached Maryton and opened service in 1855; it became a major railroad focus.

In 1882, the Castle and Clark Company (a fictitious name) moved from Philadelphia to Maryton because of the rail facilities, available water power, and abundant labor. By World War I, Castle and Clark was the world's largest manufacturer of asbestos and magnesia products, in addition to being the borough's primary employer. Not only did Dr. Clark control all the community and cultural facilities, he also operated a company store and built housing for his employees—large imposing residences for the executives, three-story structures for the superintendents, and modest homes for the laborers. For this purpose, in the 1890s, Dr. Clark recruited Italian stone masons and laborers. He used this labor for the building and maintenance of his 400-acre estate (which included a working farm and quarry), numerous industrial buildings, Trinity Memorial Church, and 400 stone homes to house his employees.

The initial labor recruitment and the expansion of Castle and Clark in the subsequent decades resulted in a single migratory stream from one town in the southern Italian district of Catanzaro, Calabria to Maryton. Italian-Americans moved into the white Anglo-Saxon Protestant community where they became the major minority group. Many Italian-American families continue to sponsor relatives from the town and provide other assistance in immigration.

The nature of the company-controlled town meant that Italian-Americans were residentially, occupationally, and socially segregated from the larger community (which was predominantly northern European). The only housing available to this group was in South and West Maryton, immediately adjacent to the manufacturing buildings operated by Castle and Clark. The housing in these areas of town (which are also immediately adjacent to the railroad line) was often without indoor plumbing or heat. Dr. Clark would not rent homes to Italian-Americans in other areas of Maryton.

Since Castle and Clark was the primary employer in the borough for seventy-five years, Dr. Clark also exercised considerable and significant occupational control. He hired Italian-American stone masons, laborers, and a few foremen. This pattern of enforced residential and occupational segregation was combined with social segregation. Italian-Americans did not participate in local government or community-wide voluntary organizations.

A number of "ethnic institutions" (Italian entrepreneurs serving an Italian clientele) developed in South and West Maryton. These included grocers, butchers, bakers, bootleggers, and huckster routes, as well as an Italian bank, travel agency, local notaries, a second Catholic parish, several fraternal organizations, and the celebration of the feast of St. Francis, the patron saint of the town in Italy.

The forced sale of the Castle and Clark property, after financial difficulties, in the 1930s was responsible for changes in patterns of residential distribution in the borough. At this time, Italian-Americans were able to purchase homes in previously denied neighborhoods in Maryton. These purchases resulted in the formation of secondary residential clusters. Many also bought their homes in South and West Maryton and rented them to new migrants.

The dissolution of Dr. Clark's control also marked the beginning of changes in occupation and social structure in the borough. Italian-Americans began to expand small businesses to serve a wider clientele and participate in local government and nonethnic-based voluntary organizations. By the end of World War II, most Italian-Americans had moved their residences and commercial operations out of South and West Maryton. These areas are now predominantly populated by blacks.

By the 1970s (the period of this study), Italian-Americans could be found in all residential areas and occupational categories. They participate in local government and voluntary organizations. They are, however, residentially and occupationally clustered. They tend to live near other Italian-Americans (to a greater extent than their non-Italian counterparts) and are concentrated in retail commercial enterprises (groceries, butcher shops, and retail shops) and services (landscaping, contracting, masonry), as well as political patronage positions. The proportion of Italian-Americans holding elected and appointed positions in local government has, since the 1950s, been substantially greater than that of non-Italians.

There is a decidedly Italian ambience in the borough; Italian is spoken in many local stores since many older residents and recent immigrants speak no English; many Italian products are sold. The local branch of the Sons of Italy owns and operates a combination meeting hall, bar, and bowling alley, where St. Francis Day continues to be celebrated. The Italian-Americans are viewed by many outsiders as controlling the borough.

The Italian-Americans in Maryton are a classic example of an ethnic group initially bounded by imposed residential and occupational segregation. Today, they maintain their separateness as a means to protect their increasing control over local business and government. Their identity and the persistence of symbols of tradition and distinctiveness are important in maintaining boundaries and control. Food patterns can be such a significant symbol.

THE HOUSEHOLDS OBSERVED

It became evident that within this relatively closed community individual households differed in what they ate and when and how they ate. Some of these differences were the result of particular household characteristics: stage in life cycle, scheduling of work and school activities, the presence or absence of a male head of household, and so forth. Other differences seemed to be the result of particular household norms and traditions.

Individuals within each household also exerted pressures on the food decisions. Individuals could be strongly influenced outside the home and community, both as a result of social pressure (school, workplace) and as a result of situational pressure to eat or avoid items which were expected parts of the community or household system.

Thus, the community-wide pattern, which was largely normative—transmitted through clubs, church, and friendship—was affected both by household patterns generated by structural features and normative traditions and by individual likes and dislikes (as opposed to socially shared models). Patterns were the result of both situational pressures and a set of strongly internalized socially mediated cognitive models about what is right and proper and aesthetically pleasing. The community-wide pattern was perceived as "Italian," although it included a large number of new elements. Household patterns were often explicitly recognized with pride as being different from the general community rule as a result of family tradition. Individual preferences were recognized and honored as such.

From the inside, the Italian-American community appears less tightly structured. It was in the process of selection of families that it became obvious that the community was, in fact, a series of articulated personal networks. Our first and key informant was well placed in the center of her community. Her generational position, family background, job, and personality made her special. Through her, we were able to sketch the social linkages in the Italian-American community in Maryton and to select our other families from different segments. Most of the community today consists of descendants of immigrants from the Calabrian town. However, continuous immigration means that many individuals born in the town are also present. Most of the Italian-Americans in the community have at least one parent descended from the town, but several of these parents were married to individuals from other localized enclaves in Philadelphia. A few families have moved to Maryton from other local ethnic segments and have no connection with the town. However, they, too, have become linked to the community through the ethnic stores, parish, and clubs.

The most significant core and maintenance group in the community was the generation of women close to the age of fifty who were first-generation American-born and who had been raised in Maryton. They had known each other since childhood and maintained a vast set of interlocking clubs and cliques—both formal and informal. Often they had also become related through marriage. These women and the households they controlled were the dominant community force. Their children had more ties outside the ethnic group. Newcomer families were also less integrated. They had fewer local kin and were tenuously tied through church, business, and children's social relationships.

What is the place of the families we have worked with within this context?

Family 1. The Fiore household is composed of a middle-aged working mother and two working daughters in their early twenties. Mr. Fiore has recently separated from the household and does not contribute to the support of the family. Both parents were born and grew up in South and West Maryton. Mr. Fiore is the child of immigrants from Calabria; Mrs. Fiore is the child of American-born parents whose regions of origin include Calabria and Abruzzi. Mrs. Fiore's Italian-born paternal grandparents were entrepreneurs (small grocery and butcher shop), as was her father, who was involved in a number of food-related commercial concerns. Mrs. Fiore's natal extended family, because of its entrepreneurial activities, was economically more secure than many of the other Italian-American families in South and West Maryton. Her natal family moved into a more desirable section of Maryton (the house where she now resides) while she was in elementary school. This position of her family is one factor related to her extensive social network.

Mrs. Fiore is high-school-educated and works in a local county office, a position she obtained through political patronage. Mr. Fiore is not a high-school graduate and works for the borough in the highway department. Both daughters attended high school, and the older one is a college graduate. They work in semiprofessional and manufacturing occupations. The older daughter was married at the close of the fieldwork to an Italian-American from Philadelphia and she now lives outside Maryton. A third daughter is married (recently separated) with a two-year-old son. She lives in a nearby town (virtually local) and is employed as a food-related service worker. Mrs. Fiore owns her home, which is in a middle-income section of the borough with primarily Italian-American residents, and has a rental income from an apartment.

Mrs. Fiore, because of her personality and the nature of her job (providing access to information and government services), her parent's entrepreneurial activities, her long residence in Maryton, and her large family (five siblings, four of whom live in Maryton), has a very extensive social network. She also participates actively in several political and church-affiliated organizations. Her role in the community was very fortunate for the project.

Family 2. The Cooper household is composed of a mother in her forties who works, a working son in his mid-twenties, and a daughter who is in her last year of high school and works part time. Mr. Cooper does not live with the family but contributes to their support. Both parents were born and grew up in West Maryton. Mrs. Cooper is the child of Italian-born parents who migrated from the Calabrian town. Mr. Cooper is of non-Italian descent. Mrs. Cooper's father worked for Castle and Clark as a laborer; her mother was not employed outside the home. Mrs. Cooper's natal household was impoverished in comparison with other Italian-American families in South and West Maryton because of her father's intermittent unemployment. Mr. and Mrs. Cooper lived in West Maryton after their marriage until the middle 1950s, when they purchased their present home. Mrs. Cooper's parents lived in this new home with the Cooper family until their death.

Mr. Cooper owns and operates a large service establishment. Both children who live at home work for him (as mechanic and secretary, respectively), as does a second son, who is married and has a one-and-a-half-year-old daughter. He and his wife (who are both college graduates) live in another neighborhood in the borough. Mrs. Cooper works part time in a service occupation. She owns her home, which is in the same neighborhood as Mrs. Fiore, and has rental income from an apartment. Mrs. Fiore's youngest daughter and Mrs. Cooper's middle son have been seeing each other regularly for about five years. Mrs. Cooper has nine siblings who live in Maryton and a much smaller nonkin social network than that of Mrs. Fiore. While her siblings provide the basic framework of her network, she also is part of the clubs and social circles of other women her age whom she has known all her life.

Family 3. The Felice household is composed of Mr. and Mrs. Felice (in their late thirties) and three school-age children. This past year a female foreign exchange student has also resided with them. Mr. Felice is high-school-educated and owns and operates a business which he began about ten years ago. Mrs. Felice has training in a health care profession and works part time outside the home. The older daughter is a senior in high school, as is the exchange student. The younger daughter is a freshman in high school; the son attends junior high school.

Both parents were born and grew up in Italian neighborhoods in other parts of the Philadelphia metropolitan area and moved to Maryton about twelve years ago. Both Mr. and Mrs. Felice's parents migrated from Abruzzi. Mr. Felice's parents worked in the carpet and garment industries. Mrs. Felice's father is employed as a skilled craftsman; her mother does not work outside the home. Mrs. Felice's natal household lived on the same block as other members of her extended family. The Felices own their home, which is in an upper-middle-income neighborhood of Maryton. This neighborhood has fewer Italian residents than the neighborhood where the Fiores and Coopers live.

Mr. Felice has a large local extended social network developed through contacts in his business. Mrs. Felice's network is largely composed of kin, many of whom live outside of Maryton. The social situation of this family is different from the two preceding families. The Felices have no roots in Calabria (although they share Abruzzi origins with Mrs. Fiore's maternal kin). They have no kin in Maryton and are oriented to a nonlocalized kinship network. However, they are linked to the other families in this study by some common friendship ties, children in the same school cohorts, and a common church membership. They also have local ties through business activities.

Family 4. The Weaver household is composed of Mr. and Mrs. Weaver, who are in their mid-twenties, and a two-year-old son. Mr. Weaver is northern European and recently immigrated. Mrs. Weaver is the child of native-born American parents; she was born and grew up in the neighborhood where the Felices live. She is of Italian (maternal, Calabria) and non-Italian (paternal, northern European) descent. Mr. Weaver works in a managerial position in retail trade in a nearby shopping center. Mrs. Weaver, who is pregnant, does not work outside the home. The Weavers own their home, which is in the same neighborhood as those of the Fiores and the Coopers. Mrs. Weaver has two siblings, who are married and live in Maryton, as do her parents. The Weavers' social network is largely composed of maternal kin.

Families 1 and 2 are headed by women of the generation which is central to Italian-American community life in Maryton. Family 4 includes the daughter of one of this generation, who is known to the children of families 1 and 2. Since much of our work involved extended family meals, we also were able to observe the wife's mother in family 4 and the married children's households, as well as the potential spouses for families 1 and 2, thus exposing us to two generations. Family 3 was interesting because of its more attentuated ties to the community and its age position between the two generations represented by the other families.

SIGNIFICANT HOUSEHOLD DIFFERENCES

While the households we have studied are different in several ways, the most significant differences for our analytical purposes seemed to be the following:

1. *Presence or absence of husband.* The most important of these variables is the presence or absence of a senior male, for menu negotiations rely heavily on his preferences and activity patterns. His presence also requires precedence in seating arrangement and service order. If absent, his role will be filled by another member of the household or a guest. The two households in which the male is absent often have present a married son or potential son-in-law who frequently plays the role.

2. *Stage in family cycle.* Two of these families have adult children, whose aesthetic (and in some cases metaphysical) preferences and activity patterns produce variations in the culinary decision-making process. The other two families are composed of school-age children and an infant, respectively, who were less influential. It is not only the variation in ages, number, and gender of children but also the compatibility of their preferences (a variable which can be measured) which contribute to differences in the nature of menu negotiations.

3. *School and work schedules.* The work patterns of males, the activities of the senior female (employment outside the home, participation in voluntary organizations, and other social relationships) and the schedules of children create contrasts in the scheduling and content of eating events. Older children's activities become increasingly more autonomous. This in turn exerts pressure on food planning.

4. *Social networks.* The nature of social networks includes factors such as whether close ties are predominantly kin and childhood friends, all mutually known (frequently observing food activities and exerting strong normative pressure), or whether ties are diverse, less intimate, of shorter duration, and not mutually known.

5. *Generational cohort of the senior female.* Differences in local, national, and world events and trends affected the initial socialization of the senior female as wife and mother.

These structural characteristics can be identified, measured, and expected to affect food decision dynamics in a uniform way. In addition, there are unique family characteristics, such as taste preferences and linear family traditions, which are not uniform or group patterned. Each household has a distinctive aesthetic and metaphysical tradition which is a combination of the general set of rules and practices of both natal and affinal households and individuals' idiosyncratic characteristics. These include preferences for certain sensory qualities (and food items), concerns about diet-related health status, and the importance of religious symbolism.

Finally, the senior females in these families have varying degrees of expertise (self-identified and reputed) as cooks. In this community, food is a requisite of all forms of social interaction. The women we have worked with express this shared pattern in different ways.

Instead of looking at class—an abstract notion whose indicators are some combination of income, education, and occupation—we are looking at relatively closed subcommunities which cannot be fragmented by the ascription of class labels since the members are all of the same general levels of income, education, and occupation. It is our contention that as individuals significantly change their incomes, educational and occupational levels, they tend to move away from the closed group socially (increase in the number of meaningful outside social ties for norm-sharing and exchange-relationships) and geographically. Class, as an abstract phenomenon, is not important to this study except insofar as we believe that it is the political economy which ultimately creates the relatively closed lifestyle groups which share a food system.

We found that income was not very significant to food patterning since it tended to be an unimportant factor in a community with substantial discretionary income and a high priority on food. When income exerted an influence, it seemed to affect only choices of particular items rather than formats or food patterning. Occupation was important mostly as it affected the scheduling of time and activities.

In fact, it was difficult to get useful income and expenditure figures for the households we worked with in spite of the close relationships between ethnographers and informants. One problem lay in the multiple sources of household income and its variation over time. The Fiore household received income from the jobs of Mrs. Fiore and her daughters, although the proportion of daughters' income contributed varied over time. In addition, there was sporadic rent from one apartment and boarders. The Cooper household received income from Mrs. Cooper's part-time work, her children's work for their father, contributions from the father, and rent. The Felices' income varied, coming from Mr. Felice's business, which was not predictable, and from Mrs. Felice's irregular employment. The Weavers' income came from Mr. Weaver's steady salary. But much of this income, as well as almost all his leisure time, was spent in renovating their old home. This was part of the family's entrepreneurial strategy of investing sweat equity in improving a house, eventually selling it for a profit, buying another old house, and repeating the process.

In Maryton, a socially transmitted pattern of meal formats dominates; it is acted upon by structural constraints; but only if economic circumstances change significantly and for the long term will they permanently affect the food system. While income directly affects content (food item) choice, change in time and the scheduling of activities exert a more direct influence on changes in meal formats and large-scale patterns.

METHODOLOGY

By comparing the distinctive phases of the long-term project we can learn about the differences between the kinds of information derived from the distinctive field techniques used in each phase.

The first phase of the research in Philadelphia began in 1973. Goode, along with several anthropologists and geographers at Temple University, decided to collaborate in an interdisciplinary study of the food patterns of an urban ethnic group. The objectives were

1. to study a food system holistically by tracing the whole chain of food-related activities from procurement through cooking, eating, and, finally, disposal
2. to assess the relationship of ethnicity to food
3. to look at the formation of ethnic communities (localized segments) as a differentiated process which varies from place to place because of different group experiences in varied local contexts

Italian-Americans in South Philadelphia were selected as the group with which to begin. This particular ethnic group was identified by the individuals themselves as well as by outsiders as strongly interested in food.

A comprehensive questionnaire was devised to be distributed by a Temple student who lived in the neighborhood and operated a food delivery route. Questionnaires were to be filled in by "respondents" and returned to the student. In spite of the individual mediation by the student, residents in the community seemed unwilling to respond to the impersonal questionnaire. In a second effort, one of us

(Theophano) who had affiliations in South Philadelphia used the questionnaire as an interview schedule. Later, other Temple students from the neighborhood were trained as interviewers. We obtained data on the following:

1. household composition (age, number, sex)
2. occupation
3. education
4. area of origin of residents
5. daily, weekly, seasonal, and yearly regularities of food intake
6. shopping patterns
7. special observances such as ritual events (feasts and fasts)
8. frequency of items consumed
9. preparation techniques; by whom, when, how, and where learned
10. ideas about food and health

We then constructed an open-ended interview schedule. Indirect questions were asked and the interviews electronically recorded. This interview was designed to elicit information about such concerns as conceptions of the meal, childhood food experience, current child socialization practices, and the use of kitchen space.

A final project component was added in an effort to correlate cultural patterns with the nutritional status of the group. The appropriate dietary research methods—dietary histories, twenty-four-hour recall, seven-day recall, and seven-day dietary record—were surveyed, evaluated, and tested before an approach was selected. At the time, the literature suggested that seven-day measurements and dietary records were the most accurate and useful method for assessing the *variability* of dietary patterns of *groups* rather than individuals. Moreover, our initial data indicated that the weekly cycle was a significant structure in the system.

Thirty-five families participated in this phase of the project. They weighed and measured their food (familial and individual) for one week. In addition, anthropometric measurements were taken of all family members and hematological analyses were performed on the adults. Health indices were reviewed by a hematologist, and a general assessment of health and nutritional status was offered. The Cornell Medical Index was completed for each family. Preliminary analysis indicated no significant incidence of diet-related pathology, but the intensive analysis of the data is still in process.

In the initial phase of research, observation of meals or other eating events occurred randomly; only if the fieldworker happened to be present at such times. This was largely a consequence of the difficulties of doing urban anthropology (time, commuting to informants, emphasis on domestic privacy, and the cost of participant observation) rather than a researchers' choice. Regrettably, this lack of systematic observation created a formidable gap in our knowledge of the "actual" food patterns of the community. As we were to discover, the loss of observational data in the South Philadelphia community made later comparisons with Maryton difficult. We plan to videotape sample meals and food preparation to provide us with comparative material.

After this stage in the research the interdisciplinary team dispersed and Goode remained to direct the project. We began to work in another localized ethnic segment which had undergone a different process of ethnic group formation. We wished to examine the effect of community difference on the development of modifications in the ethnic food system. Curtis, who was residing in Maryton, carried out both first and second interviews with thirty families. Five of these families maintained seven-day food diaries. Again, participation in food events was sporadic and uneven. Through this comparison, several interesting community differences emerged (Curtis 1977).

Long eager to be able to collect data through participant observation, we were able to accomplish this as part of the Russell Sage project directed by Mary Douglas. Our interview data had already provided us with a view of the idealized meal cycle in the community. We wanted to know more about the way that these stated ideals differed from actual practice and *why*. In other words, we wanted to understand why certain rules were overridden under certain conditions. While Douglas encouraged participant observation without elicitation, we wanted to observe as well as talk with informants about decision-making and the process of choice among available alternatives. As Trow notes: "participant observation is a relatively weak instrument for gathering data on sentiments, behaviors, and relationships which are *normatively* prescribed by the group under observation" (1969; p. 334; italics ours).

Involvement with the Russell Sage project necessitated a shift in our original research method, which we made eagerly. Initially, we limited ourselves to observation without discussion. Questions were regarded as intrusive because of their potential to alter "typical" behavior. However, after a week or more of continuous presence, we believe the effect of the observer to be minimized. Simultaneously, the relationship had become intimate enough to generate a stream of volunteered information explaining choices and decisions.

One of the stipulations of Douglas's proposal was that the fieldworkers reside in each home during the period of research. This was not possible in Maryton or in South Philadelphia. Families with adult males in the home would not eagerly accept a woman alone as a boarder. Even families without men were hesitant about "outsiders" living in. The fieldworkers commuted to the households on a daily basis and were present during all shopping, food preparation, and eating activities. Of the two sites—South Philadelphia and Maryton—the latter seemed to offer the most convenient and reasonable circumstances for doing fieldwork. Curtis contacted one of her former interviewees and friends, who is the center of a large network of relations and friends. It was her suggestion that while we could stay with her for two months, we limit our stay with other families to one month; a lengthier stay would require more tolerance on the part of our hosts. It would be easier to convince families to participate in a one-month study.

At the end of the participant observation phase, we were in a position to evaluate three very different types of information about the food system. It is our view that the data sets are complementary and even necessary for mutual illumination; each set of data alone provided misleading information about the system.

1. *Interviews.* We have interview data from 208 households, 178 in South Philadelphia and 30 in Maryton. This information provides us with a clear-cut picture of ideal food intake patterning which is a shared, normative phenomenon. Moreover, we have indications that two distinct, noninteracting enclaves from one traditional macro-cuisine do continue to practice certain common traditional patterns. Moreover, they have undergone certain changes and modifications in the same way. However, local conditions have also led to differences in the rate of some changes and the nature of others.

The interview data were sufficient to provide us with group-shared patterning. However, this information was the ideal; it told us nothing about real behavior. *And* we later discovered it was biased toward childhood, to the remembered past and not to contemporary practice. Moreover, there were new patterned events which were not explicitly recognized by the population and thus not reported. One of these was the weekend cycle of meals—a response to the American work and leisure pattern which was very different from weekly meals.

2. *Recorded meals.* The seven-day diaries and intake records kept by a small subsample of families provided us with a means to use actual meal patterns to test the stated ideals. For example, we could see that stated rules for Friday dinner and Sunday dinner and gravy/platter alternation were often overridden. However, we could also see that such ideals were also often observed. It was also possible, using this data, to discern the mini-weekend cycle, which was not reported in the interviews.

It is our contention that nutritional studies which collect actual meal data without comparing the information with perceived ideals will be likely to miss any patterning that exists. Since actual meal planning is the result of interaction between normative ideals and situational constraints, looking at the outcomes alone provides a view of highly random, individualized behavior. However, looking at actual food intake in conjunction with shared ideals enables the researcher to see that normative patterning exists.

3. *Participant observation.* Direct observation of food-related activities provided the bridge between the interview data and food records and informed us about the way the system operates. Watching the acts of shopping and meal preparation, we could see the points at which external constraints (financial resources, time, competing activities) impinged on shared rules for patterning food intake. We began to see that there were alternative choices or models for breakfast, Friday dinners, Sunday dinners, and so forth, which were also normatively approved under particular constraining conditions. Some rules bent easily; others did not.

The most serious weakness of the data gathered from participant observation is the number of households represented. Given the impact of both household structural features *and* unique household preferences (traditions) on day-to-day decisions, the use of only four households weakened our ability to make reliable generalizations. The problem of restricted cases is not at all significant for our interview data and is much less significant for the dietary record data.

However, the insights provided by the intensive observations were our only exposure to such significant aspects of the system as

1. the actual process of menu negotiation—selecting formats and content

2. the relative significance of different household roles in the process

3. the evaluative comments, discussions about food, and significant feedback to the key kitchen person which influences her actions

4. the influence of other women in the social network on choices

All in all, these observations provided us with significant insights which can be tested by follow-up interviews and food intake records. For example, if we can state our insights about the role of husbands, the principle of equity in menu negotiations, or the significance of intraweekly periodicity—as hypotheses—we can test these hypotheses through higher-level interview instruments and large samples of records for particular types of meals on a large sample of households.

The Italian-American Food System as Shared Patterning

Our early work had pointed to an Italian-American food system, similar in many parts of the northeastern United States, which could be described both in terms of items and in terms of a cyclical patterning of meal types. We described these patterns earlier.

A basic assumption which we have developed from the work of Douglas, and which was further developed in the Russell Sage project, was that the food system of an ethnic group consists of a shared repertory of eating events along with notions for their appropriate use. In our research, the events were initially differentiated by specific socially defined occasions which seemed to call for distinctive meal formats (menus), recipes, food items, and accouterments of the meal (place, utensils, and types of nonfood activity). After creating an inventory of food events, we discovered that several occasions were, in fact, celebrated by similar eating events. Thus, we were able to categorize several types of events each calling for similar menus, personnel, and types and modes of food preparation and presentation.

A *meal format* or menu structure refers to a way of patterning dishes and items in time and space. Meal formats can be differentiated by the number of courses, the number of dishes in each course, and the types of dishes required for particular courses. Not all meal formats are constructed with course sequences, however, and a format can consist of a prescribed number of simultaneously presented dishes. Such a format can specify the number of dishes, the types of dishes, and the way they are presented, served, and eaten (often indicating the way they are rank-ordered or otherwise related to each other). Thus, a *food system* consists of a repertory of particular meal formats and rules for when each is appropriate in terms of occasion and social audience.

A *meal cycle* refers to the patterning of food events over time. A food system will consist of a cycle of expected events cued by the time of the day, day of the week, season, or life-cycle stage. Such temporal cues are strong influences on meal format selection. However, there will also be many external unanticipated circumstances which also influence meal planning.

In the following analysis, we will look first at the community-shared pattern and then at the process of menu planning among Italian-Americans. Menu planning is a two-stage process involving a selection of format and a selection of content (items). It is in the selection of format more than the selection of content that we see the continuity or direct modification of the historically persistent pattern. It is in the format repertory that we can locate what is socially transmitted and normatively reinforced within an interacting community for both everyday and ritual meals.

SENSORY, METAPHYSICAL, AND SOCIAL ELEMENTS

In working with the group and its food system, we made a distinction between the food system itself—a series of cultural rules governing the pattern of food intake—and the sensory, metaphysical and social aspects of the system. The system itself contained meal structures and rules for their relationships and their periodicity. For example, as we will see, many formats are constructed from structural elements found in other formats or are merely elaborated or scaled down versions of them. There are rules for repetition and alternation for types of meals and for content.

Food is also used to symbolize, underscore, and mark elements of other cultural subsystems. In our analysis, we were concerned not only with the food system as an autonomous set of pattern rules, but with the use of food to mark social relationships and to underscore religious and health beliefs. In addition, we looked at the sensory aspects of food, its aesthetic nature.

The social dimension refers to the links between food use, social status, and social relationships. Here the community and the household are assumed to develop rules for the allocation of food based on social status (sex, age, kinship status), as well as for the exchange of food and hospitality between households or individuals who are linked by kinship or friendship ties.

—What are the regularized patterns of food giving and food receiving?

—Are they reciprocal or asymmetrical?

—Within the household, how is labor divided in activities of procurement, preparation, serving, and cleaning up?

—Who is served first? Last?

—Who is served most? Least?

—What is the position of a nonkin guest?

—Are there some statuses with greater freedom and autonomy in allocating food to themselves?

—Are some individuals favored in either food decisions or food allocation because of personal attributes rather than status attributes?

In attempting to isolate the sensory or aesthetic features of eating events, we looked first at the large-scale contextual aspects of a meal.

—How are accouterments of the meal (tablecloths, dishes, cutlery, glassware, and serving pieces) used to embellish it visually?

—How distinctly are types of meals differentiated by specific accouterments?

—How is food presented?

—How are dishes arranged on the table? Are the dishes garnished?

—Is the shape of the food carefully manipulated (sculptured)?

Aside from overall visual aspects of the meal, we also looked at the manipulation of sensory attributes in smaller units such as dishes.

—To what extent is color important?

—In addition to visual sensory perception, how is odor perceived and manipulated?

—What about touch, texture, and viscosity?

—Are foods directly eaten with the hand?

—What is considered hard, crisp, soft, smooth?

—How are textures and tastes (sweet, salty, sour, and bitter) combined or segregated?

—Are distinctive spices used for all dishes throughout the repertory or are there specifics for special dishes?

—Are mouth-irritating spices used and when?

These characteristics of items, dishes, and meals will demonstrate in the following discussion how individual and household preferences interact with community-shared cultural preferences.

Finally, we looked for nonsensory perceptions of foods and dishes as having properties which are not related to tasting, looking, or smelling "good" or "bad." The most common beliefs relate to food as "good for you," that is, having health-restoring or health-maintaining properties, or "bad for you," causing illness. Other foods can be spiritually pure or impure. They can be avoided in order to maintain righteousness, such as meat abstinence on Fridays, or used as ritually efficacious in communicating with the supernatural, such as taking communion.

As we will see, in this community the most significant *shared* patterns existed in the area of *social* meanings of food and food behavior. Where aesthetic ideas and metaphysical beliefs were concerned there had once been a significant amount of shared folklore, but these aspects were no longer significantly shared, transmitted, or reinforced.

MEAL FORMATS

We discovered that the current food system of this community was structured around the alternation or combination of two major types of meals. Members of the community make a primary distinction between Italian and American foods, commonly referred to as "gravy" and "platter," respectively. "One-pot" is a generic term referring to a nongravy mixture of foods conceptualized as Italian in origin or in style such as stews, greens, and soups. Gravy, a tomato-based mixture—what Americans call spaghetti sauce—is by far the most significant variety of Italian dishes. Regardless of the actual origins of a dish or its conformity to a particular dish which once existed in space and time, gravy and one-pot dishes are conceived of as Italian and connote an array of meanings. Platters are the interpretation of the tripartite, segregated meat, vegetable, and starch Anglo meal. The underlying characteristics of these two meal types emerge and reveal the distinctiveness of each: gravy or one-pot dishes are a wet, saucy slow-simmering mixture; platters are dry, segregated dishes with sauce accompaniment optional.

There were some analogues for the platter in the traditional system in the form of vegetable or egg-based platters served simultaneously with other greens and bread. These types of dishes probably were used with some degree of regularity in a traditional cycle. It is also possible that they were limited to certain regions or to urban centers.

These two meal formats today are combined and segregated in multiple and diverse combinations such that at the poles there is extreme segregation of the two formats and in between a merger of cuisines at several levels. For years, the two formats were alternated during the week, which culminated on Sunday in a multicourse meal incorporating both. Over time the Sunday meal prototype has been reduced in scale and alternation of formats has become more flexible as new types of meals enter the system.

At first, we assumed that food events could be ranked hierarchically according to the degree of *community uniformity* with which they were observed and that everyday meals would be less uniform than the highest feasts. This turned out not to be true. However, as one moves from everyday meals through the hierarchy of feasts, some aspects of food-related activity do increase—planning time, preparation time, duration of the event, the amount of cooperative labor and food exchange, and the number of other ritualized activities which occur.

Implicit in a ranking of food events is a consideration of the people who attend the event. As one moves up the hierarchy of feasts, the attendance list increases in number and status inclusion. We move from close to distant genealogical kin and from intimate network ties to less intimate friends and acquaintances.

To respond to the progression of social events, several meal formats have been developed to accommodate the different attendance lists generated by specific occasions. These meals formats are constructed from the basic gravy or platter elements. They comprise a repertory of meal types to be selected from for a given occasion. As we will see, uniformity at the community-wide level occurs mostly in the nature of the meal repertory itself, but for many feasts a negotiation takes place to select the specific format for that event from the shared repertory. This negotiation takes into account actual household circumstances. It also appears that uniform repertory selections for a given event occur most frequently at the lower levels (weekly cycle meals) and at the highest levels of calendrical and life-cycle events (Christmas Eve, Easter, weddings).

The meal repertory of this community consists of a series of formats which differ in structure and content specificity. Several of the formats are specific to particular occasions and limited to them; the occasions themselves are cued by the time of day, place in the week, calendrical holiday, and life-cycle event. The occasion triggers both a list of appropriate participants and a selection of meal format. The format results from both considerations; neither the occasion itself nor the attendance list alone cues the format. Decisions involve the interaction or feedback of one variable upon the other. The size of the network and the structure of the family play a role in the determination of format. Unique family traditions and the degree to which the family is influenced by outside forces (media, important ties outside the community) also affect the way an occasion is defined in terms of rank and analogy.

Life-cycle rituals include both traditional (historically continuous) events such as christenings, confirmations, and funerals, and events new to the American experience, such as high school graduations and wedding showers. Both traditional and new occasions are evaluated as similar to or higher/lower than other occasions. Considerable latitude exists for the ranking of middle-level feasts and their definitions as analogous to other feasts. High feasts, such as weddings and Christmas Eve, and lower feasts, such as Sunday dinner, exist as shared fixed points in the system against which all other occasions can be relatively ranked and defined. Once the format is selected, great latitude exists in the selection of content for most feast formats. Here, again, the possibilities are significantly affected by household features. In addition, unique individual preferences play a significant role in content decisions while they are less important in selecting formats.

WEEKDAY MEALS

Today, the community pattern consists of an invariable and significant structural sequence of three meals a day. The meals are the skeletal structure around which the day's activities are constructed. As meals are responsive to the day's events, so, too, does the daily cycle of meals influence the sequencing of other activities. There is one food event for morning which varies little throughout the week. Time is invariable, though different from household to household depending upon work and school schedules. Unlike the traditional Old World or New Haven breakfast, most often hot food begins each day, that is, oatmeal, eggs, waffles, and so forth. However, each household differs in the degree of regularity of adherence to the ideal that breakfast is a cooked family meal. In several households not all members participate or they participate only partially in this event. In fact, the ideal pattern is actualized only by two significant age groups—the eldest and the youngest—while adolescents and young adults frequently refrain from eating. This meal format is also selected for one other occasion: when late-night activities end after midnight and a shared meal is called for. In this case, the breakfast meal format ends an evening's activities. It is interesting to note that the cooked breakfast is not an aspect of the shared Italian macro-cuisine and yet it *is* shared widely within this socially interacting community. Ethnicity *is* significant in this practice not because there is historical continuity, but because the group definition of good maternal nurturance has led to the adoption of this Anglo-derived American practice.

Lunch is the second daily meal. American work schedules have altered the pre–World War II pattern of two main meals, with the midday meal larger in scale than the evening meal. Lunch formats today consist of several types: a celebratory form, a lunch with guests, a less social but complete luncheon meal, and an abbreviated lunch. Lunch events respond significantly to work and school schedules, yet are also shaped by the participants and the occasion. The more social and celebratory the occasion is expected to be the more elaborate is the meal format, which shifts from vending machines and solitary abbreviated eating to a full lunch in the home or at a restaurant. Lunches vary along the hot/cold dimension. A guest lunch or celebratory lunch will be marked by hot foods. Some of the lesser lunches may include a hot food item such as soup but often the less significant lunch meals are cold.

Daily dinner, the main meal of the day, today offers several choices from the repertory for which the traditional pattern of alternation applies. One choice is the gravy meal. Today, gravy types have become the most significant Italian element in the system. However, the nongravy one-pot has an interesting role to play. Nongravy one-pots are dishes which emphasize vegetable mixtures with bits of meat, for example, "savory" (savoy) cabbage and ham or organ meats, such as "kidney stew." "Beef stew" or "beef pastina" involve meat, vegetable, and starch mixtures in varying proportions cooked in a non-tomato-based gravy. These dishes are frequently used as exchange items, particularly the dishes which were once traditionally popular. The cooked food gift may be given to women of the same generation (family and nonfamily) whose younger household members may not eat the dish. It may be a gift to men of the same generation whose wives no longer cook the particular dish. An offering of "kidney stew" or "rabis and beans" may be one woman's specialty and the acceptance of the gift may signal reciprocity for favors received or jobs well done and the expectation of future services. These nongravy one-pot dishes are no longer part of the weekly alternation pattern. Because the popularity of such dishes has diminished for the young, they are rarely main dishes, but may be served as a side dish to some individuals who like them.

Gravy meals are anchor points in the weekly dinner cycle. They occur ideally on particular evenings, Tuesday or Thursday or when signaled by the presence of guests. Such an extended attendance list could include extended family and friends. Gravy meals lend themselves to a variable attendance list since the type and quantity of food prepared is divisible in ways which the other meal format, "the platter," is less likely to be. Thus, the relationship is interesting. The fact that one is having gravy because it is Thursday can affect the attendance list leading to spontaneous invitations *or* one can select gravy because of the attendance list on a day other than Thursday.

Alternating with the Sunday and secondary gravy meals are dinner events which use the platter or whole roast format. Another fixed point in the weekly meal cycle is the Friday "fast" meal which focuses on fish or other meatless dishes.

WEEKEND MEALS

Weekend meal patterns differ from those of weekdays. Except for Sunday dinner, this difference seems to be a result of American activity patterning and not a historically persistent pattern. Nevertheless, it is *shared* within this socially interacting community. Breakfasts are quite elaborate, and Saturday breakfasts serve as a gathering point for the family and friends. It is often an "occasion" for celebratory eating out. Again, this activity is gender specific. Female family members and/or segments of the friendship network will attend Saturday/Sunday breakfasts in the home or go out to a restaurant for breakfast together. Men have a counterpart event: work mates may go out to breakfast during the week or fathers and sons may do so on the weekends.

Not only is this breakfast well attended by the family in comparison with weekday breakfasts, but it is the most well-attended meal of the weekend outside of Sunday dinner. This suggests a reversal in the weekday pattern, in which ceremoniousness peaks at the end of the day. The weekend begins on Saturday with a ritualized meal, and meals decline in elaborateness and number of participants as the day progresses. The ceremoniousness of Saturday morning and Sunday evening meals seem to punctuate the weekend, marking it as time different from the mundane week. This reversal in ceremoniousness which occurs on Saturday is responsive as well to the complex and variable schedule of activities in which household members are engaged. Saturday activity patterns begin with interaction in the home with household members and move to other domains outside of the home: stores, restaurants, friends' homes, and so forth. Lunches on the weekends are either late and abbreviated or entirely eliminated. (For a description of weekly meal cycles, see table 2.)

Often Saturday evening meals are really a lunch format used in evenings; they precede leisure-time activities, are prepared at home, and consist of a hot sandwich (these hot sandwiches may be eaten in restaurants as well); neither of these events is considered "cooking," but is perceived as a "no-cooking" meal even though the preparation time might equal that for some gravy or platter meals.

It is interesting to note that informants do explicitly recognize

TABLE 2

Weekly Meal Cycles			
	Weekday	*Friday*	*Weekend*
A.M.	Breakfast or partial breakfast	Breakfast or partial breakfast	Elaborate breakfast	
Lunch	Full lunch or abbreviated	Full lunch or abbreviated	Late and abbreviated lunch	
Dinner	Gravy or platter	Fish or meatless Gravy or platter	Saturday "noncooking" meal in home or celebratory eating out	Sunday Gravy and/or whole meat
Postdinner	Club: Simple party or Dessert and coffee	Late night breakfast	Late night breakfast	Dessert and coffee

some of these formats, while others were defined by the analysts based on consistent practices which they observed. The gravy/platter distinction was almost universally evident in the interview data. The sandwich, no-cooking expedient meal was also recognized and consciously labeled as a type. Moreover, Sunday dinner was recognized as unique. The differences within lunch formats and between weekend meals, that is, Saturday breakfasts and other breakfasts, were not explicitly labeled in any way.

EATING OUT

It also became obvious to us after analysis that eating-out activities themselves were highly differentiated and various types were reserved for special circumstances. Eating out can be divided into occasions in other homes and those in restaurants.

During the week, after-dinner leisure activities often trigger an eating event. Women of one generation in the community belong to social clubs, the meetings of which begin and end with a modified meal consisting of several appetizers, dishes, and dessert. Very often it is a second dinner meal, and it does not replace the earlier event. Other activities such as demonstrations (tupperware, cosmetics) trigger a "simple party" format, which includes drinks, appetizers, coffee, and cake. Finally, visiting patterns which often focus on a specific activity—that is, visiting the sick, going to see a new household item, and so forth—will warrant dessert and coffee.

Visiting is a gender-specific activity carried out by female kin and the extended female network. Women rarely visit men unless they are accompanied by other females or another woman is present in the household. Infrequently men visit families other than their own during or following a meal and, if possible, accompanied by a woman.

Eating out (in a restaurant) basically consists of two types of occasions: expedient and celebratory. Expedient eating out occurs when other activities interfere with regular meal schedules or a respite from cooking is desired. The meal selected is similar to meals which are prepared at home or perhaps more elaborate versions of them. The Saturday sandwich meal and the simple platter are examples. Planning for the occasion is minimal, or it is spontaneous. The meal is only a portion of the other activities and is given no priority. The types of restaurants used for these events are diner-type establishments and fast-food restaurants.

Celebratory eating out is usually planned in advance. It occurs in more formal settings, and the meal itself consists of foods and dishes which are rarely served at home. The meal is virtually the entire event and is given emphasis. Celebratory meals such as these can occur at any point during the week but more frequently take place on the weekends.

The restaurants used for such events are of two types: the large franchised American establishment, which features beef and seafood dishes along with a salad bar, and locally-owned establishments featuring such well-known "continental" fare as veal parmigiana, veal Cordon Bleu, and wiener schnitzel.

Celebratory eating out most often entails selecting foods which are consciously and deliberately different from those eaten at home. The exception is the Saturday breakfast eaten in restaurants. These breakfasts bridge the gap between expedient and celebratory meals. At the least, these are more elaborate affairs, though not significantly different in format, from what is eaten in the home.

The weekly dinner cycle is the outcome of the intersection of two patterns: (1) a historically continuous internal rule system which encourages alternation of format and provides fixed points (Friday and Sunday) for which specific format or specific content is expected, and (2) a cycle of work and leisure activities reflecting the five-day work week and two-day leisure pattern of industrial society. Unanticipated periods of heavy work, high stress, and special events will also trigger the use of expedient and celebratory formats at other points in the weekly cycle. The principles of format selection for dinners can be summarized as follows:

1. The Sunday gravy meal is the weekly anchor.
2. Gravy meals occur once or twice after Sunday.
3. Gravy meals and platters alternate.
4. Gravy is served when attendance is large or occasion is special.
5. The Friday fast rule (absence of meat or presence of fish) is observed.
6. Expedient meals reflect the activity cycle.
7. Celebratory and expedient meals cluster around weekend leisure.

FEASTS AND FEAST FORMATS

The community emphasis on frequent sociability leads to a tendency to celebrate many holidays and life-cycle events with feasts. High feasts are those most uniformly celebrated and involve the most preparation time and longest duration. They also engender the largest guest lists. These high holiday feasts include Christmas Eve, Christmas dinner, Easter dinner, and Thanksgiving. Middle feasts include New Year's dinner, Mother's Day, Father's Day, Labor Day, Memorial Day, July 4, St. Francis Day, and St. Joseph's Day. These feasts are celebrated less uniformly. There are choices of format and/or content to be negotiated. Attendance lists are variable; preparation time and duration are reduced.

The wedding is the highest level life-cycle feast. Slightly lower feasts include christenings, first communions, confirmations, and funerals; while birthdays, anniversaries, graduations, and wedding/birth showers form another even lower middle level tier. Weekend (low) feasts are as high in degree of uniformity as high feasts. Middle-level feasts carry the most options.

There are six possible meal format responses to these occasions. For middle-level feasts households differ in the way they define an event and construct analogies to other similar events. These unique definitions and analogies lead to decisions about the appropriate attendance list and the selection of a food event type and thus to household variation for such middle-level feasts as birthdays, anniversaries, graduations, and showers.

The six feast formats are:

1. *Elaborated Sunday dinner.* Sunday dinners today are similar to ordinary gravy meals, although formerly they included not only the gravy dish, salad, and Italian bread, but soup, a whole roast meat, wine, and a dessert. Then, the festive form of Sunday· dinner included even more courses—an antipasto, as well as post-dessert nuts, fruits, and cordials. This very elaborate version no longer exists, but a multicourse dinner reminiscent of former Sunday dinners is often selected and reserved for feasts. It is home-prepared and served to a sit-down audience. Currently, Sunday dinners differ from the two-course meals served during the week only by an extended attendance list and the variety of gravy served. A baked macaroni dish such as ravioli or lasagna (highly ranked type of gravy dish) is more frequently reserved for Sunday dinners today. In addition, to make the meal more elaborate, a whole roast meat can be added (turkeys and hams are used for Thanksgiving, Christmas, and Easter following macro-American patterning), and more than one dessert can be offered.

2. *Buffet.* The buffet is a home-prepared meal consisting of elements from both gravy and platter meals. Dishes may include meatballs, sausage and peppers, and other hot meats in tomato gravy for sandwiches on Italian rolls. Platter elements include sliced roast beef in brown gravy, potato salad, cole slaw, and other salads not in the Italian tradition. These foods are presented simultaneously on a table from which participants select their choices. The meal is eaten in small groups seated at several tables. These foods would never be served together as evening meals but are elements of both the Italian and American meal types combined in this unique format. This format is often used when there is a large attendance which ranges from 50 to 125 people. An entire extended family and intimate network can attend depending upon the occasion. Interestingly, the buffet is more item specific than one would expect from a buffet pattern. Certain dishes such as meatballs and American cold salads are rigidly expected for such a format.

3. *Buffet-style meal.* This format includes many dishes which would make up several complete menus for regular evening meals.

They consist of predominantly Italian dishes: gravy dishes, meats, tossed salad, vegetables, and so forth. The foods are displayed simultaneously and away from the dining table. A single dining table is prepared for the participants to share the meal once they have helped themselves from the service table. The menu represents several Sunday meals, offering several choices for each course in such a meal. The number of participants is in the middle range, generally the extended family. This format is not item specific at all and allows a wide range of choice reflecting family preferences and specialties.

4. *Simple party.* The simple party format consists of drinks, appetizers, dessert, and coffee. It may be selected for weekly women's leisure activities and can be chosen and embellished to celebrate any middle-level feast. This format is easily recognizable as the dominant American party format today.

5. *Sit-down, catered meal.* This format is reserved for the highest level feast: the wedding. Though rigid in structure, the content of the meal, the number of courses, and the timing of the subsidiary events are variable and respond to the large attendance list and the particular resources of the hosting family. The participant list for the occasion is the largest of any and includes work mates and other "outsiders." Finally, the preparation of this event is not done by the hosting family but is contracted and paid for. The items in this format tend to be generated by the catering industry and follow its fads and trends. Very little Italian content occurs.

6. *Content-specific events.* Calendrical holidays tend to be celebrated by elaborate Sunday dinners. Two calendrical events which are occasions of abstinence also require meal formats and food items specific to those occasions. These two formats are never used for any other event.

Christmas Eve is a meatless meal, in keeping with a former church prohibition. The meal consists of an odd number of dishes, either fish or meatless, served to the immediate family or a slightly extended gathering. Such dishes as baccala, calamari, fried smelts, broccoli, and cauliflower are most favored; however, each household will select the menu with consideration for personal taste and in keeping with family tradition. The number of dishes can range from three to as many as eleven, thirteen, or fifteen. Modern practice has reduced the number served to the minimum.

Good Friday, another fasting event, has a unique set of foods associated with the holiday, which are never served together on other occasions: omelettes, fish, pisadi (a ricotta cheese pizza), and several Easter breads and pies.

Another series of foods specific to a particular calendrical event are those which are prepared and consumed continuously during a holiday period. There are a few specific Easter dishes—bread, pies, and sweets—which are served throughout the holiday season. Similarly, the Christmas season is accompanied by specific sweet baked goods.

Menu Negotiation: Linking Ideal Pattern to Structural Constraints

We have now described the repertory of food events for the Italian-American community at large. We will now link this pattern—elicited by interviews and backed by historical material—to the actual process of meal planning in the community we studied. Our discussion of menu negotiation is based on insights from the intensive ethnography of four families.

The locus of difference between families lies in two areas: the degree to which they observe a uniform community notion of appropriate format and the way that they select specific items for each format. Thus, we will look at two processes: (1) the choice of *format* (generated by the definition and rank ascribed by the occasion and the structural constraints of the household); (2) the choice of *content* (generated by individual preferences, network specialties, family tradition, and resources). We call the process of decision-making regarding format and content *menu negotiation.*

FORMAT NEGOTIATION FOR WEEKLY MEALS

When we look at the weekly dinner meal cycle, many formats are item specific. Thus, the choice of format includes the choice of the content so that here individual preferences and the role influence of the individual play an insignificant role. For the purpose of this discussion, we will consider the following as the weekly repertory from which choices are made: gravies, platters, whole roasts, quick meals (in the home and in restaurants), and celebratory restaurant meals.

Gravy and one-pot meals are different from platters or whole roasts. Gravy meals can feature baked macaroni (high rank) or boiled macaroni. One-pots include soups or stews. Gravy meals tend to be restricted formats (content specific) since they always include macaroni mixed with the household's meat-based tomato sauce. The alternative platter formats are open in content in regard to meat, starch, and vegetable. Whole roasts, quicky at-home meals (sandwich, no-cooking), and expedient eating out tend to allow a moderate range of choice. Celebratory restaurant meals usually follow the platter format and are more than two courses (entree and dessert). There are certain content rules for this format. Foods are eaten that are rarely if ever eaten at home. Although preferences develop, such foods are usually *not* added to the home repertory.

Selecting a gravy format precludes further content negotiation but a platter requires more decisions as to both content and style of preparation. More variables (individual preferences, items which are cheap or easily accessible) come into play in selecting content for platters. Eating in restaurants allows great individual choice; however, there are still norm expectations for choice. Gravy meals tend to be selected by day of week or by a given attendance list (if guests are present). The ideal frequency of gravy within the weekly cycle exists as a range and thus individual preferences do affect whether gravy will be eaten once, twice, or three times. The principle of alternation requires that platters or whole roasts be alternated with one-pot and gravy meals. However, the content of these meals is extremely variable. Expedient formats tend to be triggered by activity patterns. They occur at the end of the work week or when unusual activities require them.

One other weekly food rule is not a format rule at all. This is the Friday night abstinence rule. It is a content rather than a format rule since the rule can be applied to gravy, one-pot, platter, or quicky formats. However, we will see that the rule tends to be associated with specific formats in different households.

SUNDAY FORMATS

Sunday dinners ideally hold a special place as the most elaborate meal in the weekly cycle and as a model meal type for celebrating other special occasions. Ordinarily, a household will not eat Sunday dinner alone, but will either have extended family present or attend the meal at another household linked by kinship, fictive kinship, or intimate friendship. Thus, the attendance list is enlarged. In addition, the menu is more elaborate than for an ordinary gravy meal. While extra courses are no longer as widely served on Sunday, often baked macaroni dishes (lasagna, stuffed shells, and ravioli), which are highly ranked gravy dishes, are served. As we mentioned, the multi-course gravy menu which includes an antipasto and a whole meat course today is usually reserved for celebrations of a holiday or life-cycle event. We soon noted that many lesser feasts either occur on Sundays because of the nature of the calendar (Easter, Mother's Day, Father's Day) or are assigned to Sundays because it is easiest then to gather large groups. Birthdays and anniversaries are often celebrated on their nearest Sunday rather than their date. Christenings, graduations, and shower parties are scheduled for Sunday. At least once a month, a Sunday dinner will be elaborate because of its dual celebratory nature. It is thus possible to describe two types of Sunday dinner—"ordinary" and "special occasion." Table 3 lists those attending both kinds of dinners.

The use of frozen home-made gravy also means that the Sunday dinner is not at all time-consuming and it is possible to perpetuate this cultural practice even in households with busy schedules and with cooks who do not want to be chained to the stove.

In our four families, the shared ideal pattern for Sundays was strongly internalized. However, in no family did this type of meal appear every Sunday and in some families it rarely occurred. Households uniformly recognized that Sunday meals should be set off from ordinary meals, and they uniformly recognized the appropriateness of the extended attendance list. However, one way that food change was occurring was in the addition of alternatives to the gravy meal, which were viewed as normatively appropriate: the American Sunday dinner of roast meat and the celebratory eating-out format.

In the Cooper family, the meal served on three Sundays was the meal most likely to be chosen as a Sunday alternative—the American festive meal of roast meat, potatoes, and vegetable. Mrs. Cooper's network consists of Italian women who serve gravy on Sunday. However, although she has several complex, traditional dishes in her repertory of specialties, she views herself as a better American than Italian cook. The fact that she was married to a non-Italian probably contributed to her development of the non-Italian Sunday format. Also, Mrs. Cooper's family often disperses on Sunday, with each person attending a different household's meal (for example, Mrs. Cooper

TABLE 3

	ORDINARY		SPECIAL OCCASION	
Family	Number Attending	Relationship	Number Attending	Relationship

Sunday Dinner: Attendance List

Family	Number Attending	Relationship	Number Attending	Relationship
Fiore	5	Mother and daughter (subnuclear family) Married daughter and child (Ethnographer)	30	Mother and two daughters (nuclear family) Oldest daughter's fiancé and his father, married daughter and child, youngest daughter's boyfriend, wife's siblings and their spouses and children (Ethnographers)
Cooper	9	Mother and two children (nuclear family) Eldest son, spouse, and child; middle son's girlfriend and her mother (Ethnographer)	14	Mother and two children (nuclear family) Eldest son, spouse and child, middle son's girlfriend and her mother, daughter's boyfriend, wife's friend (Ethnographers)
Felice	7	Mother and father, three children, exchange student (nuclear family) (Ethnographer)	11	Mother, father, three children, exchange student (nuclear family) Wife's parents, husband's parents (Ethnographer)
Weaver	6 (8 for dessert course)	Mother and father, son (nuclear family) Wife's brother and spouse (Ethnographer), (wife's parents for coffee and dessert)	12	Mother and father, son (nuclear family) Wife's parents, wife's siblings, their spouses and child, wife's mother's friends (Ethnographer)

frequently goes to a friend's mother; her son goes to his girlfriend's home). Thus, there is less pressure to habitually think of Sunday as a day to be planned around the preparation of a gravy meal, as it is in most other households. This is a reflection of family life-cycle stage since adult children have autonomous activities and married sons often visit their wife's mother. In addition, Mrs. Cooper has a health condition which restricts her consumption of spicy foods; and her children do not have the strong preference for gravy found in other households. Moreover, her eldest son (and his family) who comes whenever Mrs. Cooper is home on Sunday has a marked preference for eye roast, and the meal is prepared in deference to his preferences as a surrogate senior male. At the end of the month, Mrs. Cooper prepared for us a most elaborate Sunday dinner—more elaborate than any we had elsewhere. It consisted of "pastacinu," an elaborate baked macaroni dish, braciole, meatballs, and sausage, the usual accompaniments, and three desserts. She did this to make up for what she perceived as the lack of real Italian meals in the month we had observed. Thus, she certainly understood the ideal and felt pressure to explain her nonobservance.

The Weaver family did not consume *any* typical Sunday dinners, except for one Sunday at her mother's home which coincided with Father's Day. The Father's Day dinner at Mrs. Weaver's mother's home was an elaborate gravy meal with an extended attendance list (the extended family).

Mrs. Weaver's mother had grown up with and remained close to Mrs. Fiore and her other generational peers. However, she prides herself on not being bound by the rules of the food system. She speaks frequently of her independence from such norms. Nonetheless, Father's Day was treated as an elaborate Sunday dinner. Other factors which affected choice in the Weavers' dinners were metaphysical. Mrs. Weaver is pregnant and her numerous cravings for a variety of foods was a significant contributing factor. This can be looked at as a group-shared metaphysical belief since the cravings of pregnant women are considered very important in Italian folklore. A major factor here was the stage in the family cycle and the occupational constraints of the father. The Weavers have a two-year-old son who exerts no direct pressure on menu selection, and the husband was often away on business during the month we were there. These circumstances decrease the adherence to rules. However, a child in the house does affect food choice indirectly since certain food consistencies and preferred foods are often chosen because a meal every-one can share is easiest. One Sunday was celebrated with beef stroga-noff. This was a clear violation. Non-Italian one-pot dishes occur very rarely in this community; Mr. Weaver is non-Italian and views the roast meat alternative as correct. He was critical of beef stroganoff for Sunday dinner. Mrs. Weaver, at this point, tends to be spontane-ous in her meal planning and to respond to her cravings. She is some-what like her idiosyncratic mother in this respect. While Mrs. Wea-ver loves gravy, she tends to serve it randomly and not when expected.

Mrs. Fiore has the reputation of being an outstanding Italian cook. In her household, the ideal Sunday pattern was obviously given high priority, but it was also frequently replaced as the result of factors generated by social activities. Mrs. Fiore has the largest number and busiest set of social ties. Six of the eleven Sunday dinners were gravy formats. Four were Sunday dinner formats, and two were other spe-cial feast formats. Of the four Sunday meal types, two were birthdays, one was a gravy meal consumed as guests in another home, and one was Easter dinner.

One feast meal was a buffet-style format featuring gravy which oc-curred on a double occasion: Palm Sunday and two kinsmen's birth-days. This format was selected because of the size of the attendance list. The final special occasion format was a buffet dinner to celebrate the daughter's wedding shower. For this meal, the food was prepared in the Fiore household ahead of time and served in a large meeting hall. On still another Sunday, one household member attended an-other buffet format meal in honor of a christening, again demonstrat-ing the selection of Sunday for feasts and the tendency for young adults to disperse.

Of the nongravy formats consumed on Sunday, one was a whole meat roast eaten as guests in Mrs. Cooper's home. Two were eat-ing-out events, one a celebratory dinner for Mother's Day and one a semi-expedient dinner out after a hospital visit. While this was not entirely a recreational event, an expensive celebratory format (sea food) was selected because it was Sunday. Another weekend involved travel out of town on Sunday so the expedient Saturday meal (no-cooking meal) was served on Sunday. One meal was scheduled to be eaten out but bad weather led to a last-minute shift to a meal at home. One of the daughters prepared chicken. This was one of the only meals eaten in the Fiore household which was almost solely determined by what was available. There is a strong normative and sensory preference for gravy in this family, and gravy is always selected when Mrs. Fiore prepares Sunday dinner at home. However, since Mrs. Fiore is a central figure in an active network, she is frequently visiting and eating away from home. In this family, celebratory eating out is the second most frequent type of Sunday dinner event.

In the Felice household, gravy was served every Sunday. The attendance list was also frequently enlarged to include extended family from the ascending generation. It was obviously the husband's choices which dominated meal decisions here. In fact, two of the gravy meals were made by his mother. One was a special meal of homemade pasta for St. Joseph's Day, and the other was prepared by the wife's mother and featured eggplant lasagna. The husband's desire for appropriate Sunday gravy was much stronger than either the wife's metaphysical beliefs about nutrition and health, which caused her concern about the use of macaroni (high carbohydrate diet), or the strong dislike of gravy on the part of the son.

FRIDAY FORMATS

Friday as a day of abstinence is interpreted differently in each household. Here, again, we can underscore the importance of social mediation. As a more public and shared event, Sunday dinners are talked about, observed, and evaluated frequently. However, observation of Friday fasting is a private event. The traditional abstinence rule is interpreted by some as a rule for the presence of fish or shellfish, and by others as a rule for the absence of meat. This rule, originally religious in nature, seems to be used today to mark the separation of the week from the weekend.

The abstinence rule for Friday is a *content* rule, not a format rule. Insofar as a format is specified, Friday tends toward the expedient formats. Meals are often "quickies" because of the position of Friday at the culmination of the work week and commencement of a minor period of leisure. Often fish is present as a symbol of Friday, but it is served among other dishes which may include meat. At other times, meatlessness is observed without using fish or shellfish at all as with pasta/legume dishes or omelets. Omelets and other meatless sandwiches can be both quick and meatless. Thus, the format could be expedient (no-cooking), platter, gravy, or one-pot.

Two of the Weavers' four Fridays were meatless, but with no indication that this was more than a coincidence. One meal was at a restaurant. Fish and shellfish were eaten, but they are favorites when eating out. One meal was expedient (soup and grilled cheese), which her husband criticized as appropriate for lunch, not dinner. At first he said it was not a "hot" meal and when the comment was made that the food was hot he said that it was not "meat" the way a dinner "should be." Here he was correctly aware of the difference between the dinner format platters and gravies and expedient sandwich meals which are analogous to lunches. The third Friday was indeed a meat dinner with her husband present, and the fourth was a hamburger cookout produced largely by some cousins who came to visit to keep Mrs. Weaver company when her husband was away. (Here, the unusual attendance list triggered the format rather than the day of the week.)

The Coopers are also ambivalent about Fridays. However, serious attention is sometimes paid to Friday as a day with special rules. Out of five Fridays, one meal was totally fleshless: no meat or fish. One meal contained both fish and other meatless dishes. The third meal at home contained meat, and the remaining two were meat meals outside home.

As with Sundays, Mrs. Cooper either prepares model meals (either the primary gravy type or secondary whole roast type) or she does not symbolize the occasion at all. The same is true for Fridays, when her meatless meals are models and her other meals do not symbolize Friday at all.

The Felices state explicitly their desire to mark Fridays with a meatless meal. However, if someone voices a strong desire for gravy or steak, both family favorites, and they have not been served recently, the convention will be abandoned. Here, the definition of the convention involves the presence of fish more than the absence of meat. Out of five Fridays, three were fish nights, one of which included meat. Two were meat meals, both family favorites. In both cases, strong statements about cravings and preferences overruled the convention. The husband's preferences are ranked first and the wife will sometimes act out one of her cravings. Children's preferences are often accommodated with supplementary dishes rather than through the basic meal structure. The Felices were the most consistent in their Sunday gravy meals. They were among the most consistent in terms of the symbolic observance of Friday abstinence.

The Fiores generally follow the convention. However, activity schedules and personnel shifts often interfere and the rule is loosened. Out of ten Fridays, seven were fish meals. One of these was a take-out fish meal, one was a restaurant fish meal, and one included meat, too. Of the other three meals when fish was not eaten, one was eaten out and two were quicky meals because the key kitchen person was alone and had no guests. One quicky meal was leftover chicken salad and the other a sandwich which happened to be meat.

Of the total number of Friday meals observed (23) in all four families, 61 percent were marked by the presence of fish or the absence of meat; 81 percent of the total Sunday dinners (22) were marked by one of the three appropriate formats. Three-quarters of the marked Sundays entailed gravy formats.

Table 4 summarizes the meal formats chosen for each day of the week on a monthly basis.

Mrs. Fiore is consistent in not having platters on Monday, having platters on Tuesday, having a secondary gravy night on Wednesdays or Thursdays and having a quicky meal on Saturday. Mrs. Cooper recognizes Monday with a particular platter, observes a secondary gravy meal (non day-specific) and observes quicky meals on Saturday. Mrs. Felice observes a secondary gravy night and consistently has platters on Tuesdays and Saturdays. The Weavers are least consistent.

EFFECTS OF WORK AND LEISURE SCHEDULES ON FORMAT

Factors which affected the scheduling of activities were very important in menu decisions. Activities include both anticipated regularities in scheduling such as work schedule and work location. They also include irregular and unpredictable social events and crises.

A widespread community norm emphasizes the importance of a family eating together, but individual work and leisure schedules often interfere. The daily meal times are scheduled around the predictable schedules of family members as much as possible. However, in every family individuals occasionally worked late or had part-time after-school jobs through dinner time. The usual response to such scheduling is for the key kitchen person to prepare the meal early for a child who leaves before dinner to work or to save a portion of the dinner for a latecomer. One-pot formats are better for this than platters. When unusual work or leisure activities affected the whole household the appropriate alternatives were the expedient meal out, the no-cooking sandwich meal, or, in some cases, leftovers.

TABLE 4

Meal Formats Chosen Over One Month

Family	Sunday	Monday	Tuesday	Wednesday	Thursday	Friday	Saturday
Fiore	1 Platter 1 Whole meat 4 Gravy	2 Whole meat 1 One-pot	4 Platter 1 One-pot	2 Gravy 2 Platter	3 One-pot 1 Gravy	4 Platter 1 Sandwich	2 Sandwich
Cooper	3 Whole meat 1 Gravy	3 Platter 1 Gravy 1 Sandwich	3 Platter 2 Gravy	4 Platter 2 Sandwich	2 Gravy 1 One-pot 1 Sandwich	1 One-pot 1 Platter 1 Sandwich	3 Sandwich 2 Platter
Felice	4 Gravy	2 Gravy 1 Whole meat 1 Platter	3 Platter	3 Platter 2 Gravy	3 Platter 1 Whole meat	3 Platter 2 Gravy	4 Platter 1 Gravy
Weaver	1 One-pot 1 Whole meat 1 Platter	3 Platter 1 Gravy	2 Platter 2 Sandwich	3 Platter 1 Sandwich	1 Platter 1 Gravy 1 Sandwich	1 Platter 2 Sandwich	2 Sandwich 1 One-pot 1 Platter

Note: Eating out in restaurants or in other homes not included.

Quicky meals, traditional for Saturday night, can also occur on Fridays. Eating out, both expedient and celebratory, is most like to occur on Friday, Saturday, or Sunday. All of these are format decisions affected by the activity cycle—the increasing desire to be free of routine and oriented to leisure at the end of the week. Gravy can occur any other night if activities prevent it from being served on a Sunday or Thursday, the preferred days.

Another set of factors relates to whether women work and whether they like to cook. Interestingly, Mrs. Fiore, who worked full time, liked to cook the most. She also had an outstanding community reputation. She really enjoyed the activity, and work did not interfere with her ability to cook elaborate meals frequently. This was largely because the location of her job made it possible to come home at midday and start dinner, and to get home early at the end of the day. Mrs. Cooper was concerned about cooking too. She worked part time but regularly. She did not feel that she excelled in Italian cooking, but she had several Italian specialities (for example, pasta ceci which is macaroni and chick peas) and often had friends come to sample them. She regularly fed a childhood friend whose work schedule was difficult and made special menus for these occasions. She also enjoyed baking and was very proud of her cake repertory.

Mrs. Felice seemed ambivalent about cooking. She often stated that she didn't like being tied to the kitchen and tried labor-saving ways to decrease her time there. Since in contrast to Mrs. Cooper and Mrs. Fiore she worked only irregularly (and part time), it seemed as if in this community working outside the home did not interfere with one's role as a cook, but even encouraged it.

However, when we look at the data, we find that Mrs. Felice in fact cooks the most! Mrs. Fiore's social schedule (not her work) necessitates her frequently eating in restaurants or preparing expedient meals. Mrs. Felice actually prepared most of the meals eaten by her family during the month of observation. This included hot breakfasts, lunches, and dinners. Her concern about being tied to the kitchen results from that very fact! Mr. Felice does not allow expedient meals and so there is little respite from preparing a whole meal format every evening and gravy every Sunday. This is also the family cycle stage which encourages the most domestic eating.

Mrs. Weaver is the most casual cook with a very casual and spontaneous attitude toward meal planning. This was probably exacerbated by the fact that her husband was away for two weeks and her child, at 2, exerts no pressure. She was pregnant and not feeling well. However, she did not feel that her activities were very different from what they had been in the past.

When we look at the degree to which gravy and platter formats are alternated throughout the week, we also find that situational variables prevent consistency. For example, we observed nine weeks at the Fiore home. Four of these weeks contained perfect cycles of alternating formats. Three contained one repetition and two contained two repetitions. Many instances of repeated formats involve the use of leftovers and can be traced to the irregular and unpredictable activities affecting Mrs. Fiore's time or those present at the meal. For example, heavy shopping and baking activities related to a wedding led to the use of leftovers as a main meal. (Leftovers are usually served to augment a new planned meal format or to feed someone who does not like the menu being served.) When her daughters do not eat at home, Mrs. Fiore eats leftovers, also.

Out of six weeks of observation, Mrs. Cooper followed the principle of alternation during three. She repeated a format once during each of two weeks. She significantly "broke the rules" during one week by serving three sequential platters followed by two sequential gravy meals. Again, rule violation occurred each time because of unusual activities, the absence of household members or the presence of guests.

Both Mrs. Felice and Mrs. Weaver, who are not closely tied to the core women's group, observe the principles of alternation less stringently.

Patterning is still evident within the week in all four families except when the Weavers operate as an independent nuclear family household. Marking Sundays and Fridays, observing second or third gravy nights, and alternating formats are keys to the pattern.

WEEKLY MEALS: VARIABLES IN CONTENT NEGOTIATION

Tables 5–8 illustrate the outcomes of household differences in *content* negotiation within the shared meal formats. Just as each family follows a distinctive weekly cycle of choices from the shared meal formats, selection of ingredients and dishes within these formats also differ.

While formats are influenced by community norms, activities, and attendance, the most important factor in content selection for weekly meals are *individual preferences* in terms of taste, health beliefs, and cost.

TABLE 5

Meals	Meat	Starch	Vegetable/Salad	Accompaniments
Platter	Fried chicken	Rice	Green beans, applesauce, tossed salad	
	Meatloaf	Potatoes	Corn, applesauce, tossed salad	
	London broil	Potatoes	Mushrooms, tossed salad	
	Breaded chicken		Corn, applesauce, tossed salad, beets, eggplant	
	Monkfish		Cole slaw, applesauce	
	Liver	Sweet potatoes	Green bean salad	
	Fried smelts		Cole slaw	
	Whiting			
Whole Meat	Roast pork	Potatoes, rolls	Spinach, corn, cole slaw, applesauce	
One-pot and gravy	Lasagna, gravy, meatballs			Italian rolls, tossed salad
	Beef stew			Italian rolls, bean salad
	Minestra			Italian bread, tossed salad
	Lasagna			Tossed salad
	Gravy, meatballs			Italian rolls, tossed salad
	Gravy, ravioli			Rye bread, tossed salad
	Minestra, ravioli			Italian bread
	Fried pork chops, potatoes, and eggs			Tossed salad
	Kielbasa with sauerkraut and pork			Biscuits
	Spaghetti with clam sauce			Tossed salad
Sandwich	Steak sandwich with cheese and mushrooms			Tossed salad
	Spiced beef			Cole slaw

TABLE 6

Meal Content Chosen Over One Month: Coopers				
Meals	*Meat*	*Starch*	*Vegetable/Salad*	*Accompaniments*
Platter	Filet mignon	Potatoes	Mushrooms, peas, spinach, applesauce	
	Veal cutlets	Potatoes	Peas, greenbeans, corn	
	Stuffed chicken breasts	Potatoes, rolls	Peas, greenbeans, corn	
	Fried chicken	Potatoes	Peas, green beans, corn, spinach	
Whole meat	Roast beef	Potatoes, sweet potatoes, rolls	Peas, green beans, corn, broccoli, applesauce, tossed salad	
	Ham	Potatoes, sweet potatoes	Greenbeans, asparagus, cole slaw	
One-pot and gravy	Pastacinu, gravy, braciole, meatballs			Italian bread, tossed salad
	Bean soup, stuffed peppers with gravy			Italian bread, tossed salad
	Gravy, meatballs			Rolls, tossed salad
	Macaroni and ceci			Tossed salad
	Gnocchi, gravy, meatballs			Rolls, tossed salad
	Beef stew			Bread, tossed salad
	Baked macaroni			Sweet potatoes, stewed tomatoes, tossed salad
Sandwich	Cheese steak			Tossed salad, macaroni salad, olives, potato chips
	Grilled cheese			
	Creamed chipped beef on toast			Peas, tossed salad

TABLE 7

Meal Content Chosen Over One Month: Felices

Meals	Meat	Starch	Vegetable/Salad	Accompaniments
Platter	Steak	Potatoes	Green beans, corn, broccoli, tossed salad	
	Baked chicken	Potatoes	Carrots, green beans, broccoli, tossed salad	
	Meatloaf	Potatoes	Green beans, corn, tossed salad	
	Fried chicken	Potatoes	Green beans, broccoli, corn, tossed salad	
	Hamburgers	Rolls	Green beans, corn, tossed salad	
	Hot dogs	Macaroni and cheese, rolls	Sauerkraut	
	Monkfish, turbot, whiting	Spaghetti, rolls	Green beans, cauliflower, tossed salad	
	Fish sticks, fish cakes	Macaroni and cheese	Artichokes, corn, tossed salad	
	Pepper steak, sweet and sour pork	Rice	Corn, squash	
Whole meat	Leg of lamb	Potatoes	Carrots, peas, corn, tossed salad	
	Roast beef	Potatoes, rolls	Corn, tossed salad	
One-pot and gravy	Soup, gravy, meatballs, sausage			Italian bread, tossed salad
	Soup, lasagna, gravy			Italian bread, tossed salad
	Soup, macaroni, and ceci gravy, meatballs, sausage			Italian bread, cole slaw
	Raviolis, gravy, breaded chicken			Italian bread, tossed salad
	Gravy, sausage, meatballs, chicken			Italian bread, tossed salad
	Lasagna rollups			Italian bread, carrots, green bean salad

TABLE 8

Meals	Meat	Starch	Vegetable/Salad	Accompaniments
		Meal Content Chosen Over One Month: Weavers		
Platter	Fried chicken	Macaroni and cheese	Peas, green beans, tossed salad	
	Breaded chicken	Potatoes	Peas, mushrooms, green beans, cucumbers	
	Meatloaf	Rice	Beets, macaroni salad	
	Pork chops		Italian vegetables, baked beans	
	Hamburgers, hot dogs	Potatoes, rolls	Mushrooms, tomatoes, cucumbers, macaroni, salad	
	Breaded fish	Potatoes	Peas	
One-pot and gravy	Beef stroganoff			Rolls, tossed salad
	Rigatoni with tomato sauce			Bread, tossed salad
	Gravy, meatballs, sausage, pork chops, stuffed shells			Italian bread, tossed salad
	Macaroni and cheese			Spinach
	Egg pastina			
Sandwich	Grilled cheese			
	Bacon, lettuce and tomato			Potatoes, peas, corn
	Soup, grilled cheese			Potato chips
	Peppers and eggs			English muffins
	Fried eggs			English muffins
	Soup, scrambled eggs			English muffins

In this discussion, both strong likes and strong dislikes are considered. We must also make a distinction between basic and supplementary dishes. The way of handling the strong likes and dislikes of non-influential household members is to make them supplementary dishes or serve them leftovers which are not conceptualized as part of the menu. This is a distinctly modern American pattern. However, it is important to note that most of the time and money are invested in the main menu rather than the supplementary dishes which might often feed a larger number. In other words, the distinction between main menu and supplementary foods is not arbitrary. However, the use of leftovers and supplements affect the integrity of the meal format. Many evening meals appear to the observer to be a number of bits and pieces of leftover and supplementary dishes in spite of the planned central format.

1. *Husbands' preferences.* His preferences are most often the primary filters for decisions about basic menu structure. Their relative strength varies across households. For example, Mrs. Felice almost always accedes to her husband's desires, while Mrs. Weaver verbally describes her freedom from her husband's control (but still acts to please him). Mr. Weaver's preferences are important in her choices although she often will disagree with his stated preferences. Compared with the three other women we studied and with Mrs. Weaver's mother's household, Mr. Weaver's preference is given less priority in menu negotiation. Mrs. Fiore and Mrs. Cooper often recalled the strong influence of their former husbands in meal planning.

A food strongly disliked by the husband will usually not become part of a basic meal structure, while favorite foods of the husband are often part of the menu even though other household members will not eat them. For example, only Mr. Felice liked oysters, but they were often part of a platter meal. In the Cooper household, the married elder son's preferences dominate menu planning when he is present. In the Fiore household, prospective sons-in-law exert similar influence.

2. *Others' preferences.* In spite of the senior male's strong influence, there is also an effort made to see that all other household members get their preferred foods sometime during the week. Thus, a child's strong preference—if not disliked by the senior male—can become part of the basic meal structure (menu) and the fact that a child complains of being ignored can strongly influence decisions about meals—even Friday and Sunday meals. Finally, the key

kitchen person herself occasionally seizes the upper hand and makes content decisions with regard to her own likes, cravings, mood, or desire for cooking experimentation. The degree to which she does this can probably be related to the number of influential members of the household (senior males and adult children). A more common pattern is for the key kitchen person to make her own preferred foods frequently and serve them over and over as supplementary leftovers until they are finished.

We have seen that sex is important in ranking the priority of preferences of the adult household members. Sex is not that significant among younger age groups. In fact, young children's preferences are unimportant. As a child grows older, his or her preferences become more influential. Children show preferences for sweets and other treats, but these are given only at strategic times in order to control and manipulate children's behavior.

An example of the importance of age over sex in children occurs in the Felice family where the son (youngest) is a fussy eater. He dislikes gravy, yet gravy is most frequently served in this household. His likes and dislikes are not influential in meal planning when they conflict with those of the senior male. However, the eldest daughter—almost an adult—and the foreign-exchange student (guest) do influence menu decisions.

3. *Household compatibility.* Each household we studied could be said to have a different compatibility factor. Aside from the senior male's dominance, the compatibility of the likes and dislikes of children was significant. If children liked roughly the same foods, their preferences were easier to accommodate than if they were very disparate. Not every family had a "fussy" eater, and the process by which such a role is developed (physiological and social etiology) is an interesting phenomenon in itself.

Guests supercede all household members in influencing food items. Guests in this sense do not include former children of the household who are now grown and married since they are likely to be present at the table several times a week and continue in their family roles. Often a key kitchen person prepares a specialty she is known for during the week. She will then invite members of her family or circle of friends. Since guests are always people whose taste preferences are well known, they play a dominant role in particular menu selections. Guests for weekly (Sunday or weekday) meals are rarely nonintimate kin or friends. They are most often parents, siblings, or childhood friends of the key kitchen person or friends and potential spouses of the children of the household.

4. *Cash resources.* In this community, we are dealing with a population that has discretionary income. Thus, the relationship between cash resources and food is not clear or direct. In general, the older generation tended to be least cost-conscious in menu planning. They shopped for "good" food rather than cheap food. In many ways, the Fiore household had the greatest constraints on its income and yet good food was a major priority. For Mrs. Cooper also, concern with cost was not a major factor in food acquisition.

However, for Mrs. Weaver and Mrs. Felice, cost consciousness was very important. Mrs. Weaver spends a great deal of her time shopping. Her shopping activities are highly oriented toward bargain hunting. She travels to a discount packaged goods store and selects most foods by price rather than brand. She is very concerned about quality and experiments with generic brands and unknown brands before she buys large quantities. She compares meat for fat content and taste as well as price. Many of her menu decisions are set by the items she has bought at significant cost savings.

Mrs. Felice's cost concerns are reflected, for example, in the use of sausage, which she sees as "going further" than other meat. She also recycles leftovers at every meal, even Sunday. This is both a cost- and a labor-saving device. Cost considerations seem to vary by generation, with the older women less concerned than the younger. Income was not significant.

We found that there was little relationship between shopping activities and basic meal planning in all of the households except the Weavers'. Only Mrs. Weaver tended to plan her meals primarily according to what was "on special" when she shopped. However, her cravings often led her out to do menu-specific shopping. Shopping activities were either of the long-term type or they were menu specific (picking up an item for a particular meal). All the women maintained large inventories of frequently used items—dried, canned, and frozen—for gravy meals, quick meals, and favorite platter elements.

5. *Sensory preferences.* Taste preferences are more determined by household tradition and generation cohort than by community consensus. There is a significant generational difference in that members

of the older generation still like many traditional Italian one-pots which their offspring will not eat. There is a repugnance among the offspring in all the households (adult children and school-age children) for foods that suggest their natural forms. Pigs' knuckles, organ meats, and smelts are popular only with the older generation. The younger generation requires that foods be disguised and processed, heads removed, and so forth. However, the younger generation also avoids mixtures like one-pots in which the contents may be too small or too mixed together and thus unrecognizable. Gravy is the only mixture which has retained its preferred status in the younger generation.

Taste preferences vary greatly from household to household. Salt and strong spices, particularly garlic, are used differently in different households. Each household has a very distinct gravy taste and such differences are well recognized. The outsiders' perception of a single "Italian" taste in gravy does not exist.

Visual attributes of food are also very important. In most households, there are enough strong likes and dislikes for particular ingredients so as to significantly modify the composition of gravies, salads, and other universally present dishes. Family members are very verbal about aesthetic qualities: color, texture, greasiness, and spiciness.

6. *Metaphysical beliefs.* There are both community-shared metaphysical beliefs about nonaesthetic properties of food and household and individual differences. Examples of community-shared notions are (1) beliefs in the importance of food in determining acidity in blood and the relationship between blood acidity and health and (2) beliefs about garlic which involve its ability to purge or "clean out" the system, lower high blood pressure, and improve complexion. While differences in aesthetic preferences among individuals and households is largely a result of idiosyncratic experiential variables, health beliefs are the result of the collision of traditional health beliefs with other systems of belief. In other words, external systems enter the household as a result of the outside socialization of members and affect the household beliefs and practices. In the Felice household, Mrs. Felice's training as a health professional is the significant competing system and greatly affects menu decision-making.

The metaphysical views about food differ for the two spouses in this family. The husband feels that good eating preserves good health and says he would rather put his money "on the table" than give it to the doctor. The wife feels that they eat too much and are over-weight and would like to streamline the diet. In actual deci-sion-making, the husband's wishes are paramount.

In the Cooper household, two adult children are concerned about avoiding additivies and not polluting or contaminating their bodies. This strong set of beliefs internalized outside the household now greatly influences the mother (key kitchen person) and her decisions.

ILLUSTRATION: HOUSEHOLD VARIATIONS IN GRAVY

Household variation in the community-wide pattern is exhibited in the various forms of gravy. Often, a family tradition is passed from mother to daughter; in some cases, the recipe may be learned from a mother-in-law. This basic procedure is then modified to please the tastes of the individual household members.

While the basic ingredients and procedure for making gravy are the same, each female head of household has perfected a variation to suit her household.

Mrs. Fiore makes a relatively "spicy" gravy. Though hot Italian sausage may be used in the preparation, only small amounts are ac-ceptable. She browns a combination of pork (country-style pork ribs), mild sweet Italian sausage, and infrequently some beef (usually a cheaper cut suitable for stewing) in oil. She then adds basil (home-grown), Italian parsley, garlic, salt, and pepper, which are browned along with the meat. (Mrs. Fiore alleges that the secret to a good gravy is browning the spices.) After this, she adds tomato sauce and paste and water (this varies according to the quantity she is making). Half an onion is added for sweetness. The mixture is simmered for at least four hours, usually an entire day. Meatballs or bracciole are added a bit later if they are made.

Mrs. Cooper learned how to make gravy from her mother. She uses the same wooden spoon her mother used, for she feels that the use of the spoon helps to recreate her mother's recipe. Mrs. Cooper's gravy is not spicy. Because of her ulcer she refrains from using too many spices, and she never adds hot sausage. Rather than use fresh garlic, she uses garlic powder, which she claims disturbs her system less. Frequently, she adds tomato paste to her gravy if she feels it is not thick enough.

In both the Cooper and Fiore households the children have a dis-dain for organ meats and parts of pork such as pigs' feet and knuckles.

It is claimed that these now unacceptable parts of the pig make the best tasting gravy; if these parts are used, they are removed from the gravy and never shown to the children, who would reject them.

Mrs. Felice learned to cook after her marriage. Her own mother was never fond of cooking and kept it to a minimum. Therefore, many of Mrs. Felice's skills were learned either from her mother-in-law or through her own experimentation. Interestingly, although Mrs. Felice, Sr., prepared her gravy with onions and garlic while raising her family, her son developed a dislike for these ingredients early in childhood. Since his marriage he insists that neither of these items be used in the preparation of food. On most occasions Mrs. Felice modifies her method to accommodate her husband's preference. (There have been times when she has attempted to disguise her use of these ingredients, either by rendering them to a pulp or removing them before serving). Mr. Felice also enjoys hot and sweet sausage, so both of these meats are usually cooked for his benefit.

Mrs. Weaver has adopted an American way of cooking gravy, which she calls sauce. Though she learned cooking from her mother, who prepares a variety of the gravy described above, Mrs. Weaver has virtually abandoned this method of preparation. Her gravy consists of ground beef, browned, to which she adds tomato sauce and spices. She also—as we saw above—has abandoned the rules for when gravy is appropriate. She is fond of gravy; it is probably one of her favorite meals; however, her husband considers "meat and potatoes" an authentic dinner.

FORMAT NEGOTIATIONS FOR FEASTS

Selecting format and content for a feast involves different factors than those discussed for everyday meals. The evaluation of the occasion—the size and nature of the participating group—influences format choice. Are they close kin, close friends, members of the Italian-American community, or outsiders? Evaluations of the occasion lead to analogies with other occasions for which formats are specified. The size of the group limits choices in terms of logistics. The nature of participants affects the way that ethnic formats and ethnic foods are used to communicate meaning.

In the following illustration, two families observing their daughters' graduations from high school selected both different formats and different attendance lists because each defined the event differently. This is an example of the latitude allowed for middle-level feasts.

In both the Cooper and Felice households, a daughter graduated during the research. The Coopers invited about forty people and selected a "simple party" format. The attendance list included extended kin and long-term friends from the locality. (In the Cooper household, the kinship network and friendship network are largely coterminous.) For this occasion, invitations were issued by word of mouth.

In the Felice household, 130 people were invited by written invitation. The list was dominated by kin, particularly matrilateral kin, but there were also several members of the extended network of the friends and acquaintances. Many of the kin were from outside the community. The format of the occasion was a buffet, for which preparation began long before the event. The menus for both formats can be seen in table 9.

The Coopers accorded this event lower status than did the Felices; they also responded with a more American format than did the Felices. This response is consistent with other behavior. For example, the Cooper household is biased toward the American format for Sunday dinner, while the Felice household always selects gravy. The ascription of different status to the event relates to the evaluation of the event. The Felices place greater emphasis on educational achievement than the Coopers. Mrs. Felice recently went back to school and received a degree. She celebrated her own graduation in much the same manner as her daughter's celebration. Her daughter also performed well in school and was awarded a prize at graduation. While Mrs. Cooper's eldest son and his wife are college graduates, college is not thought of as an inherently desirable and necessary part of the life cycle in this household, while Mrs. Felice views it as desirable for her children. In addition, Mrs. Cooper, who did not graduate from high school, feels some ambivalence about her daughter's educational achievement.

For the Felices, the occasion triggered an attendance list which, in turn, led to the selection of the buffet format. Earlier, a confirmation was celebrated for the two younger Felices. This occasion was equal in rank to the graduation, but the attendance list had been smaller, limited to grandparents and to close extended kin. The con-

TABLE 9

Two Graduation Formats

Family	Format	Menu	Invited Number	Attendance List Relationship
Cooper	Simple party	Beer, wine, mixed drinks, coffee Raw vegetables with several dips Cheese and crackers Pistachio cake, German chocolate cake, white cake with cream filling, cherry cheese cake	40 (word of mouth invitation	Extended family, intimate network, and graduate's friends
Felice	Buffet	Potato chips, pretzels, mints, peanuts Stuffed shells Meatballs in gravy Hot roast beef in brown gravy Rolls Potato salad, cole slaw, macaroni salad, olive salad Green and black olives, hot peppers American and swiss cheese, boiled ham, pepperoni, salami Pumpernickel bread Beer, wine, soda Tray of cookies Italian cream cakes Jello molds Coffee, tea	130 (written invitation)	Extended family, intimate network, and graduate's friends and school network

firmation was celebrated with a buffet-style dinner. The larger attendance list for the graduation called for a buffet format as the only
logistically feasible format.

The two graduation celebrations were not greatly different in cost
because of the alcohol consumption at the "simple party." However,
they varied most in the degree of advance planning and preparation
time as well as the use of gravy as opposed to American foods.

This comparison says nothing about differences in affective ethnic
identification between the households nor the degree to which they
are socially approved participants in the ethnic community. It
merely demonstrates the complex factors which affect the definition
of middle-level feasts, choices of formats, and choices of content.

The highest level life-cycle feast is the wedding. Traditionally,
weddings were elaborated versions of Sunday dinner or buffet-style
meals, with kinsmen bringing dishes. In some Italian-American communities such as South Philadelphia, the growth of delicatessen caterers after World War II led to the use of the buffet for larger weddings with extended attendance lists. In Maryton, this was not the
case, and homemade buffet-style meals continued until recently; the
use of formal caterers for sit-down dinners has increasingly replaced
the homemade wedding. The meal itself thus reflected whatever format was used.

The formal catered dinner often does not include any Italian items
on the menu. However, an important *item* in this feast occurs within
the dessert course. Not only is the wedding cake an item specific to
this event, but the tray of cookies serves a major role. Although they
are often served along with a cake at other feasts, they are mandatory
at weddings. The tray of cookies is a classic example of the use of food
in maintaining social relationships. The tray consists of a wide variety
of different types of cookies, each type baked by a different network
member (kin or friend). The mother handles brokering in the assignment of who will bake which cookie. Cookies are delivered to the
bride's house before the wedding and the trays are prepared by close
friends and relatives. Certain cookies are always present—pizzelles,
tarales, white pepper cookies, and so forth. The trays are prepared
to look as sumptuous as possible. They are decorated with lace, rib-
bons, and wrapped candies and delivered to the place of celebration.
They serve as main conversational items and indices of evaluation
for the wedding itself. The tray of cookies is a major element of feasts
in both South Philadelphia and Maryton. However, in South Phila-

delphia, the trays are now often commercially prepared and lose their exchange function.

If we compare two daughters' weddings in the Fiore family, we can see that format choices are determined by the circumstances of each wedding and messages which the family wishes to convey to the social audience. Wedding meals are not always "ethnic" in food content. When the eldest Fiore daughter married a non-Italian in a marriage not highly approved by the family, the wedding was a buffet-style event incorporating only Italian dishes. It was home-prepared and served at home; it resembled a traditional Old World celebration. On the other hand, when the second daughter married into a good Italian family, the food was catered to a seated audience at a country club. No Italian items were included except the trays of cookies baked by kin and friends. This celebration did not need to convey the message of strong ethnic traditions while the first did. (Note: A third marriage occurred after fieldwork between a Fiore daughter and a Cooper son. Again, this wedding was celebrated at a country club dinner. For this wedding, the trays of cookies were commercially purchased, as they are in South Philadelphia.)

CONTENT VARIATION WITHIN FEASTS

While community norms are very significant in selecting a feast format, household variables and individual preferences do operate in choosing content. However, feasts are relatively public events in comparison with weekly meals and more social norms and positive and negative sanctions are involved.

In selecting the content for formats, some menu structures are more content specific than others. While the party format calls for the most American selections, all other formats are mixed and include both Italian and American items. Families differ in this respect. The Felices consistently use only Italian items in their buffet-style format, while the Fiores tend to mix items.

The buffet format is more content specific and offers fewer choices than buffet-style. Sandwiches of meats in Italian gravy and roast beef in American gravy, as well as combinations of both American salads (with mayonnaise) and Italian vegetables and both Italian and American cold cuts and cheeses, are standard items.

The dessert course in both buffet and buffet-style formats is the broadest in its openness. Desserts are a domain in which one finds

Italian items much less frequently than in other segments of the event. Even the tray of cookies allows for content negotiations and not all cookies are Italian in origin, although such obvious American cookies as the tollhouse variety are excluded.

Buffet-style content offers great choice throughout the meal. One of the most important variables taken into account are the specialties of members of the extended family for these specialties become family traditions as individuals develop reputations and specialized roles for feasts. Taste variables which enter into these decisions are the preferences of both the planner (key kitchen person) and her perception of what foods are universally liked. Both network and intra-household dislikes are obviously incorporated in decisions and tend to be avoided.

Table 10 compares two different buffet-style celebrations. This format is selected for special occasions, like special birthdays, anniversaries, and confirmations when the attendance list is small (grandparents, aunts, uncles, cousins). The two occasions were different.

The Fiore menu included three chicken dishes. Chicken is still associated with ceremonious occasions and is a particular favorite in this household. The dishes were of different styles—some Italian and others not (breaded chicken, baked chicken with vegetables, and barbecued chicken). Two relatives brought chicken to the Fiore house and prepared it there (cooperative labor). Another relative brought a prepared chicken dish. All of these dishes were composed of parts, rather than a whole roast.

The specific St. Joseph dish of macaroni and sawdust was unfamiliar to most guests. It is a *sweet* dish served within the main course. Mrs. Fiore was concerned about people eating it because of its unusual sweet nature (sweet dishes are usually reserved for dessert). Other starch dishes served were macaroni and cheese (a sister's specialty) macaroni and ceci, and sweet potatoes. This non-Italian item is a specialty of a close friend, a network member who frequently is present at buffet-style occasions in the Fiore household. Mrs. Fiore has developed a strong taste preference for it and incorporates it as part of special occasion celebrations. Wine was served. Desserts were predominantly specific to this feast: a special St. Joseph's rice pudding, a holiday-specific baked good: cavazumes (St. Joseph's pants), and Dunkin Donuts.

While the Fiore buffet-style contained several platter components,

TABLE 10

| | | Two Buffet-Style Celebrations | | |
Family	Occasion	Menu	Number Invited	Attendance List
Felice	Confirmation	Stuffed shells Lasagna Baked chicken Tossed salad Rolls Wine, soda Italian cream cake Tray of cookies Jello mold Fruit salad Coffee, tea Liquers	17	Extended family including ascending generation (wife's parents, husband's parents, wife's sibling and girlfriend) plus two (intimate network) for coffee and dessert
Fiore	St. Joseph's Day	Spaghetti and sawdust* Macaroni and ceci Baked macaroni and cheese Baked sweet potatoes Tossed salad Baked chicken (two kinds) Barbequed chicken Wine, soda Cavazumes* Rice pudding* Doughnuts Coffee, Tea	13	Extended family, same generation (wife's siblings and their nuclear families)

*Holiday-specific foods: "sawdust" is a sauce made with bread crumbs, walnuts, raisins, sugar, and oil; "cavazumes" are a fried dough filled with ceci (chick peas), orange rind, honey, and oil of cinnamon.

the Felice format consisted largely of gravy components. Once again, the Felices are consistently Italian in content, even down to the dessert. At the Felice celebration, all the food was prepared at the Felices', but there was advance preparation when Mr. Felice's mother came to help prepare the large quantities of festive dishes.

While the buffet format is a standardized menu used for occasions when large segments of the ethnic community are present, the buffet-style format helps to develop solidarity for the subcommunity networks of close kin and friends. The relatively stable sets of households who celebrate life-cycle feasts develop menus which incorporate the exchange of cooked dishes as well as cooperative labor. Network members develop reputations for particular dishes, which leads to the relatively constant but unique menus found in each network.

The Complexity of Continuity and Change

Any assumption that ethnic food persistence is measured by the frequency of use of traditional food items is seriously questioned by this research. The belief that ethnic feasts remain the major residue of an ethnic pattern is also not supported.

In this community, the major locus of continuity in the food system is not the frequency of pasta or tomato sauce, but the rules for constructing and scheduling gravy meals which persist over time. Such rules do not involve the use of particular foods (tomatoes or spices), but the rules for combining them in a variety of distinct dishes, one of which (the meat-based gravy) is basic to the structure of particular weekday, Sunday, and elaborated feast meals.

Much of the continuity and change in the system is related to the manipulation of the repertory of formats. Some formats have been reduced in scale (for example, all three gravy meal structures are diminished from their former scale). New formats have been added such as the platter, the lunch, the celebratory restaurant meal and a variety of expedient forms which respond to new activity patterns. New feast forms such as the party and the commercially catered meal have been added. Some formats have been almost deleted such as the nongravy one-pot meals. The buffet-style format is traditional in origin while the buffet is an amalgamation of gravy and platter components, Italian and American in content.

Other types of changes include shifts in the occasions for which particular formats are appropriate, enlarging the range of permissible formats (as for Sunday dinner) and shifts in content rules (as for Friday dinner).

The bulk of what is shared and socially reinforced within Maryton consists of the patterned formats and the consensus regarding which occasions and which social audiences suggest their use.

The areas of great variability in the community include the degree to which day-specific format rules are observed (Sunday and Friday), the selection of formats for middle-level feasts, and the selection of content, particularly for platter meals, parties, and buffet-style formats.

Some formats, such as gravy meals and buffet feasts, are highly content specific. Other formats such as the platter, the party, or the buffet-style feast are open to broad content negotiation. It is through these open formats that many new American food items enter the system. In many ways, factors that influence format choice or content choice within open formats are most significant to understanding the frequency of food item use. Thus, household structural features related to activity patterns, stage in family cycle, and participation in social networks are more salient to individual food intake than such indicators as intensity of ethnic identification or degree of acculturation.

The degree to which one follows the rules for weekly patterning bears no direct relationship to the frequency with which traditional food items are eaten. Yet the former is a better indicator of participation in the ethnic community than the latter.

Another common assumption about ethnic persistence emphasizes the significance of religious or health ideologies in the retention of traditional patterns. While our informants could state some shared folk beliefs, these were not significant to food choices. (Note: There is some indication that Mrs. Weaver followed pregnancy beliefs, suggesting that for vulnerable states such folk beliefs still operate.)

Instead, social structure was the major cultural subsystem which accounted for whatever was historically continuous and/or shared in the community. Food persistence could be traced directly to the marking of occasions special to the family, extended family, and female peer group with special meals and food exchanges. The frequency with which this group celebrates special occasions and the emphasis on hospitality and food exchange for each celebration accounts for the way that the repertory of food formats remains a continuing focus of discussion, gossip, interest, and manipulation among the women. The female peer group and the intricate linkages between households accounts for both the shared traditions and the shared innovations.

In some cases, the persistence of traditional social roles has even led to a *decrease* in the use of traditional formats and items. A concern with nurturance led to the Anglo hot breakfast replacing the traditional cold meal. Mrs. Cooper talks about trying to make platters more often because they are "healthier" (in line with the negative image in the American media of high carbohydrate gravy meals). Thus, ethnic persistence lies in the social role rather than the food item.

This complex relationship between ethnicity and food patterns is also illustrated by the weddings described above. Italian items are more important in a disapproved marriage to an outsider than in a highly approved marriage between those with strong identities. For insiders, format and item choices had more to do with social status and prestige than ethnicity.

Identifying the process of menu negotiation provides insights about how structural constraints and individual preferences interact with shared models. They also provide us with clues about how change occurred over time. Long-term shifts in food technology and activity cycles in the post–World War II period led to permanent changes in formats (reduction, addition, deletion) in the same way that these variables affect individual meal plans in the short run.

Menu negotiations for weekly meals are the accommodation of ideal expectations to the realities of cycles of heavy and light work, leisure activities, as well as illness and other crises. These affect both available food preparation time, the absence of family members, and the presence of guests. Menu negotiations also incorporates the differential impact of social roles within the household: the senior male, older child, key kitchen person, and young child. Participation in social networks outside the home influences the feast cycle: the number of special events to observe, the frequency of eating away from home, the frequency of guests, the size of the guest list for feasts, and the menus for buffet-style events.

THE SIGNIFICANCE OF PARTICIPANT OBSERVATION

Our experience with three sources of data has demonstrated that we would know far less if we had used only one kind of data. Moreover, without participant observation, we would have missed the interaction between the shared community pattern (emerging from interview data) and household structure and/or individual preferences which we call menu negotiation.

Table 11 indicates the different information provided by each kind of data. Interview data which were taken from a large sample of the population do reveal a perceived distinct pattern, stronger for Sundays than Fridays. However, the frequency with which this ideal was observed is unknown.

The seven-day dietary records use a more limited sample. Only one Friday and one Sunday occurred for each family. The Friday rule is strongly observed while Sunday appears less marked. However, after participant observation, we know that alternative formats can be used to mark Sundays. With this knowledge, Sundays can now be said to be marked by all families. It is possible that the high marking of Fridays and Sundays emerged because the families wanted to be observed following the ideal and were able to do this for the single occasion involved.

The ethnographic data took place over at least four weeks, and it is obvious that the ideal is not consistently followed. However, the ethnography revealed the reasons for not marking Fridays and Sundays so that we better understand the process of menu negotiation.

Interview data do not include meal patterns which are not consciously perceived and labeled, such as weekend patterns or Sunday alternatives. Actual dietary records analyzed to indicate the frequency of Italian items would have been misleading. Pattern rules would also be masked by meals which reflected unusual situational constraints which interfere with ideal rules.

COMMUNITY VARIATION

We do not have space here for a detailed community comparison. The fact that similar elements of a historical pattern persist and similar modifications take place in both communities further underscores the pattern. Rules for Sundays, Fridays, gravy meals, and platters are shared. The buffet as a hybrid feast format exists in South Philadelphia where it is also called a "set-out" or "lay-out." Catered dinners are also common.The more traditional buffet-style format used for small feasts with extended family is less significant in South Philadelphia.

One difference between the two communities is in the *rate* of change as opposed to its nature. Life cycle feasts and holiday celebrations seem to have changed early in South Philadelphia. This can be

TABLE 11

Information Provided by Three Kinds of Data

	Survey (N = 208)			Seven-Day Record (N = 40 families)			Ethnography (N = 4 families)		
	Basic Rule	Other Rule	No Rule	Basic Rule	Other Rule	No Rule	Basic Rule	Other Rule	No Rule
Fridays	42%	16%	42%	82%[a]	—[b]	18%	61%	—	39%
Sundays	59	18	23	59	41	—	59	23[c]	18

[a] 50% fish or seafood, 50% meatless dish
[b] 67% celebratory restaurant, 33% Anglo roast meat
[c] 67% Anglo roast meat, 33% celebratory restaurant

explained largely by the nature of ethnic mix and interethnic relations in both communities.

Italian-Americans in Maryton are a closed community. This was due first to enforced segregation in work and residence. Later, boundaries were maintained to protect their local political and economic power. Holidays and life-cycle feasts were celebrated within the local community and change was slow. The small numbers in the population were not sufficient to develop large commercial food enterprises, and most celebrations were home-prepared.

In the multiethnic community of South Philadelphia, Italian-Americans developed political alliances with other white Catholic groups. They also became more dispersed in the occupational structure, thus lessening the bonds which would be developed by the common occupational interests in Maryton (local small entrepreneurs with local political control). Frequent intermarriage with other white, Catholic ethnic groups led to mixed extended families which accommodate many cultural backgrounds and espouse loyalty to the South Philadelphia community more than the ethnic group. The local delicatessens and caterers which developed in South Philadelphia served multiethnic clientele and developed open formats. The rate at which buffets and catered dinners replaced elaborated Sunday dinners and buffet-style meals was more rapid in the less bounded enclave. However, Maryton is now undergoing the same shifts.

CONCLUSION

This research has been concerned with what happens to an immigrant food pattern after several generations within a fast-changing new environment. We have included in our study the effects of linear time, generation turnover, changes in the food supply and technology of preparation, changes in activities (women in the labor force, greater emphasis on scheduled leisure time), increased autonomy of household members, and the increased diversity of households within the community. In spite of these major changes, we can still point to a community-shared, socially reinforced continuity in meal patterns and social participation in menu negotiation.

What is shared is a repertory of formats, and rules for when and for whom to use them. Some rules are specific; others allow alternatives. Some formats specify content, while others allow for significant menu negotiation in which preferences and situations dominate outcomes. Menu negotiation is a process in which factors can be measured (such as the degree of household preference compatibility) and ranked in significance. Obviously much food intake is influenced by such decisions about format and content. We need to understand more systematically, for many communities, how they are made.

Acknowledgments

We would like to express our appreciation to many individuals and organizations who were essential to the success of this research. David Feingold and Karen Kerner of the Institute for the Study of Human Issues first conceived of the food study and played a major role in the initial phases. Two geographers, Kenneth Meyer and Marilyn Silverfein, also helped us to formulate the initial research design. Temple University was very generous in supporting the work throughout with a Biomedical grant (College of Arts & Sciences), two study leaves, and two grants-in-aid. The women of Maryton were extraordinary in their interest, patience, generosity, and affection. Their lasting friendship has been very important to us. They have contributed enormously to our ideas and our analysis.

Bibliography

Allen, J. B. *The Company Town in the American West.* Norman: University of Oklahoma Press, 1966.

Anderson, E. N., and Anderson, M. L. "Cantonese Ethnohoptology." *Ethnos* 34 (1969): 107–11.

————. "Penang-Hokkien Ethnohoptology." *Ethnos* 37 (1972): 134–47.

Bennett, J. "Food and Social Status in a Rural Society." *American Sociological Review* 8 (1943) 561–69.

————; Smith, H; and Passin, H. "Food and Culture in Southern Illinois." *American Sociological Review* 7 (1942): 645–60.

Chang, K. C. *Food in Chinese Culture: Anthropological and His-*

torical Perspectives. New Haven: Yale University Press, 1977.

Curtis, K. "Food and Ethnicity: An Italian American Case." Unpublished master's thesis, Temple University, 1977.

Douglas, M. "Deciphering a Meal." Daedalus 101 (1972): 61–82.

—— and Nicod, M. "Taking the Biscuit: The Structure of British Meals" New Society 30 (1974): 744–47.

Freedman, M. R., and Grivetti, L. E. "Effects of Generation on Dietary Change in Greek-Americans." Paper presented at the 12th International Congress of Nutrition, San Diego, 1981.

Gans, H. The Urban Villagers: Group and Class in the Life of Italian-Americans. New York: Free Press, 1962.

Gillett, L. "Factors Influencing Nutrition Work Among Italians." Journal of Home Economics 14 (1922): 14–19.

Jerome, N. "On Determining Food Patterns of Urban Dwellers in Contemporary United States Society." In Gastronomy: The Anthropology of Food and Food Habits, edited by M. L. Arnott. The Hague: Mouton, 1975.

—— "Diet and Acculturation: The Case of Black-American In-Migrants." In Nutritional Anthropology, edited by N. Jerome et al. New York: Redgrave, 1980.

——; Kandel, R.; and Pelto, G, eds. Nutritional Anthropology: Contemporary Approaches to Diet and Culture. New York: Redgrave, 1980.

King, A. "A Study of the Italian Diet in a Group of New Haven Families." Master's thesis, Yale University, 1935.

MacDonald, J. S., and MacDonald,

L. D. "Chain-Migration, Ethnic Neighborhood Formation and Social Networks." Milbank Memorial Fund Quarterly 42 (1964): 82–97.

Mead, M. Manual for the Study of Food Habits. Report of the Committee on Food Habits. National Research Council, Bulletin No. 111. Washington, D.C.: National Academy of Sciences, 1945.

——. Food Habits Research: Problems of the 1960s. Publication No. 1225, Washington, D.C.: National Academy of Sciences, 1964.

Mudge, G. G. "Italian Dietary Adjustments." Journal of Home Economics 15 (1923): 181–85.

Nicod, M. "A Method of Eliciting the Social Meaning of Food." Master's thesis, University College, London, 1974.

Nizzardini, G., and Joffe, N. "Italian Food Patterns and Their Relationship to Wartime Problems of Food and Nutrition." Mimeographed. National Research Council, Committee on Food Habits. 1942.

Rozin, E. The Flavor Principle Cookbook. New York: Hawthorn Books, 1973.

Spiro, M. "Acculturation of American Ethnic Groups." American Anthropologist 57 (1955): 1240–52.

Trow, M. "Comment on Participant Observation and Interviewing: A Comparison." In Issues in Participant Observation, edited by George McCall and J. L. Simmons. Reading, Mass.: Addison-Wesley, 1969.

Wood, B. Foods of the Foreign Born in Relation to Health. Boston: Whitcomb & Barrows, 1922.

5

Measurement of Calendrical Information in Food-Taking Behavior

Jonathan L. Gross

The program Gastronomic Categories provided an opportunity to study the possibility of measuring the amount of information expressed by a behavioral system. In particular, several aspects of food-taking behavior were considered as indicators of calendrical information. The empirical pattern was that the rank of a household for information quantity was largely consistent across the various aspects. Thus, beyond the obvious fact that one household may have qualitatively different ways from another of supporting public categorical distinctions, there is evidence that its distinctions may be quantitatively stronger or weaker than those in another household. The information-theoretic measure adapted here to cultural analyses serves to refine the "grid-group" model introduced by Mary Douglas.

How to Measure the Quantity of Information

In an ordinary sense as well as a technical sense of cultural anthropology, food-taking behavior contains information. For instance, under circumstances likely to be familiar to the reader, dry cereal and milk means morning, sandwiches means noon, and turkey means a holiday. Perhaps eating in the dining room, rather than the kitchen, or using a tablecloth means that invited guests are present.

However, food-taking signs are often ambiguous or uncertain. Dry cereal and milk might be a midnight snack, or perhaps lunch is sometimes omitted. Nonetheless, ambiguity or uncertainty does not render a sign worthless. From a concrete mathematical viewpoint, the information value of a sign depends only on the extent to which it improves a guessing strategy, not on whether it guarantees a correct guess. There is also a mathematical sense in which one may appraise the information value of a sequence of signs without any knowledge of what they represent.

Showing the applicability of formal information-theoretic models to a cultural context was the main objective of the research described here. This first section explains information-theoretic models. The second section describes how they were adapted to a cultural context. The third section discussed the results and conclusions. An appendix shows the coding guide and data forms.

THE SHANNON MODEL

Suppose that there exists a known set X of possible outcomes of a random event and that the optimal *a priori* guessing strategy has probability p of choosing the correct outcome. Suppose also that some information I would enable us to revise our strategy to have an improved probability q of guessing correctly. According to the information model invented by C. E. Shannon (1948),

$$\text{value } (I) \;=\; \log_2 \,(q\,/\,p) \text{ bits}$$

Two examples demonstrate how to calculate the value of information.

Example 1. A crime has been committed by one of eight persons, each presumed equally likely *a priori* to be the culprit. Thus, there is probability $p = 1/8 = .125$ of guessing correctly. A remarkable clue

C narrows the investigation down to two suspects, thereby improving the prospects of a correct guess to $q = .5$. Then,

$$\text{value } (C) = \log_2 (.5/.125) = \log_2 (4) = 2 \text{ bits}$$

Example 2. An ethnographer is completely isolated from all external time cues, except for the food eaten by an experimental subject. The *a priori* probability of guessing the hour of the day is $p = 1/24 \approx .0417$. From prior experience, it is known that this subject eats smoked fish at 7 A.M. daily and also at 4 P.M. on Tuesdays. The ethnographer sees the clue *F* that the subject eats smoked fish. The optimal *a posteriori* guess is that it is 7 A.M., which is correct with probability $q = 7/8 = .875$. Thus,

$$\text{value } (F) \approx \log_2 (.875/.0417) \approx \log_2 (20.98) \approx 4.39 \text{ bits}$$

The units of information measurement are called bits, as if they were the binary digits 0 and 1 of computer science. One might imagine that the members of the set *X* of outcomes are determined by the presence or absence of various attributes. Suppose that there are five attributes. Then each possible outcome can be denoted by a string of five binary digits, such that a 1 indicates presence of an attribute while a 0 indicates absence. Thus, the string 01101 is the outcome that has attributes two, three, and five, but not attributes one or four. There are $2^5 = 32$ possible outcomes, if all combinations of attributes can occur. Thus, the *a priori* probability of a correct guess is $1/32 = 2^{-5}$. If the information *I* tells which of three attributes is present or absent in the outcome to be guessed, then the revised probability of guessing correctly is $q = 1/4 = 2^{-2}$, because now there are only two undetermined attributes, each with two possibilities. Therefore,

$$\begin{aligned} \text{value } (I) &= \log_2 (2^{-2}/2^{-5}) \\ &= \log_2 (2^3) = 3 \text{ bits} \end{aligned}$$

THE KOLMOGOROV MODEL

Another model for information content was developed by A. N. Kolmogorov (1965). A Kolmogorov model assigns an information value to a sequence *S* of symbols, without knowledge of the range of possible signs or their "meaning". Relative to a fixed algorithmic language *L*, the information content of *S* is the minimum number of instructions in language *L* needed to produce the sequence *S*.

Omissions or errors in a sequence would usually tend to inflate the

Kolmogorov score of a sequence. However, there are regularization methods, largely due to Baum et al. (1967, 1970) that can be used to reduce the error introduced by small perturbations down to tolerable proportions.

REASONS FOR ADOPTING A SHANNON MODEL HERE

The advantages of a Shannon model over a Kolmogorov model are an interval scale, rather than an ordinal scale, freedom from the need to design and justify an algorithmic language that corresponds to a cultural context, and relative simplicity of the scoring method. The extensive prior experience of the ethnographers with their communities permitted a Shannon model for the data analysis.

TO THE READERS

This report has been difficult to write, since it is simultaneously aimed at social scientists and mathematicians. What is obvious to an experienced ethnographer can be bewildering to a mathematician and vice versa. On the other hand, the ethnography is not the usual descriptive analysis, and the mathematics is not standard statistics, since neither standard approach would have answered the questions posed. Accordingly, some patience is required in more than one respect. Additional discussion of the general approach is given by Douglas and Gross (1981).

Adapting the Model to a Cultural Context

The scores in this experiment were based on the extent to which various aspects of food-taking behavior carry information about calendrical categories. Within each of three communities, several households were measured for the information content in each of the aspects of behavior. The details of the experiment, including the exact method of scoring, are now described.

CALENDRICAL CATEGORIES

Based on our interest in public meanings, we defined three classes of culturally significant occurrences that precipitate food events.

These classes are astronomical and meteorological phenomena, life-cycle phenomena, and reciprocity phenomena.

Days of the week, for example, are predictable from the revolution of the earth on its axis. The only mathematics required is counting to seven. Predicting Thanksgiving, on the other hand, requires knowledge of a more complicated rule. Yet it is still determined by astronomy. Births, weddings, confirmations, and deaths are life-cycle occurrences. A party that represents reciprocated hospitality or hospitality that is to be reciprocated is a reciprocity event.

There exist many anecdotes relating instances of the possible overlap of these classes on a theoretical basis and also instances of actual events of multiple significance. No such problems arose during the periods of observation.

Collectively the three classes of phenomena are called calendrical events. Each of the ethnographic teams listed the specific kinds of calendrical events that occurred during the observation period. These kinds were the same for all households in a community, but differed from one community to another. Table 1 lists the types of events that were observed in each of the three communities.

INFORMATION SUBMEDIA

Various aspects of food-taking behavior were isolated in the expectation that they would individually provide clues about the type of event. Each of these aspects was scored separately as a submedium

TABLE 1

Event Types Observed in Three Communities		
North Carolina	*Pennsylvania*	*South Dakota*
Weekday	Weekday	Weekday
Saturday	Saturday	Saturday
Sunday	Sunday	Sunday
Christmas Eve	Holiday	Wake
Christmas day	Confirmation	Party
Christmas other	Graduation	Curing
New Year's Eve	Christening	Memorial
New Year's Day	Shower	Farewell
Mother's Day		Sun dance
Anniversary		Powwow
Family reunion		*yuwipi*
Birthday		

of information, wherever the quality and quantity of the data permitted such scoring. Table 2 indicates the submedia.

Each submedium is to be understood as a range of possibilities for behavior. We shall consider briefly the definition of each submedium and also the general approach by which within each community each submedium was analyzed into a system of coded outcomes suitable for information-theoretic analysis.

Duration (DUR) is the length of the consumption phase of the food event. In particular, it begins when the consumption phase begins, not when the preparation begins, and it ends when the consumption phase ends. The possibilities for measurement problems are seemingly endless, yet all resolvable in practice by a reasonable rule for competent ethnographers. For instance, what if a child starts nibbling before anyone else gets to the table? What if one person lingers for hours over cold coffee at the end?

In deciding which starting and stopping times to record, an ethnographer must be sufficiently familiar with the community to decide those times according to community standards. Do they behave as if the meal begins when the little child sneaks a nibble or when the others arrive? Do they behave as if it stops when everyone else leaves or not until the last person finally abandons the cold coffee?

The ethnographer cannot ask the participants in the experiment what their behavior means. As Douglas and Nicod (1974) report, verbal interactions between the observer and the participants with reference to the purpose of the experiment substantially change the behavior. Moreover, since the participants are not ethnographers fully

TABLE 2

The Submedia of Information Used for All Three Communities

Submedium	Abbreviation
Duration of the event	DUR
Number of persons attending	ATT
Number of courses	CRS
Number of food varieties	VAR
Courses/varieties vector	C/V
Equipment combinations	EQP
Dispensing system	DSP
Position system	POS
Precedence system	PRC
Food quantity	QTY

prepared for this experimental approach, it is unreasonable to expect that they are able to analyze their own behavior according to our technical standards.

The working rule was that within each community the ethnographers were responsible for deciding which variations of behavior were meaningful and for applying consistent standards in recording data. Obviously, poor ethnography would lead to useless data, just as bad experimental practices in biology or chemistry might lead to useless data.

The number of persons attending (ATT) means the number of persons interacting in the food consumption phase of the event. In trying to anticipate problems of data collection, the ethnographers asked about such possibilities as an uninvited person dropping in briefly and joining the main group. In practice, the number of anecdotes about possible difficulties was vastly greater than the number of difficulties actually encountered during the experimental period. Moreover, the rule that the ethnographers decide what matters and apply a consistent standard resolved the problems that did arise. Minor discrepancies of ethnographic interpretation were no more troublesome in this experiment than minor differences of measured values in any natural science.

The number of courses (CRS) provided very little information in these communities, as the ethnographers anticipated, because there was scarcely ever a meal with more than two courses. The number of food varieties (VAR) was a somewhat more clearly differentiated submedium. Combined into a courses/varieties vector (C/V), it was a rather rich source of information.

By a food variety, we mean the outcome of a recipe, however simple or complex. For instance, a glass of water is a food variety. So is candied yams. So is a decorated cake. Ingredients are not counted. What mattered was the outcome in the form it might be discussed within the communities. Thus, if carrots, potatoes, and meat in gravy are served separately, that is three varieties, since one requests them individually. If they are served as a stew, then that is one variety.

The courses/varieties vector is an ordered list of the number of varieties in each course. For instance the list 2,4,3 means two varieties in the first course, four in the second, and three in the third.

Given the large number of constituents of equipment used in food taking and the different possibilities for each constituent, it is obvious that the number of possible equipment combinations (EQP) is large.

What matters here is only overt public distinctions such as paper plates versus china or plastic drinking cups versus glass. Most of the theoretical possibilities for combinations such as crystal stemware with paper plates are ethnographically meaningless or statistically insignificant or (most likely) both.

Possible dispensing systems (DSP) included overt distinctions such as buffet, one server serves all, or food passed around at the table. This was a very weak information submedium in the communities studied. Two of them used only one system during the experimental period, although the ethnographers reported the existence of others observed at other times.

The order in which various persons were served (PRC) was considered, as was the quantity of food per person (QTY).

WHAT MATTERS IS MEANINGFUL DIFFERENTIATION: SOME EXAMPLES

To try to impart some intuition about high information scores, we now consider several examples.

Example 3. Family A always eats a lot, no matter what the occasion. Thus, their QTY score is low, because you cannot guess the occasion from the quantity. There is no variation in quantity.

Example 4. Family B eats little on weekdays and Saturdays, moderately on Sundays, and in great quantity on special occasions. Indeed, the more important the occasion to them, the more they eat. At the high points of their gastronomic year, they consume vast quantities. Their QTY score is high, since by watching how much they eat, you can greatly improve your chances of guessing the date.

Example 5. Family C eats at random. They diet at random. If you were at their house for a holiday dinner, you might leave hungry. On the other hand, one night at 3 A.M., they all got up for a huge turkey dinner when someone said "Let's do it." Their QTY score is low, because even though the variation is extensive, it does not correspond to the public categories (calendrical event types) under consideration.

FREQUENCY TABLES AND RATIO TABLES

The range of possible signs of each submedium is partitioned into ethnographically meaningful subranges of cases. Then a *frequency table* is constructed. Suppose that there are m different event types in a community and n subranges of signs in the submedium. The frequency table for each household has *m* rows, one for each event type, and *n* + 1 columns, one for each subrange of signs and one for totals.

The entry in row *r* and column *c* of the frequency table is denoted *f(r,c)*. Its value is given by the following rules:

If $1 \leq c \leq n$, then

$f(r,c)$ =   the number of times that event type *r* was represented by a sign in subrange *c* during the observation period;

if $c = n + 1$, then

$f(r,c)$ =   the total number of times that event type *r* was observed.

For purposes of illustration, we now examine a simplified example of a household in a hypothetical community. In this community there are five types of events: weekday, Saturday, Sunday, wedding, and birthday. The submedium is the color of the tablecloth, which is either blue or red. Each of these colors is regarded in itself as a separate subrange of signs. Table 3 is an example of a frequency table.

For instance, the top row tells us that 62 weekdays were observed. On 60 of these days a blue tablecloth was used, and on the other two red.

From an $m - by - (n + 1)$ frequency table it is easy to derive an $(m + 1) - by - (n + 1)$ *ratio table.* The entry in row *r* and column *c* of the ratio table is denoted *p(r,c)*, and its value is given by this rule:

$$\text{If } 1 - r - m, \text{ then } p(r,c) = f(r,c) / f(r,n + 1);$$
$$\text{if } r = m + 1, \text{ then } p(r,c) = \Sigma_{i=1}^{m} p(i,c).$$

In other words, the entry *p(r,c)* is the proportion of occurrences of event type *r* that were represented by a sign in subrange *c*, except in the bottom row. The bottom entry in each column is simply the

TABLE 3

	A Hypothetical Frequency Table		
	Blue	*Red*	*Total*
Weekday	60	2	62
Saturday	11	1	12
Sunday	4	9	13
Wedding	0	7	7
Birthday	2	2	4

TABLE 4

A Hypothetical Ratio Table			
	Blue	Red	Total
Weekday	.97*	.03	1.0
Saturday	.92	.08	1.0
Sunday	.31	.69	1.0
Wedding	0.00	1.00*	1.0
Birthday	.50	.50	1.0
Total	2.70	2.30	5.0

*The maximum entry in a subrange column, excluding the bottom row of totals.

sum of the other entries. Table 4 is the ratio table derived from table 3.

SIMPLIFIED INFORMATION SCORES

Suppose that there are m event types and n possible sign types. Thus, the ratio table has $m + 1$ rows and $n + 1$ columns. Suppose one believes that each of the m event types is equally likely to occur, so that an optimal guessing strategy is to select one of the m event types at random, each with equal probability $1/m$. Then the probability of a correct guess is $1/m$. Given n trials believed to be independent, the expected number of correct guesses is n/m.

Now suppose instead that one has at hand a copy of the ratio table and what actually occurs is a sequence of n events, one for each sign type, and that the distribution follows the conditional pattern derivable from the ratio table. Then for each sign type, the optimal strategy is to guess the event type with the maximum entry in the column of the sign type. The probability of a correct guess is the quotient of the maximum entry by the column total. Thus, the sum of those quotients is the expected number of correct guesses, using the signs as clues. The Shannon information value of the clues in this model is obtained by dividing the sum of the quotients by n/m and taking the base 2 logarithm.

Since we are only comparing households within the same community in this experiment, we do not bother to take the base 2 logarithm to divide by n/m. This has no effect on the rankings. Every household in a single community has the same event types and sign types available, under the model adopted.

Of course, the event types are not equally likely to occur. However, treating them as if they were is equivalent to assigning higher payoffs to the less frequent event types. In effect, we are assuming that the institution of Sundays, for example, is only as important as the institution of weddings, even though one sees more Sundays than weddings. Such equal treatment seemed appropriate for a pilot experiment.

For our hypothetical example, the optimal strategy is to guess "weekday" if you see a blue tablecloth and "wedding" if you see a red one. The probabilities that these guesses are right are .97/2.70 and 1.00/2.30, respectively. That is, it is the quotient of the starred entry by the bottom entry, for each subrange of signs. Thus, the information score used to rank this household is

$$\frac{.97}{2.70} + \frac{1.00}{2.30} = .36 + .43 = .79$$

If we really wanted to have a score in bits, we would use the value

$$\log_2 (.79/.4) = \log_2 (1.975) \approx .98 \text{ bits}$$

Converting the scores to bits would not change the rankings within a community and might tempt someone to make an inappropriate comparison across communities. The experiment would have to be designed differently for such a comparison to make sense.

Results and Conclusions

In three different communities, we identified public categories of calendrical event types and public signs in various submedia within the general medium of food-taking behavior. We selected several households in each community and ranked them for information transmitted in each submedium. The fact that the ranking of households in each community was generally consistent across the various submedia is support for the development of a model of a social unit that explicitly admits quantitative differences of information transmission rate.

TABLES OF RANKING ACROSS THE SUBMEDIA

Tables 5, 6, and 7 show the ranks of the households within the three communities studied. If the raw scores of two or more households in a community were sufficiently close, the households were

TABLE 5

Information-Transmission Ranks for Four Households in an Italian-American Community

Submedium	Household			
	1	2	3	4
DUR	4	1	3	2
ATT	2	1	4	3
CRS	2–3	1	4	2–3
VAR	2	1	4	3
C/V	2	1	4	3
EQP	3	1	2	4
DSP	1–2	1–2	3–4	3–4
PRC	2–3	1	4	2–3
QTY	2–3–4	1	2–3–4	2–3–4
Composite	2	1	4	3

TABLE 6

Information-Transmission Ranks for Four Households in an Oglala Community

Submedium	Household			
	1	2	3	4
DUR	1	3–4	3–4	2
ATT	1	3	4	2
CRS	1–2–3–4	1–2–3–4	1–2–3–4	1–2–3–4
VAR	1	3–4	3–4	2
C/V	1	3–4	3–4	2
Composite	1	3–4	3–4	2

TABLE 7

Information-Transmission Ranks for Eight Households in a Southern Community

Submedium	Household							
	1	2	3	4	5	6	7	8
DUR	6	4–5	2–3	2–3	4–5	1	7	8
ATT	5–6	4	2–3	1	7–8	2–3	5–6	7–8
VAR	5-6-7	4	5-6-7	2	3	1	8	5-6-7
C/V	7–8	4	5–6	2	3	1	5–6	7–8
Composite	6–7	3-4-5	3-4-5	2	3-4-5	1	6–7	8

considered to have tied. Notation such as 3-4-5 suggests a three-way tie for those positions.

CONSISTENCY OF INFORMATION RANK

This was a pilot study, concerned exclusively with the information value of food-taking behavior as a medium of expression of signs for types of calendrical events. The consistency of information rank across the various submedia is obvious from a glance at tables 5, 6, and 7.

An important feature of this mode of cultural analysis is that it makes absolutely no judgments of the cultural categories themselves, nor of the relative importance that a community assigns to the various categories. It simply measures the extent to which their behavior provides information that enables one to distinguish the categories.

Even within a single community, no preference is given to approved behavior, not even to whether a person or household matches the signs to the categories in the accepted manner. In principle, the information score would be just as high for a household that has an elaborate system of desecration of important occasions as for one that has a system of reverence. All that matters is the consistency of differentiation of categories. Thus, highly differentiated desecration would outrank poorly differentiated reverence.

The immediate importance of information scores to cultural analysis is that they are inherently a cross-cultural concept. In particular, even if the design of an experiment does not permit a comparison of the mean information scores, it might permit a comparison of the distribution patterns. At the least, the information transmission concept creates a general framework for qualitative comparisons.

Conclusions from this limited experiment are necessarily tentative, even though the results seem so positive. A more comprehensive test of the consistency of information rank would include additional classes of categorical information, for which major activities (as determined by ethnographic study of the particular communities) and principal roles (also to be determined by ethnographic study) are suggested. It would also include additional information media, for which space allocation or clothing is suggested.

A BROADER CONTEXT: THE GRID-GROUP MODEL

At a limited level, the results of this experiment support the grid-group model for cultural analysis that was defined by Mary

Douglas (1970, 1978). In this model, *grid* is defined to be the amount of control that the public system of categorical distinctions—such as male and female, edible and inedible, or workday and weekend—exerts on individual behavior. *Group* is defined to be the amount of control that arises from a person's experiencing his or her identity through membership in a social unit.

Douglas conceives of grid and group as orthogonal coordinates, and she associates certain attributes of social environment with various combinations of grid and group strength. For instance, she associates competition among individuals with the combination of low grid strength and low group strength. Gross and Rayner (1984) have developed an operational procedure for measuring grid and group that is independent of reference to such cultural attributes. Within this context, the information score for a household is one of several contributing factors to the grid coordinate.

The usefulness of the grid-group model depends largely on two things, which are the reliability of grid-group measurements and correlation of specific cultural attributes with various combinations of measured values. The consistency of information rank across submedia of a single information medium, food-taking behavior, is first evidence of the reliability of measurement.

Acknowledgments

Thanks are due to Bruce Styne, who wrote and ran the computer programs that analyzed the data, as well as to Aaron Gross and Joel Stein, who assisted him.

Bibliography

Baum, L. E., and Eagon, J. A. "An Inequality with Applications to Statistical Estimation for Probabilistic Functions of Markov Processes and to a Model for Ecolo-gy." *Bulletin of the American Mathematical Society* 73 (1967): 360–63.

Baum, L. E.; Petrie, T.; Soules, G.; and Weiss, N. "A Maximization

Technique Occurring in the Statistical Analysis of Probabilistic Functions of Markov Chains." *Annals of Mathematical Statistics* 41 (1970): 164–71.

Douglas, M. *Natural Symbols.* (1970): Penguin, 1970.

———. *Cultural Bias.* London: Royal Anthropological Institute, 1978.

——— and Gross, J. "Food and Culture: Measuring the Intricacy of Rule Systems." *Social Science Information* 20 (1981): 1–35.

Douglas, M. and Nicod, M. "Taking the Biscuit: The Structure of British Meals. *New Society* 30 (1974): 744–47.

Gross, J. L. and Rayner, S. F. *"Measuring Culture: A Paradigm for the Analysis of Social Organization.* New York: Columbia University Press, 1984.

Kolmogorov, A. N. "Three approaches to the Quantitative Definition of Information" (in Russian). *Problemy Peredachi Informatsii* 1 (1965): 3–11.

Shannon, C. E. "A Mathematical Theory of Communication." *Bell System Technical Journal* 27 (1948).

A Coding Guide for Gastronomic Categories

Some of the data collected under the 1978–79 culture program will be keypunched into computer cards. In order to help prevent errors and omissions, special forms are provided in which to record these data. Copies of these forms appear at the end of this coding guide.

Forms A1 to A13 are for recording community-wide information; forms B1 to B5 are for recording the observations at a single food event. All the forms except A13 and B5 adhere to the standardized 80-column computer card format. The two exceptions are for providing supplementary information that might not fit, for reasons either of size or content, onto the other forms.

Part A: Community-wide Information

For each of the four communities, there are twelve forms to be completed. Although some of the information could be entered in advance by any person adequately familiar with one of the communities, much of what is to be recorded depends on what is actually observed.

FORM A1

COMMUNITY CARD

Columns 13–26: Each community is to be identified by the name of the state of its principal location, such as PENNSYLVANIA, SOUTH DAKOTA.

Columns 69–70: State abbreviation, such as PA, SD.

UNIT CARDS

Column 6: Each of the four commensal units in a community is to be designated by a letter of the alphabet. For instance, if the names of the key kitchen persons all begin with different letters, those letters would be a good choice. If no more meaningful choice is possible, the letters A, B, C, and D will do.

Columns 10–26: A little more information to identify each unit, such as the name of the key kitchen person.

Columns 69–70: State abbreviation, as on the COMMUNITY card.

FOOD VARIETIES CARD

Columns 17–21: The total number of different food varieties observed at all food events for all commensal units during the experimental periods. This number must agree with the number of FOOD cards completed. (See form A12.)

Columns 69–70: State abbreviation, as on the COMMUNITY card.

FORM A2

FOOD EVENT TYPE CODES CARD

Columns 25–26: The *number* of food event types. A food event type is a designation such as breakfast, tea, lunch, brunch, dinner, or supper. It may be necessary to distinguish between a vending machine dinner and a kitchen-prepared dinner. Other types might be a snack or an office party. Each project must determine the ethnographically correct categories for its community. It is preferable to include every possible type, which may be obtained by outside knowledge and questionnaires, not only the ones actually observed.

Columns 69–70: State abbreviation.

TYPE CARDS

Columns 6–10: A code name, exactly five characters long including blanks, for a food event type. The idea here is to choose five characters that immediately suggest the name of the food event. For instance, one might use BREAK, DINNER, TEAℏℏ, and OFFPR for breakfast, dinner, tea, and office party, respectively. It is not necessary for observers in two different communities to use the same code names for food event types. However,

coding consistency

it is *absolutely necessary* for the same code to be used consistently within a single community. For instance, if an observer sometimes writes BREAK and sometimes BREKF for breakfast, the computer will think these are two entirely different

about blanks ℏℏℏℏℏ

types of food event. The character ℏ, used twice in TEAℏℏ, is a blank. The computer thinks that TEAℏℏ, ℏTEAℏ, and ℏℏTEA are completely different event types. The safest general rule is to left justify all your alphabetic codes and to omit interior blanks.

Columns 14–26: A name for the food event type, such as BREAKFAST, DINNER, TEA, or OFFICE PARTY. The idea here is to provide a brief explanation of the code. For instance, the code OFFPR is not completely self-explanatory. If thirteen characters are insufficient, then attach a form A13 with a more complete explanation.

Columns 69–70: State abbreviation.

TYPE CARDS (CONTINUATION, TO SHOW METAPHYSICAL REQUIREMENTS)

Each of fourteen metaphysical indicators is to be recorded as required or not. These indicators are described in Douglas's working paper *Metaphysical Meanings in Food* (February 1979).

how many TYPE cards?

The number of TYPE cards completed must be the number supplied in columns 25–26 of the FOOD EVENT TYPE CODES card. Although form A2 provides room for at most eight TYPE cards, there is no

what if there are too many food event types for one page of form A2?

such limit on the possible number of types. If an observer happens to be in a community with nineteen separate types of events, the observer should use three copies of form A2. The number 19 should be

Column	Metaphysical Requirement	Marker, If Needed for This Event	Marker, If Not Needed
29	exhortation	X	. (period)
31	prayer	P	.
33	archaic language	A	.
35	witnessing, testifying	W	.
37	reciting the code	R	.
39	singing	S	.
41	joking	J	.
43	significant member, or quorum	Q	.
45	dress	D	.
47	food, positive	F	.
49	significant objects, besides food or dress	B	.
51	physical state (of consciousness)	C	.
53	efficacy, positive ("mana")	M	.
55	efficacy, negative ("taboo")	T	.

recorded in columns 25–26 of the FOOD EVENT TYPE CODES line on the first form A2. The FOOD EVENT TYPE CODES lines on the second and third forms A2 should be crossed out. All eight TYPE lines should be used on the first two forms A2, and three TYPE lines should be used on the third form A2. This same general rule applies whenever there are too many codes to fit on a one-page form.

better to have too many categories than too few!

If an observer is not certain whether dinner and supper are really separate food event types in some community, the rule is that it is better to treat them as separate types. It is much easier for the computer to combine two types into one than to pull one apart into two.

FORM A3

CALENDRICAL EVENT CODES CARD
Columns 25–26: The *number* of different kinds of calendrical event. This number tells the computer

how many CALEN cards to expect. Christmas, homecoming, George Washington's Birthday, harvest moon, and volcano eruptions are all examples of calendrical events. It is preferable to include every calendrical event that affects food events, not just the ones actually observed. (The computer will know from the EVENTS cards, form B1, which ones were actually observed. This is an opportunity to provide additional information, to be obtained by outside knowledge and questionnaires.)

Columns 69–70: State abbreviation. One reason the state abbreviation is to be written on every card is to avoid the serious errors that might result if a card got out of order.

why write the
state abbr. on
every card?

CALEN CARDS

Columns 7–11: A code name, exactly five characters long including blanks, for a calendrical event. Choose five characters that immediately suggest the calendrical event, such as XMAS♭, THANX, GWASH, HARVM, and HOMEC for Christmas, Thanksgiving, George Washington's Birthday, harvest moon, and homecoming. As for food event types, it is necessary to be completely consistent within the same community, but unnecessary for two different communities to use the same codes. Be sure to left justify short codes, such as XMAS♭.

Columns 15–26: A brief explanation of the code name. If a brief explanation would be insufficient, then attach a form A13.

Columns 69–70: State abbreviation.

number of
CALEN cards

The number of CALEN cards must be the number specified in columns 25–26 of the CALENDRICAL EVENT CODES card. If there are more than eight different calendrical events (and there probably are for most communities), then use several forms A3, crossing out the CALENDRICAL EVENT CODES line on all forms A3 after the first. This is essentially the same rule that is used for form A2.

FORM A4

LIFE CYCLE EVENT CODES CARD

Columns 25–26: The *number* of different kinds of life-cycle events. This number tells the computer how many LIFE cards to expect. Births, weddings, deaths, Bar Mitzvahs, school graduations, birthday anniversaries, wedding anniversaries, and golden wedding anniversaries are all examples of life-cycle events. Fraternal lodge initiations might also be included here. In general, include anything that affects the food events, and call two events different if they affect the food events differently (for example, ordinary wedding anniversaries versus golden wedding anniversaries) or if they are commonly regarded as different. Once again, it is preferable to list all possible kinds of life-cycle events in the community, not just the ones actually observed. The computer will know from the forms B1 which ones were actually observed.

Columns 69–70: State abbreviation.

LIFE CARDS

Columns 6–15: A code name, exactly ten letters long including blanks, for a life-cycle event. As for TYPE cards and CALEN cards, choose meaningful codes, such as WEDDINGƄƄƄ, CONFIRMATI, or BDAYƄANNIV, for wedding, confirmation, or birthday anniversary. As for TYPE cards and CALEN cards, it is necessary to be consistent within the same community, but unnecessary for two different communities to have the same codes. As always, too many categories is better than too few.

Columns 17–26: A brief explanation of the code name. If a brief explanation would be insufficient, then attach a form A13.

Columns 69–70: State abbreviation.

how many
LIFE cards?

The number of LIFE cards must be the number specified in columns 25–26 of the LIFE CYCLE EVENT CODES card. If there are more than eight different life cycle events that affect food behavior, then use several forms A4, crossing out the LIFE CYCLE EVENT CODES line on all forms A4 after the first. This is the same rule as for forms A2 and A3.

FORM A5

PARTICIPANTS CARD
Columns 15–16: The *number* of persons an observer cares to specify by name, at most ten. The names go on WHO cards.
Columns 69–70: State abbreviation.

WHO CARDS
Columns 5–13: A nine-letter abbreviation of a person's name, chosen as meaningfully as possible. If two persons happen to have the same name, then they might be designated, for example, PETE-JONE1 and PETEJONE2.
Columns 17–50: The person's name. If two persons have the same name, give some distinguishing information also. If it does not fit, then fill out a form A13.
Columns 69–70. State abbreviation.

purpose of
WHO cards

number of
WHO cards

The purpose of WHO cards is to permit an observer to make special mention of persons whose attendance at a food event is most likely to affect the outcome. The number of WHO cards must be the number specified in columns 15–16 of the PARTICIPANTS card. If more than four persons are to receive special mention, then use additional copies of form

A5, crossing out the PARTICIPANTS line on those additional copies.

FORM A6

COURSE STRUCTURES CARD
Columns 20–21: The *number* of different course structures a meal can have in this community, not just the ones actually observed.
Columns 69–70: State abbreviation.

C-STR CARDS
Columns 7–15: A nine-letter code for a course structure.
Columns 19–50: A brief description of the course structure.
Columns 69–70: State abbreviation.

For each of the C-STR cards, fill out a form A13, giving details of the course structure identified on that card. The number of C-STR cards must be the number in columns 20–21 of the COURSE STRUCTURES card. If there are more than four possible course structures, use extra forms A6, crossing out the COURSE STRUCTURES line on the extras.

FORM A7

EQUIPMENT COMBINATIONS CARD
Columns 25–26: The *number* of different combinations of food service equipment that might occur, paying particular attention to utensils, plates, glassware, tablecloths, and such things. Two

when are two combinations the same?

roughly similar combinations of equipment, either in the same household or in two different households, are to be regarded as the same if their public meanings are the same.

apply the public meanings rule

Columns 69–70: State abbreviation.

EQUIP CARDS

Columns 7–15: A nine-letter code for an equipment combination. It seems to be a lot harder to think of meaningful codes here than with most other kinds of cards. Try to use a code that will help recall the particular combination of equipment.

Columns 19–50: A brief explanation of the code. A form A13 is almost certainly necessary to describe a combination of equipment.

Columns 69–70: State abbreviation.

The number of EQUIP cards must equal the number given in columns 25–26 of the EQUIPMENT COMBINATIONS card. If there are more than four possible combinations of equipment, then use extra forms A7, crossing out the EQUIPMENT COMBINATIONS line on the extras.

***

1

*** The categorizing of equipment combinations may be one of the more difficult aspects of an observer's work. However, it should be possible to build a firm foundation for this, based on a discussion of examples, at the next Project Directors meeting.

FORM A8

DISPENSING SYSTEM CODES CARD

Columns 25–26: The *number* of different food-dispensing systems used in the community. To clarify this point, a few different food-dispensing systems are now described: (a) Each person at the food event takes a plate into the kitchen as often as he or she wishes and takes the food him-self/herself. (b) Each person takes a plate into the kitchen once, where a kitchen person serves the food. (c) Each person is permitted to go back to the kitchen as often as he or she wishes for more food, which is always served by a kitchen person. (d) Food is passed around at the table. (e) Everyone at the table passes plates to a serving person. (f) First servings are put on the plates in the kitchen and served to seated persons; addi-tional helpings are obtained by going back to the kitchen.

In general, a food-dispensing system is the com-plete set of rules for dispensing food at a single event. In the same commensal unit, different systems may apply to different occasions. Breakfasts may be "come and get it," while dinner foods may be care-fully apportioned by a serving person. The food-dispensing system is closely connected to the precedence system, in certain cases, so it may be nec-essary to repeat oneself on the forms A13.

what is a good dispensing sys-tem?

Two of the most important distinctions in food-dispensing systems are whether persons serve themselves, or whether someone else serves, and whether they get only one helping, or more. It is also important to observe whether persons help them-selves in full view of others at the event, or whether they may take their food unwatched.
Columns 69–70: State abbreviation.

important dif-ferences be-tween dispens-ing systems

DISP CARDS
Columns 6–14: A nine-letter code for a food-dispensing system, as meaningful as possible.
Columns 18–50: A brief description of the system. It is certainly necessary to attach a form A13 with a complete description, giving all the rules.
Columns 69–70: State abbreviation.

Although it may not seem important whether it is the mother or the father, for example, who is serving the food, the general rule to follow in establishing the

too many dis-
pensing system
categories is
better than too
few!

different food-dispensing system types is that too many types is better than too few. Again, the computer can easily combine types. It cannot separate what the anthropologist has put together, because it wasn't at the event.

FORM A9

PRECEDENCE SYSTEM CODES CARD

Columns 25–26: The *number* of different precedence systems used in the community. A few different possible precedence rules are now described: (a) No one begins eating until the kitchen persons are seated. After that, everyone waits until the father begins to eat. (b) The order of food service is first the mother; then the daughters, eldest first; then the father; last the sons, eldest first. (c) As soon as the third person is served, everyone may begin to eat. (d) No one eats until the guest begins to eat.

what is a prece-
dence system?

A precedence system is the collection of all the precedence rules in effect at a single food event. Thus, there might be one precedence system for weekday dinners, another for Sundays, and perhaps yet another when there is a guest.

Columns 69–70: State abbreviation.

PREC CARDS

Columns 6–14: A nine-letter code for one of the precedence systems.

Columns 18–50: A brief description of the precedence system. A form A13 will be necessary to give a complete description, mentioning all of the rules.

Columns 69–70: State abbreviation.

The number of PREC cards must be the number given in columns 25–26 of the PRECEDENCE SYSTEM CODES card. As always, use extra forms A9 if necessary, crossing out the top line on the extras.

FORM A10

POSITION SYSTEM CODES CARD

what is a position system?

Columns 25–26: The *number* of different position systems used in the community. As always, it is preferable to list all those that exist, not just those observed during this experimental period. Position systems have to do with the rooms in which the food events take place, the shape of the tables, the seating arrangement, the standing arrangement, and the movement of persons from place to place during the event.

Columns 69–70: State abbreviation.

POSI CARDS

Columns 6–14: A nine-letter code for one of the position systems.

Columns 18–50: A brief description of the system. Complete details should be given on an attached form A13.

Columns 69–70: State abbreviation.

the public meanings rule again

The number of POSI cards must be the number specified in columns 25–26 of the POSITION SYSTEM CODES card. If there are more than four position systems in use in the community, use extra A10 forms, crossing out the top line on the extras. The general rule in categorizing is that two roughly similar systems are the same if they do not differ in public meaning.

245

FORM A11

INGREDIENT COUNTS CARD

Columns 19, 21, 23, 25: List the same four unit codes given on form A1 in column 6 of the four UNIT cards, in alphabetic order.

Columns 69–70: State abbreviation.

INGR CARDS

Column 6: One of the unit codes. (Each of the four INGR cards on form A11 corresponds to a different commensal unit.)

Columns 10–16: A calendar date, in the form 04MAR79, indicating the first of three occasions on which the observer counted the number of ingredients in the kitchen of the specified commensal unit.

Columns 18–20: The number of ingredients in the kitchen on that occasion.

Columns 23–29: A calendar date, in the same form, indicating the second of three occasions on which the observer counted the number of ingredients in the kitchen (including the pantry, of course, and other locations in the house in which food is stored—this rule applies to all three occasions for counting).

"kitchen" includes pantry, etc.

Columns 31–33: The number of ingredients counted on the second counting.

Columns 36–42: A calendar date for the third and final counting of ingredients.

Columns 44–46: The number of ingredients in the third counting.

Columns 69–70. State abbreviation.

***
2

***The purpose of counting the ingredients three times is to avoid the hazard of an unrepresentative single measurement. One obvious standardization is to count in the middle of weeks one, two, and three of the observational period. The goal is to obtain an average count. Since some communities have elaborate occasional events, or periods of unemployment, the extreme counts, high or low, are not to be neglected. A look ahead to form B1 shows that in columns 61–63 of the EVENT card, the number of ingredients used in particular meals is also to be reported.

FORM A12

FOOD CARDS

In columns 17–21 of the FOOD VARIETIES card on form A1, there was specified the total number of different food varieties used in the four commensal units during the experimental periods. A separate FOOD card is now required for each variety.

Qu: when are two food varieties to be considered different?

Although it was suggested at one time that two varieties were identical only if they had the same recipe, it is now suggested that two roughly similar varieties are different only if they have different public meanings. Thus, while a boiled potato and a mashed potato are different, apple pie with cinnamon flavoring is probably not different from apple pie with nutmeg. One might say that a veal stew differs from a beef stew if the difference in taste is obvious, and it should be noted that they have different names, not just different modifiers. It might be ventured that different names are tangible evidence of different meanings.

Ans: if in doubt, apply the different names rule.

Columns 6–14: A nine-letter code name for a food variety, as meaningfully chosen as possible.

Columns 18–50: A brief description of the food variety. If it might not be clear to other persons associated with this study, or to persons interested in the results, what the food variety is, then attach a form A13.

Columns 69–70: State abbreviation.

FORM A13

Form A13 is a means to provide supplementary information for any other group A form. Sometimes, several pages of form A13 might be needed to give an adequate description, for instance, of a combination of food service equipment or of a position system. The notation 2/5 in line 3 of form A13 would indicate that this is the second page of a five-page supplement.

A form A13 should always be attached to whichever form (that is, A1 to A12) it supplements.

Part B: Observations at a Single Event

For every food event observed, whether it is kitchen prepared, vending machine dispensed, restaurant served, or catered, there are four forms to be completed.

FORM B1

EVENT CARD

Columns 6–13: The calendar date, in the form 24JUL79.

Columns 15–21: The starting time of the event, in the form 02:45PM. The colon (:) and the "M" for AM or PM are already supplied.

Columns 26–32: The stopping time of the event, in the same form, if the event ends that same calendar day. If the event ends the following calendar day, then add 24 to the number of hours. For instance, if it ends at 04:21AM or 07:33PM the next day, then record it as 28:21AM or 31:33PM, respectively. If it ends two or three calendar days later, then add 48 or 72, respectively, to the hour number. Also, attach a form B5, explaining the circumstances of the extra long event.

Columns 35–39: The event type. Enter one of the food event type codes from columns 6–10 of a TYPE card on form A2. The entry here must agree, character for character, with one of those prespecified codes for a food event type.

Columns 42–46: A calendrical event code. Enter one of the codes from columns 7–11 of a CALEN card on form A3. They must agree character for character.

Columns 49–58: A life-cycle event code. Enter one of the codes from columns 6–15 of a LIFE card on form A4.

***

3

what is counted as an ingredient?

Columns 61–63: The number of different food ingredients used in the preparation of this event. *Do not count the number of ingredients on the label of a can or a package.* For example, a home-baked apple pie has about a dozen ingredients, but a store-bought apple pie has only one ingredient. Remember to count "incidental items" like water and salt. If some ingredients are used in two or more recipes, they should *not* be counted two or more times, only once.

Columns 69–70: State abbreviation.

Column 71: Code for this commensal unit, as in column 6 of some UNIT card on form A1.

Columns 73–74: The event number for this unit. The events for each commensal unit are to be numbered 1, 2, 3, and so forth, corresponding to the chronological sequence.

ATTENDANCE CARD

Columns 13–17: The number of persons that the food preparers expect to attend the event. If a range is given, enter the middle value. This entry should be flush right, that is, ҍҍ147, not 147ҍҍ, or ҍ147ҍ.

Be sure to *ask in advance* how many are expected.

Columns 20–24: The number of persons who did attend, flush right.

Columns 29–30: Enter the number of persons who attended listed on WHO cards from form A5.

Columns 69–70: State abbreviation.

Column 71: Unit identification letter.

Columns 73–74: The event number, that is, the same number that appears on the EVENT card for this food event, *not* necessarily the sum of the following (since the same variety—for example, water—can occur in more than one course.

COURSES: VARIETIES CARD

Columns 21–22: The number of courses in this event.

Columns 24–26: The total number of different varieties served during the event.

Columns 30–31: The number of varieties served in course 1.

Columns 33–34: The number of varieties served in course 2.

Columns 36–37: The number of varieties served in course 3.

Columns 39–40: The number of varieties served in course 4.

Columns 42–43: The number of varieties served in course 5.

Columns 45–46: The number of varieties served in course 6.

Columns 48–49: The number of varieties served in course 7.

Columns 51–52: The number of varieties served in course 8.

Columns 54–55: The number of varieties served in course 9.

Columns 57–58: The number of varieties served in course 10.

Columns 60–61: The number of varieties served in course 11.

Columns 63–64: The number of varieties served in course 12.

If the food event has more than twelve courses, then use additional COURSE: VARIETIES cards in the following form.

Columns 21–22: The letters CC.

Columns 24–26: The letters CCC.

Columns 30–31: The number of varieties served in course 13.

Columns 33–34: The number of varieties served in course 14.

.

.

.

.

Columns 69–70: State abbreviation.

Column 71: Commensal unit code, as on the EVENT card and on the ATTENDANCE card.

Columns 73–74: Event number, as on the EVENT card and the ATTENDANCE card.

FORM B2

ATTEN CARDS

ATTEN cards provide the opportunity to track the persons specified in WHO cards on form A5. One or more ATTEN cards may be used. However, if none of the special persons named on WHO cards is in attendance at a particular event, then a zero should be entered in columns 29–30 of the ATTENDANCE card, and no ATTEN cards should be filled out.

Column 6: The first six special participants are to be listed on ATTEN card 1 for this event, the next six on ATTEN card 2, and so forth. Enter a number 1, 2, and so forth.

Columns 9–17: The code name of a special participant, from columns 5–13 of a WHO card on form
A5.
Columns 19–27: The code name of another special
participant.
Columns 29–37: The code name of another special
participant.
Columns 39–47: The code name of another special
participant.
Columns 49–57: The code name of another special
participant.
Columns 59–67: The code name of another special
participant.

If there are fewer than six special participants,
then their code names should be packed contigu-
ously from the left, that is, the obvious way to do it.
Columns 69–70: State abbreviation.
Column 71: Commensal unit code letter.
Columns 73–74: Event number.

FORM B3

FDVAR CARDS

Each food variety at the food event is to be recorded
on a FDVAR card. The number of these cards must
agree with what is specified on the COURSE: VA-
RIETIES card of form B1.
Columns 6–7: The course number in which the variety was served. (If the same variety is served in two
or more courses, then it is necessary to give it two
or more FDVAR cards, that is, one for each course
in which it occurs.)
Columns 9–10. The varieties in each course are to be

numbered 1, 2, 3, and so forth. Enter a number. These numbers are used mainly to ensure that FDVAR cards do not get lost. Whereas the number in columns 6–7 should be entered flush right, the number in columns 9–10 should be entered flush left. Thus, the numbers will have the form 5.2, 6.13, and so forth.

Columns 12–20: Code name of the variety, that is, one of the nine-letter codes listed in columns 6–14 of a FOOD card on form A12.

Columns 22–26: The number of persons attending the event who had first helpings of this food variety.

how to estimate the average quantity

Columns 28–30: An estimate of the average quantity in a first helping. In some communities, persons will have larger portions at feasts, not just more portions, or different food. In some communities, the size of a first helping is always approximately the same. What matters here is *not* absolute quantities, but variations in quantity from meal to meal.

***

4

use any consistent standard

Using any consistent standard of quantity as the basis by which all persons at all events are to be measured, give the average number of multiples of that quantity. If your own dietary habits are consistent, use the amount you would ordinarily take yourself as a standard. If persons seem to be taking about half as much as you would, or half of whatever consistent standard you adopt, then record the number 0.5. If they seem to be taking about a third more than you would, then record the number 1.3, and so forth.

perhaps your own normal quantity

or perhaps the size of a highly standardized restaurant portion

Another consistent standard of quantity might be the amount that a quantity-control restaurant (such as Howard Johnson's) would serve of this variety in a single portion if it served this food variety. The most important thing is to use the same estimation basis at every event.

Columns 32–34: Minimum quantity estimate. Among all nonempty portions, what was the size of the smallest portion of this food variety in any first helping? Record this entry in terms of the number of multiples of the standard size portion.

Columns 36–38: Maximum quantity estimate. Among all portions, what was the size of the largest portion of this food variety in any first helping.

Columns 40–44: The number of persons who had second helpings of this food variety,

Columns 46–48: Estimate the average quantity in a second helping, again in terms of a number of multiples of a standard portion (not a standard second portion, but a standard first portion).

Columns 51–55: The total number of additional helpings, including thirds, fourths, fifths, and so forth.

Columns 58–60: Of the amount of this food variety prepared for this event, what *percentage* was *left over?*

Columns 69–70: State abbreviation.

Column 71: Commensal unit letter code.

Columns 73–74: Event number.

FORM B4

OTHER CARD

Columns 8–16: Equipment combinations code for the combination observed at this event, that is, one of the codes from columns 7–15 of an EQUIP card on form A7.

Columns 19–27: Dispensing system code, that is, one of the codes from columns 6–14 of a DISP card on form A8, for whichever dispensing system was used at this event.

Columns 30–38: Precedence system code, that is, one of the codes from columns 6–14 of a PREC card on form A9, for whichever precedence system was used at this event.

Columns 41–49: Position system code, that is, one of the codes from columns 6–14 of a POSI card on form A10.

Columns 52–60: Course structure code, that is, one of the codes from columns 7–15 of a C-STR card on form A6, for whichever course structure was used at this event.

Columns 69–70: State abbreviation.

Column 71: Commensal unit code.

Columns 73–74: Event number.

FORM B5

Form B5 is a means to provide supplementary information for any other group B form or additional information about the food event of any other sort. A form B5 should be attached to whichever form (that is, B1 to B4) it supplements.

FORM B6

PROTOTYPE AND DUPLICATES CARDS

Powers reported that within a given commensal unit of the South Dakota community, one secular breakfast tends to be exactly like another. The same persons are present, the same food varieties are eaten, the quantities are the same, and so on. If he were to transcribe the information from his notes onto the type B forms, the ATTENDANCE card, COURSE: VARIETIES card, ATTEN cards, FDVAR cards, and OTHER card for any one of these secular breakfasts would be identical to the corresponding cards for many of the others, except for the event numbers in columns 73–74. He recommended that a form be designed to enable him to record this exact duplication without having to recopy the same information over and over again. Form B6 is designed to reduce the paperwork.

Columns 7–8: The prototype event number, that is, the first of the sequence of identical events. Suppose, for instance, that events 2, 5, 8, 11, 14, 23, 26, 29, 32, 35, 44, 47, 50, 56, 68, and 71 were the standard bacon/eggs/coffee secular breakfast. Then event 2 is the prototype.

Columns 16–21: The word ENTIRE, for the case of absolute duplication, as reported by Powers. The number of strips of bacon does not vary. Nor do the numbers of eggs or cups of coffee. Everyone present sits in the same seats. The acronym *acafos* is designed to anticipate somewhat less complete duplication of events in other communities.

Columns 24–25: The first duplicate event number. For the example described here, it would be 5.

Columns 27–28: The second duplicate event number (abbreviated den 2). For the example given, it would be 8.

.

.

.

Columns 57–58: The twelfth duplicate event number (abbreviated den 12). For the example given, it would be 50.

For this example, one would create a second PROTO card, again specifying event 2 as the prototype, with events 56, 68, and 71 as the duplicate events.

Caution 1. Since the day and time of two different events cannot be the same, a separate EVENT card is needed for each event. However, there is no need to complete the other two cards on form B1 if the information is identical to a previous event.

Caution 2. The coding instructions just given apply only to the case of exact duplication, not to near duplication or to partial duplication.

Form A1

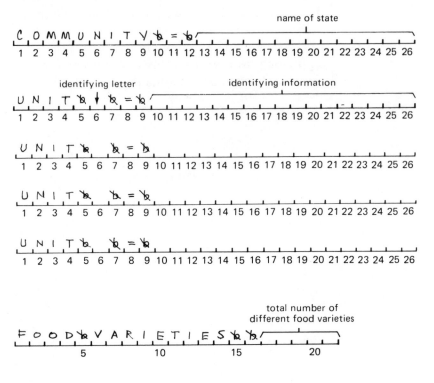

Measurement of Calendrical Information

Form A2

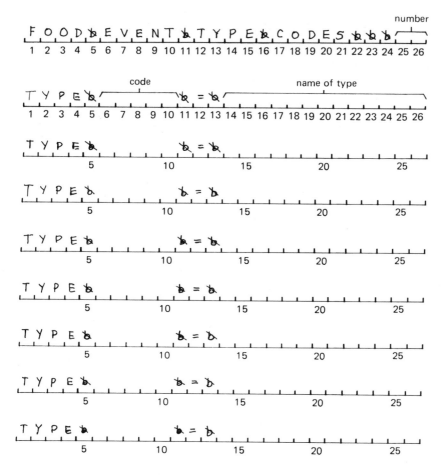

number

F O O D ♭ E V E N T ♭ T Y P E ♭ C O D E S ♭ ♭ ♭

1 2 3 4 5 6 7 8 9 10 11 12 13 14 15 16 17 18 19 20 21 22 23 24 25 26

code   name of type

T Y P E ♭   ♭ = ♭

1 2 3 4 5 6 7 8 9 10 11 12 13 14 15 16 17 18 19 20 21 22 23 24 25 26

T Y P E ♭   ♭ = ♭

     5   10   15   20   25

T Y P E ♭   ♭ = ♭

     5   10   15   20   25

T Y P E ♭   ♭ = ♭

     5   10   15   20   25

T Y P E ♭   ♭ = ♭

     5   10   15   20   25

T Y P E ♭   ♭ = ♭

     5   10   15   20   25

T Y P E ♭   ♭ = ♭

     5   10   15   20   25

T Y P E ♭   ♭ = ♭

     5   10   15   20   25

Form A2 (with metaphysical categories)

F O O D   E V E N T   T Y P E   C O D E S

number

name of type

T Y P E

X   P   A   W   R   S   J   Q   D   F   B   C   M   T

1 2 3 4 5 6 7 8 9 10 11 12 13 14 15 16 17 18 19 20 21 22 23 24 25 26

27 28 29 30 31 32 33 34 35 36 37 38 39 40 41 42 43 44 45 46 47 48 49 50 51 52 53 54 55

T Y P E

5   10   15   20   25   30   35   40   45   50   55

T Y P E

5   10   15   20   25   30   35   40   45   50   55

T Y P E

5   10   15   20   25   30   35   40   45   50   55

T Y P E

5   10   15   20   25   30   35   40   45   50   55

Measurement of Calendrical Information

Form A3

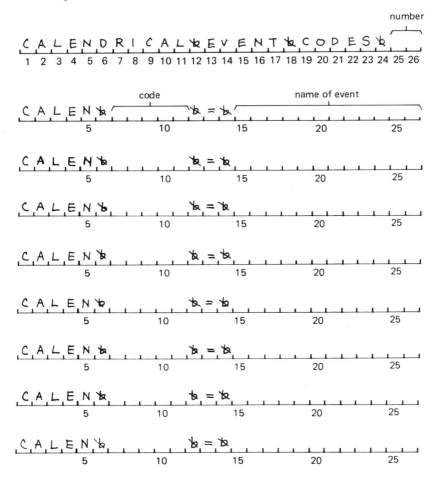

Form A4

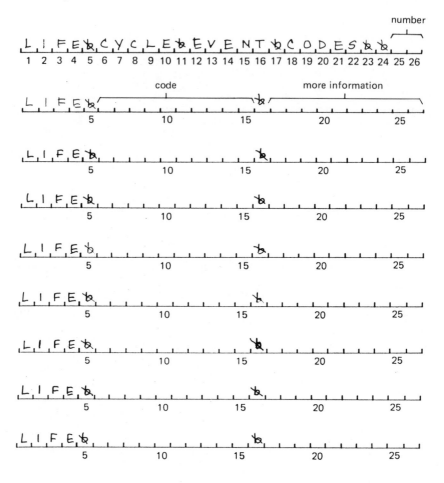

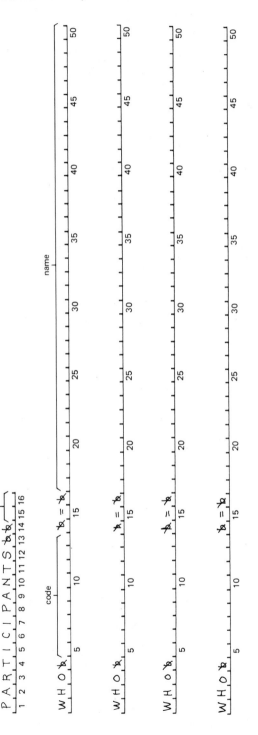

Form A5

Form A6

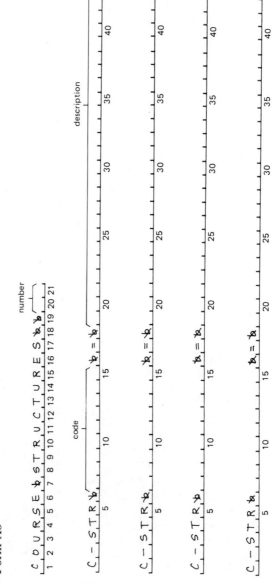

Form A7

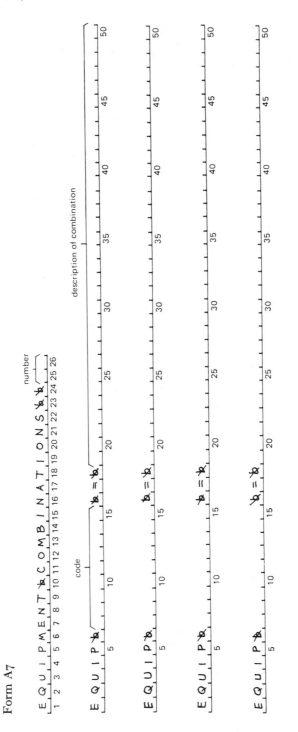

Form A8

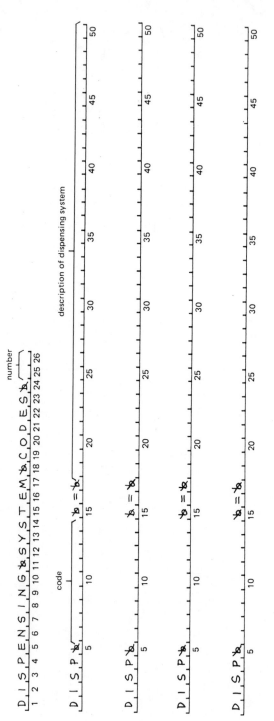

Form A9

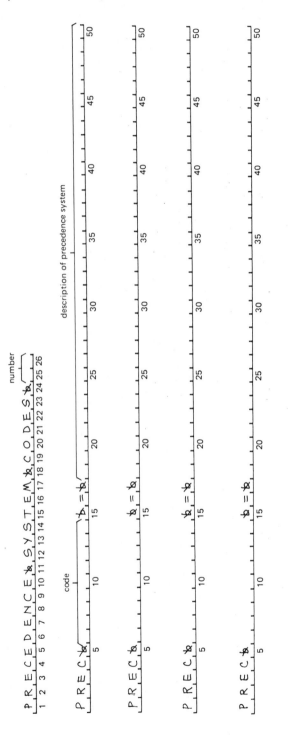

Form A10

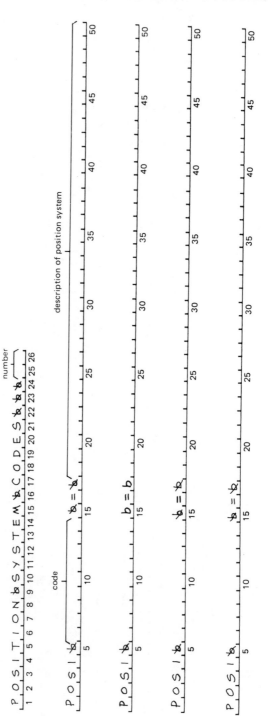

Form A11

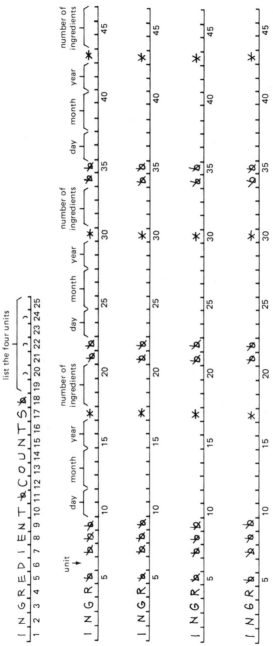

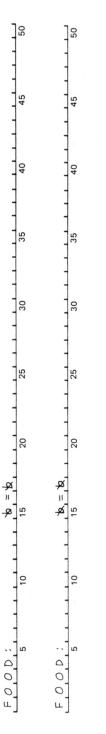

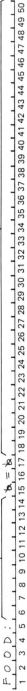

Form A12

Measurement of Calendrical Information

Form A13.   Supplementary information for Group A forms.

|___|___| State abbr.

|_A_|___|___| Which form does this information supplement?

|___|___|___/___|___| Page number / Total number pages in this supplement

Form B1

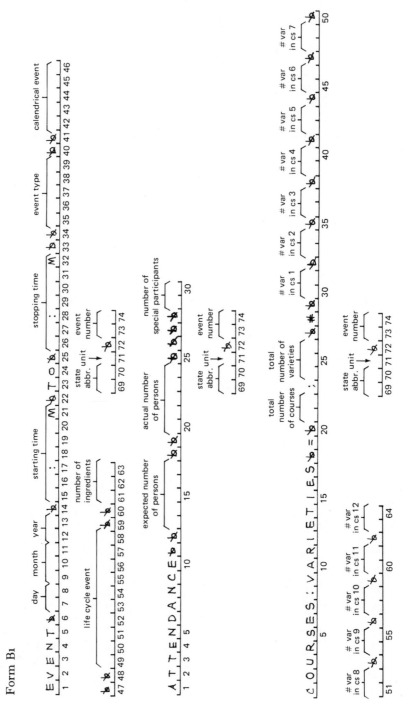

Form B2

Measurement of Calendrical Information

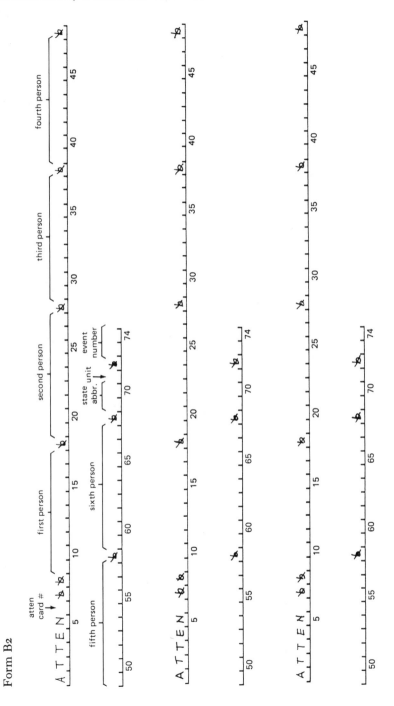

273

Form B$_3$

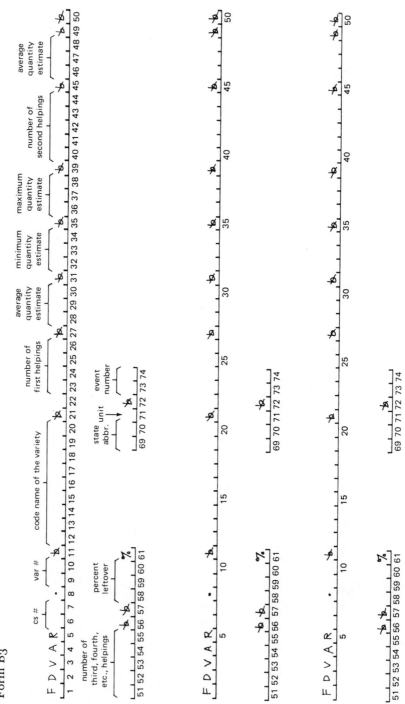

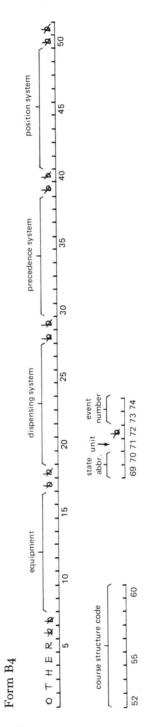

Form B4

Form B5. Supplementary information for Group B forms.

⌴⌴⌴ ⌴⌴ ⌴⌴⌴ Same as columns 69–70, 71, 73–74 of any group B form
state   unit   event
abbr.   number

B⌴⌴⌴ Which form does this information supplement?

⌴⌴⌴/⌴⌴⌴ Page number / Total number pages this supplement

Form B6

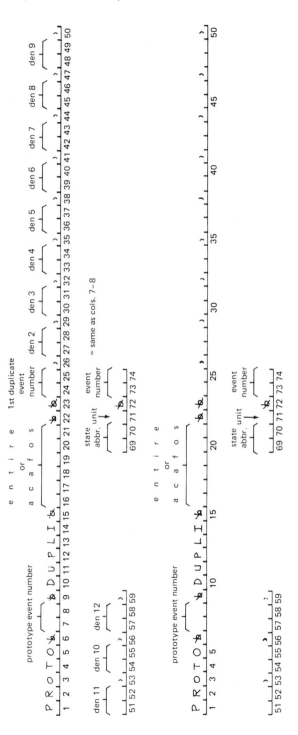

Index